THE CANADIAN ELECTION STUDIES

THE CANADIAN ELECTION STUDIES
Assessing Four Decades of Influence

Edited by Mebs Kanji, Antoine Bilodeau,
and Thomas J. Scotto

UBCPress · Vancouver · Toronto

21 20 19 18 17 16 15 14 13 12   5 4 3 2 1

Printed in Canada on FSC-certified ancient-forest-free paper
(100% post-consumer recycled) that is processed chlorine- and acid-free.

Library and Archives Canada Cataloguing in Publication

The Canadian election studies : assessing four decades of influence /
edited by Mebs Kanji, Antoine Bilodeau, and Thomas J. Scotto.

Includes bibliographical references and index.
Issued also in electronic formats.
ISBN 978-0-7748-1911-4 (cloth); 978-0-7748-1912-1 (pbk)

1. Elections – Research – Canada. 2. Voting research – Canada. 3. Elections – Canada
– History. 4. Voting – Canada – History. I. Kanji, Mebs, 1969- II. Bilodeau, Antoine,
1976- III. Scotto, Thomas J.

JL193.C3579 2012	324.97106	C2012-901114-2

Canada

UBC Press gratefully acknowledges the financial support for our publishing program of the Government of Canada (through the Canada Book Fund), the Canada Council for the Arts, and the British Columbia Arts Council.

This book has been published with the help of a grant from the Canadian Federation for the Humanities and Social Sciences, through the Aid to Scholarly Publications Program, using funds provided by the Social Sciences and Humanities Research Council of Canada.

UBC Press
The University of British Columbia
2029 West Mall
Vancouver, BC V6T 1Z2
www.ubcpress.ca

We respectfully dedicate this volume to John Meisel,
the pioneer of the Canadian Election Studies

Contents

Illustrations

Figures

Tables

Acknowledgments

This volume has benefited enormously from the efforts of many, all of whom deserve to be properly acknowledged. The Canadian Political Science Association and especially Lisa Young in her role as program chairperson were among the first to throw the wind behind our sails. Lisa enthusiastically championed our idea to host a workshop on the Canadian Election Studies during the 2007 Annual Conference of the Canadian Political Science Association, held in Saskatoon between 30 May and 1 June.

Then came all those who agreed that this was an important intellectual exercise and walked the talk by taking us up on our offer to participate, either in the workshop and/or by contributing a paper to this volume. Without the support of John Courtney, Mildred A. Schwartz, Allan Kornberg, Harold D. Clarke, William Cross, Barry Kay, Elisabeth Gidengil, Joanna Everitt, Kenneth Carty, Richard Johnston, Brenda O'Neill, André Blais, Gisèle Yasmeen, Alain Pelletier, John Meisel, Lawrence LeDuc, Andrea M.L. Perrella, Richard Nadeau, Éric Bélanger, and Jon H. Pammett, this project would simply lack substance. We particularly express our deepest appreciation to our contributors for their outstanding co-operation and the incredible patience that they have exhibited from start to finish.

Lastly, there have been a number of extremely capable people who have played a significant role behind the scenes in advancing this volume along the way. Research assistants such as Soheyla Salari, Nicki Doyle, Julie Stephens, Nada Fadol, Alain Deschamps, Meaghen Annett, and Dennis

Molina Tapia have worked tirelessly on compiling references and shaping components so that they conform to the appropriate standards. Four anonymous reviewers provided us with excellent feedback and suggestions for improvement. And without the superb professionalism and experienced advice provided by Emily Andrew from UBC Press – well, let's not even go there!

Mebs Kanji,
Antoine Bilodeau, and
Thomas J. Scotto

THE CANADIAN ELECTION STUDIES

Introduction
Four Decades of Canadian Election Studies

MEBS KANJI, ANTOINE BILODEAU,
AND THOMAS J. SCOTTO

The Canadian Election Studies (CES) are an impressive body of survey data that have been gathered and analyzed for over four decades. The primary objective of this collection of surveys has been to investigate why Canadians vote the way they do. The CES are designed and administered by academics, and they have been paid for largely through public funding agencies such as the Canada Council and the Social Sciences and Humanities Research Council of Canada. They are made freely available to the general public but are used most extensively by scholars and university students in the field of political science.

This volume brings together several researchers, most of whom have served as principal investigators on various CES research projects conducted over the past forty or so years to tackle three main objectives. The first is to document the evolution of these studies as there is much about the beginning, development, and current state of the CES that is not widely shared or understood. For example, how did the CES first come into being? Who were the key players? And what were the driving theoretical underpinnings? Also, how has the methodology of these studies advanced over time? Has the implementation of these surveys resulted in notable payoffs? And what are the most pressing challenges that lie ahead?

The second objective is to highlight some of the major findings and advances in thinking that have emerged from researching the CES. Forty years

is a considerable period of time in which to be repeatedly injecting significant amounts of public research dollars into a single set of projects without
taking stock of how these investments have contributed to our understanding and the prospects for further study. What have we learned from the
CES? Do we know any more about why Canadians vote the way they do than
we did four decades ago? And do these surveys inspire new investigative
opportunities?

The third objective of this volume is to project forward after taking a
systematic and reflective look at the past. Here, our intentions are mainly
twofold. The first is to attempt to synthesize what has been achieved as a
result of conducting the CES over four decades. The second is to flag ways
in which this research endeavour might be improved, based on what we
have gathered from the various contributions to this book and the insights
that we have developed along the way. Our hope is that this exercise can
provide some added perspective to the ongoing debate about where to steer
the CES in the years ahead.

The idea for this volume was conceived initially at a one-day workshop
that was scheduled prior to the Annual Conference of the Canadian Political
Science Association, held at the University of Saskatoon in June 2007. The
workshop was entitled *Assessing the Canadian Election Studies' Contribution
to Canadian Political Science.* The purpose of this workshop was to provide
a formal occasion for dialogue between the principal investigators from the
various CES research teams and others who were interested in examining
and assessing the CES's contribution to Canadian political science.

The degree of interest and debate sparked by this workshop suggested
that this project might be worth following up. As a result, we asked the principal investigators who attended, as well as others who were not able to at-
tend, if they would be willing to participate as contributors to an edited
volume on the subject. The reaction was very positive and encouraging. The
road since has been long, but the end result of this collaborative undertaking is now complete and is laid out on the pages that follow.

What Are the Canadian Election Studies?

The place to begin is with a more elaborate description of the CES. These
surveys have been randomly administered (mostly over the telephone) to
eligible Canadian voters primarily during and/or after federal elections. As
Table I.1 indicates, the studies were launched in the mid-1960s and have

TABLE 1.1

Principal investigators of the Canadian Election Studies, 1965-2006

Year	Principal investigators	Specialization
1965	1. John Meisel (Queen's University)	Political Science
	2. Philip Converse (University of Michigan)	Political Science/ Sociology
	3. Maurice Pinard (McGill University)	Sociology
	4. Peter Regenstreif (University of Chicago)	Political Science
	5. Mildred Schwartz (University of Chicago)	Sociology
1968	1. John Meisel (Queen's University)	Political Science
1974,	1. Harold Clarke (University of Windsor)	Political Science
1979,	2. Jane Jenson (Carleton University)	Political Science
and	3. Lawrence LeDuc (University of Windsor)	Political Science
1980	4. Jon H. Pammett (Carleton University)	Political Science
1984	1. Ronald D. Lambert (University of Waterloo)	Sociology
	2. Steven D. Brown (Wilfrid Laurier University)	Political Science
	3. James E. Curtis (University of Waterloo)	Sociology
	4. Barry J. Kay (Wilfrid Laurier University)	Political Science
	5. John M. Wilson (University of Waterloo)	Political Science
1988	1. Richard Johnston (University of British Columbia)	Political Science
	2. André Blais (Université de Montréal)	Political Science
	3. Jean Crête (University of Laval)	Political Science
	4. Henry E. Brady (University of California, Berkeley)	Political Science
1992	1. Richard Johnston (University of British Columbia)	Political Science
and	2. André Blais (Université de Montréal)	Political Science
1993	3. Henry E. Brady (University of California, Berkeley)	Political Science
	4. Elisabeth Gidengil (McGill University)	Political Science
	5. Neil Nevitte (University of Toronto)	Political Science
	6. Joseph Fletcher-1992 only (University of Toronto)	Political Science
1997	1. André Blais (Université de Montréal)	Political Science
and	2. Elisabeth Gidengil (McGill University)	Political Science
2000	3. Richard Nadeau (Université de Montréal)	Political Science
	4. Neil Nevitte (University of Toronto)	Political Science

▶

◄ TABLE I.1

Year	Principal investigators	Specialization
2004	1. André Blais (Université de Montréal)	Political Science
and	2. Elisabeth Gidengil (McGill University)	Political Science
2006	3. Neil Nevitte (University of Toronto)	Political Science
	4. Patrick Fournier (Université de Montréal)	Political Science
	5. Joanna Everitt (University of New Brunswick)	Political Science

Note: Some of these researchers have since relocated to other universities.

been conducted several times since over a span of more than forty years. During this period, the CES were steered and implemented by eight different teams of researchers, most of which were made up of four to six political scientists, from different universities in Canada and occasionally from the United States.

The more exact breakdown reported in Table I.2 shows that a total of fourteen separate CES projects were administered between 1965 and 2006. Of these, twelve were conducted during federal elections and two during major referendums – the Quebec Referendum in 1980 and the Charlottetown Accord Referendum in 1992. Thus, the CES are not exclusive to covering just elections. With these data, it is possible to explore Canadians' survey responses across a variety of political and electoral contexts.

Note too that the total number of surveys conducted and available for study is even more extensive. From the mid-1960s to the mid-1980s, the standard methodological approach for most CES research projects was to implement one cross-provincial post-election survey immediately after every federal electoral contest. The only exceptions to this rule came in 1972, the one federal election year during this period when no such election study was attempted,[1] and in 1980, when one additional provincial survey was administered more than three months after the 1980 federal election, during the time of the first Quebec Referendum. In total, there were seven surveys administered during this initial twenty-year period (see Table I.2).

Following the mid-1980s, however, the total number of surveys conducted almost quadrupled. The research team designated to study the 1988 federal election brought with it a more expansive research agenda, which included both the desire to study campaign dynamics and a variety of broader topics, not all of which dealt directly with voting and elections. In order to accommodate their research interests, the 1988 CES research team introduced a new three-wave survey methodology, which included a campaign

TABLE 1.2

Canadian Election Studies, 1965-2006 – events covered, survey types, and number of interviews completed

Event	Survey type	Canada (N)	Number of interviews completed — Provinces and territories												Gender	
			PEI	NS	NFLD	NB	QC	ON	MA	SA	AB	BC	YK	NWT	Male	Female
1965 FE (8 November)	PES	2,118	24	73	24	108	643	723	130	94	171	128	–	–	1,036	1,082
1968 FE (25 June)	PES	2,767	17	116	–	99	754	970	139	139	235	250	–	–	1,388	1,379
1974 FE (8 July)	PES	2,562	97	180	102	134	702	702	113	101	179	252	–	–	1,191	1,371
1979 FE (22 May)	PES	2,761	108	191	113	148	734	741	127	113	196	273	–	–	1,312	1,431
1980 FE (18 February)	PES	1,748	82	133	73	78	446	488	89	67	110	182	–	–	846	902
1980 QR (20 May)	QRS	325	–	–	–	–	325	–	–	–	–	–	–	–	161	164
1984 FE (4 September)	PES	3,377	112	132	134	136	779	967	251	252	263	351	–	–	1,467	1,910
1988 FE	CPS	3,609	127	109	113	213	835	968	179	193	446	426	–	–	1,792	1,817
(21 November)	PES	2,922	109	90	90	172	637	783	145	162	379	355	–	–	1,481	1,441
	MBS	2,115	85	66	68	134	452	565	98	119	272	256	–	–	1,082	1,033
1992 CAR	REFS	2,530	67	64	51	53	1,001	563	124	101	236	270	–	–	1,234	1,296
(26 October)	PRS	2,223	60	57	47	43	858	491	110	93	220	244	–	–	1,102	1,121

▼ TABLE 1.2

Number of interviews completed

Event	Survey type	Canada (N)	PEI	NS	NFLD	NB	QC	ON	MA	SA	AB	BC	YK	NWT	Male	Female
							Provinces and territories								Gender	
1993 FE (25 October)	CPS	3,775	100	98	112	108	1,007	953	228	212	485	472	–	–	1,929	1,846
	PES	3,340	97	90	101	96	864	843	210	185	440	414	–	–	1,721	1,619
	MBS	2,209	57	64	75	61	563	555	132	132	300	270	–	–	1,156	1,053
1997 FE (2 June)	CPS	3,949	101	101	99	108	1,034	951	203	211	481	473	90	97	1,856	2,093
	PES	3,170	86	93	83	90	801	756	158	174	407	371	71	80	1,539	1,631
	MBS	1,851	44	64	48	58	459	453	89	96	234	225	43	38	887	964
2000 FE (27 November)	CPS	3,651	50	138	145	144	1,251	983	118	116	325	381	–	–	1,762	1,889
	PES	2,860	41	113	106	111	941	774	97	101	273	303	–	–	1,432	1,428
	MBS	1,517	23	67	68	65	457	417	52	59	154	155	–	–	739	778
2004 FE (28 June)	CPS	4,323	115	112	120	116	1,048	1,318	217	214	437	626	–	–	1,981	2,342
	PES	3,138	90	89	76	86	657	1,004	150	169	349	468	–	–	1,455	1,683
	MBS	1,674	53	47	46	41	345	512	74	96	196	264	–	–	753	921
2006 FE (23 January)	CPS	4,058	96	109	102	101	1,013	1,231	203	206	408	589	–	–	1,925	2,133
	PES	3,250	76	95	85	82	818	984	159	166	322	463	–	–	1,550	1,700
Totals		71,822 (34,553)	1,917	2,491	2,081	2,585	19,419	19,695	3,595	3,571	7,518	8,461	204	215	35,898	37,027

Note: CAR = Charlottetown Accord Referendum; CPS = campaign period survey; FE = federal election; MBS = mail-back survey; PES = post-election survey; PRS = post-referendum survey; QR = Quebec Referendum; QRS = Quebec Referendum; REFS = referendum survey. Projects: 14; Elections: 12; Referendums: 2; Total surveys conducted: 26.

period survey (designed to be administered and capable of being analyzed during election campaigns), a post-election survey (that is administered, similar to earlier surveys, immediately after elections), and a mail-back survey (which is intended to probe a more diverse array of research topics and is sent through the mail not too long after an election has been contested).

The team responsible for examining the 1993 federal election effectively took on the same three-wave survey methodology. The only distinction is that prior to the 1993 election, they also conducted two additional surveys before and after the 1992 Charlottetown Accord Referendum. Since 1993, other successive research teams have followed suit by opting not to deviate from using a multi-wave surveying approach. The net result during this second twenty-year period has been a gain of nineteen additional surveys. Moreover, during the time in which this volume was being compiled, two additional surveys were conducted, both before and after the 2008 federal election.

In individual terms, this collection of survey data amounts to nearly 72,000 completed interviews with various members of the Canadian electorate, and this total does not include the two most recent surveys conducted in 2008. Not all of these interviews constitute distinct cases because respondents in multi-wave projects are asked to participate in more than one survey, and many often comply. Still, over the course of four or so decades, the CES have accumulated a total sample size of nearly 35,000 respondents. This makes it possible to conduct fairly detailed and statistically sophisticated analyses of various types, including an examination of different subgroups within Canadian society, without instantly having to grapple with the limitations of insufficient sample sizes. For example, it is possible to mine the CES data by variables such as region or gender, just to name a couple. The downside, however, as is made clear in Table I.2, is that certain regions and provinces remain better represented than others. Moreover, to this point, the CES contain very few cases from the Northwest Territories or the Yukon and none from Nunavut since the latter's ascension to territorial status.

The CES also make it possible to probe a great many topics. As Table I.3 indicates, the 1965-2006 collection of CES encompasses nearly 6,700 variables. Questions dealing specifically with voting decisions and voting patterns, partisan attachments, political interest, political efficacy, perceptions of leaders and parties, issue and spending orientations, campaign activities, leadership debates, economic outlooks, media exposure, political knowledge, various socio-demographic characteristics, and the like are designed

TABLE 1.3

The scope of the Canadian Election Studies, 1965-2006

Event	Number of variables probed	Sample topics	
1965 FE	350	Political performance	Networks
		Political efficacy	Issue orientations and
		Personal financial	priorities
1968 FE	575	circumstances	Quebec sovereignty
		Respondent mobility	Charlottetown Accord
		Group associations	Bilingualism
1974 FE	480	Political leaders	Foreign investment
		Leadership attributes	Material satisfaction
		Perceptions of politicians	Post-materialism
1979 FE	538	Perceptions of party	Free trade
		differences	Senate reform
		Perceptions of parties	Economic attitudes
1980 FE	158	Political interest	Voter registration
		Political knowledge	Volunteerism
1980 QR	43	Campaign activities	Federalism
		Demographics and personal	Deficit elimination
		data	Social class
1984 FE	641	Life satisfaction	Constitution and rights
		Foreign affairs	Sponsorship scandal
		Religion and religiosity	Media exposure
1988 FE	547	Leadership debates	Government influence and
		Integration with the United	authority
		States	Political discussion
1992 CAR	244	Election financing	Orientations toward
		Past and present party	Canada and other sub-
		attachments	national units
1993 FE	627	Voting decision and voting	Referendum voting patterns
		patterns	Orientations toward
		Group orientations	founding peoples
1997 FE	625	Orientations toward	Confidence in the voting
		political institutions	process
		Inflation	Death penalty
2000 FE	784	Majority and minority	Waiting lists (health care
		governments	system)
		Parental party attachments	Women in politics
2004 FE	641	Party contact	Meech Lake Accord
		Spending orientations	Abortion
		Ideology	Gay marriage
2006 FE	398	Perceived electoral	Privatization
		outcomes	Voting age
		Group influence	Immigrants
Total	6,651	Protest	

Note: CAR = Charlottetown Accord Referendum; FE = federal election; QR = Quebec Referendum primarily for examining the determinants of voting. However, there are various other topics that can be explored. For example, the CES include questions on group associations, integration with the United States, orientations toward government institutions, Quebec sovereignty, the Charlottetown Accord, foreign investment, post-materialism, federalism, social class, the death penalty, human rights, health care, women in politics, and much more. Furthermore, since the implementation of computer-assisted telephone-interviewing technology in 1988, the CES have also become fertile ground for conducting various methodological experiments relating to question wording, question ordering, and the randomization of survey responses. The combination of these features makes the CES a potentially useful data source for accommodating a fairly broad array of research interests.

In addition, the CES incorporate a number of distinct study designs that contribute even further to the analytical possibilities provided by this data source. The inventory reported in Table I.4 suggests that there are at least forty-three separate study designs embedded within the 1965-2006 collection of CES, the vast majority of which were introduced after 1984. For example, twenty-six cross-sectional samples provide multiple data points for conducting various historical and cross-time analyses. Of course, it must be kept in mind that some of these studies are much smaller in size (and more parochial in focus) than others, and some have been collected in more abbreviated time frames than others. Still, in terms of overall duration, these data points cover nearly half a century, which is a considerable stretch of time to satisfy a variety of different curiosities. Moreover, the CES contain a variety of standardized variables, which means that it is also possible to explore changes and consistencies in Canadians' survey responses, especially from the late 1980s on, when larger multi-wave surveys became the norm and teams of researchers began to place a greater emphasis on cross-time comparability and continuity when contending with questionnaire design.

The CES also contain both short- and long-term panel data, so it is possible to track the same people over both abbreviated and more extended periods of time. In all, there are more than two times as many short-term panels as there are long-term ones. Still, the CES contain no less than three different longitudinal panels that vary in terms of the time frames and events that they cover. The longest extends approximately six years, beginning after the 1974 federal election and stretching past the 1980 Quebec Referendum. The second covers a more recent but much shorter period of time that spans from the 1992 Charlottetown Accord Referendum to after the 1993 elec-

TABLE I.4

The variety of study designs contained within the Canadian Election Studies, 1965-2006

Year	Number of cross-sectional samples	Longitudinal panels	Short-term panels	Rolling cross-sectional samples	Total variety
1965	1	–	–	–	1
1968	1	–	–	–	1
1974	1	–	–	–	1
1979	1	–	–	–	1
1980	2	1974 FE –1980 QR panel	–	–	3
1984	1	–	–	–	1
1988	3	–	1988 CPS-PES-MBS panel	1988 election campaign, rolling cross-section	5
1992	2	–	1992 REFS-PRS panel	1992 referendum, rolling cross-section	4
1993	3	1992 REFS – 1993 MBS panel	1993 CPS-PES-MBS panel	1993 election campaign, rolling cross-section	6
1997	3	–	1997 CPS-PES-MBS panel	1997 election campaign, rolling cross-section	5
2000	3	–	2000 CPS-PES-MBS panel	2000 election campaign, rolling cross-section	5
2004	3	–	2004 CPS-PES-MBS panel	2004 election campaign, rolling cross-section	5
2006	2	2004 CPS – 2006 PES panel	2006 CPS-PES panel	2006 election campaign, rolling cross-section	5
Total	26	3	7	7	43

Note: The sample sizes for these surveys have been presented in Table I.2. CAR = Charlottetown Accord Referendum; CPS = campaign period survey; FE = federal election; MBS = mail-back survey; PES = post-election survey; PRS = post-referendum survey; QR = Quebec Referendum; QRS = Quebec Referendum survey; REFS = referendum survey.

tion. And the third covers a period of about two years and incorporates both the 2004 and 2006 federal elections.[2]

In terms of short-term panels, there are seven in total that are distributed over a period that extends from 1988 to 2006. These short-term panels are particularly useful for examining how people's survey responses can change before and after major democratic events, such as elections and referendums. Similarly, the CES contain seven rolling cross-sectional samples that have also been collected for nearly twenty years now. These data are ideal for examining campaign dynamics and changing trends during election and referendum campaigns.

Given the immense richness of this data source, it is not difficult to see why the CES are considered by many to constitute a major research endeavour in Canadian political science. For over four decades, public research funds have contributed to developing a substantial and continuously expanding body of data that is used extensively by several researchers and students. This is precisely the reason why we think it is relevant to document the history and evolution of these studies and assess how they have contributed to our understanding of voting in Canada. Moreover, just as we feel it is important to take stock of what has been achieved, we also believe that it is equally germane to reflect on how these studies might be improved in the future.

A Brief Preview of What Is to Come

The remainder of this volume is organized into three parts. Part 1 houses the basic narrative. This discussion begins with John Meisel's brief introductory chapter, which provides his personal recollections of how the CES began. It was Meisel who effectively jump-started these surveys, and in his chapter he revisits this experience. He portrays the social and academic contexts of the time and describes how the initial funding for the 1965 study was derived. He introduces the major players who were involved and details some of the preliminary decisions that were made and the difficulties that were encountered.

In Chapter 2, Mildred Schwartz reviews the extent to which theory influenced the first study conducted in 1965. Her focus is primarily on the players involved and their theoretical motivations. Her recollections suggest that the theoretical underpinnings of the first study were neither overt nor well articulated but that all of the team members came to the table with different ideas and hypotheses in mind. Ultimately, Schwartz claims that the final questionnaire in 1965 was based on a compromise of the competing preferences of the five team members. Schwartz's chapter also briefly discusses some of theoretical motivations behind later studies and concludes that future studies should stay alert to the theoretical developments that lie beyond the boundaries of political science in order to continue advancing and deepening our understanding of the Canadian electorate.

In Chapter 3, Lawrence LeDuc further expands our appreciation of the theoretical influences on the development of the CES. More specifically, he discusses the development of survey-based electoral studies in a comparative context. By the time the first Canadian study was administered, the field had already become highly internationalized, and it was not simply the Americans who had provided theoretical inspirations but also the Western Europeans. The key point of this chapter is to remind us that both the CES and our analyses of these data have also been fuelled by broader interests in other comparative contexts through publications, collaborative efforts, and other forms of exchange.

In Chapter 4, Thomas Scotto, Mebs Kanji, and Antoine Bilodeau provide an overview of how the methodology of the CES has evolved over the last forty years. This chapter systematically highlights major design innovations and charts how the CES went from being a post-election cross-sectional survey, administered through face-to-face interviews, to adopting a multi-wave short-term panel design and other improvements. This chapter also highlights major changes in content and in sample design, and it describes how the methodological evolution of the CES has helped to expand our understanding of the Canadian voter. The chapter concludes by discussing the need for future advances in the CES methodological design and, more particularly, the pros and cons of Internet surveys.

In Chapter 5, Richard Johnston and André Blais remind us of the general contribution and relevance of the CES. They refer to these studies as a pivotal project with an extensive history, but one whose future may be in jeopardy. The main problem, ironically, is not that different from a major obstacle encountered initially by Meisel during the mid-1960s. The key distinction, however, is that the stakes are now much higher. Coming up with a consistent and reliable source of funding to sustain these studies over the long-term is an immediate, real, and pressing concern, and Johnston and Blais provide some suggestions on how we might proceed, based on how such matters are handled in other countries.

Part 2 of this volume takes stock of how the CES have contributed to our understanding of voting behaviour as well as the prospects for further research. More specifically, Chapters 6 to 11 provide some key examples of the types of insights that we have gained from our various investigations of the long- and short-term determinants of voting and, more recently, the decline in voter turnout. In many instances, these chapters also illustrate how working with the CES continuously inspires new research curiosities. For example, in Chapter 6, Elisabeth Gidengil provides a broad overview of what we have learned about the long-term sociological determinants of the vote. A major finding thus far has been that socio-demographic variables do not seem to carry all that much weight; however, there remain variables that have yet to be properly explored. Moreover, Gidengil believes that we now need to move beyond solely examining associations between socio-demographic indicators and how individuals vote and conduct additional research that investigates individuals as social beings within their networks of social interaction to see if that tells us more about why individuals vote the way they do. This advance, she suggests, may help us to explain vote choice and not simply predict it.

In Chapter 7, Barry Kay and Andrea Perrella look in more detail at social class, which they argue is one socio-demographic factor that many Canadian researchers, similar to researchers working with election studies in other parts of the world, have often turned to when examining voting behaviour. The findings, however, have not been all that robust, which seems to suggest that class may not be a very relevant factor when it comes to explaining electoral choice in Canada. In their analysis, Kay and Perrella look systematically at the link between two different objective measures of class and party preference using data from ten CES. They also compare class effects with the influences of other socio-demographic variables. Their findings lend further support to the claim that different objective measures of class have weak and inconsistent effects on vote. However, while the influence of these variables may not be as strong as the effects of other socio-demographic determinants such as region and religion, there is evidence to suggest that the impact of class might be comparable to that of gender and age. In their conclusion, Kay and Perrella provide us with additional suggestions for further research, and they remind us that the way we operationalize variables affects our results and that our current interpretations of the evidence may vary if we had more precise measures.

In Chapter 8, Richard Nadeau and Éric Bélanger turn to consider a major regional divide that many have used the CES to learn more about. The approach in this chapter is to unpack the development of the Quebec/rest of Canada (ROC) cleavage in three distinct periods so as to better contextualize how research and results have evolved over time. Nadeau and Bélanger cover over four decades worth of studies published by various CES research teams and others who have grappled with these data. Their investigation centres on the similarities and differences in the outlooks of these two communities and the motivations behind their voting patterns. The analysis in this chapter re-emphasizes that long-term influences such as region are relevant. The evidence suggests that the nature of the similarities and differences between Quebec and the ROC has shifted over time. Moreover, in terms of the determinants of voting behaviour, there are a number of important differences that emerge, but one of the most striking distinctions is the relevance of the sovereignty issue in Quebec.

In Chapter 9, Richard Johnston further expands the scope of our assessment by providing a comparative perspective on what the CES have taught us about the long-term structural determinants of party preference. His analysis shows that when data from the CES are stacked up against evidence from election studies in other Anglo-American democracies, the power of societal cleavages to explain variation in party preferences differs remarkably little from one country to the other. Canadian parties appear as structurally rooted as parties in other societies, and these structural bases have significant electoral consequences. What is unique, however, is that Canada's cleavage structure is dominated by cultural forces, which when combined with the long-term significance of the Quebec/ROC divide produce a political system that has been dominated by a party at the centre. The Liberals, Johnston argues, have historically been the dominant party of the centre in Canada because outside of Quebec they are the party of the Catholics, French Canadians, and ethnic and religious minorities, whereas inside Quebec they are the party of non-francophones and those on the right of the political spectrum.

In Chapter 10, Harold Clarke and Allan Kornberg put forward an alternative argument that suggests that voting in Canada is driven more by short-term forces than by long-term sociological factors. Since parties in Canada generally avoid real policy debate during election campaigns and focus instead on brokering deals with different elites in an attempt to ensure electoral support, voters in turn behave accordingly. For instance, data from the CES and other surveys suggest that Canadians have flexible partisan attachments to parties. The issues that they see as being relevant during elections are typically broad and one-sided, otherwise known as valence issues. And Canadian voters, it seems, rely heavily on leader images for making electoral decisions. Much of the data, Clarke and Kornberg argue, point to short-term forces such as these as being the key determinants of voting. Regardless of which party's electoral support they examine, the same three factors – flexible partisanship, valence (or one-sided) issues, and party leader images – explain much of the variance in voting patterns.

In Chapter 11, Jon Pammett examines the ways in which the CES may be more or less useful for examining the problem of declining voter turnout. He makes the case that the CES are not particularly well suited to conducting detailed investigations of why people do not vote. However, because these studies are administered across the entire country and they ask certain questions about provincial voting behaviour, they may be more useful for examining non-voting at different levels of the federal political system. To this point, there has not been much research on differential abstention, but Pammett's preliminary investigation in this volume suggests that Canadians may be becoming more consistent in their voting habits by not voting at both the provincial and federal levels. Moreover, this chapter shows that voting patterns across multiple levels are related to similar socio-demographic and attitudinal factors as well as to other types of political participation.

In Part 3 of this volume, Antoine Bilodeau, Thomas Scotto, and Mebs Kanji (Chapter 12) summarize what they feel the CES have helped to achieve over the last forty years, and they assess the publication record that has been established (see Appendix). Their synthesis suggests that we have learned a great deal from the CES about why voters vote the way they do and that the effects of this productivity have been far reaching. They are not of the view, however, that this research endeavour has been entirely problem-free, and they provide a few suggestions on how the CES might be improved in the future.

NOTES

1 See John Meisel's chapter in this volume for an explanation as to why no survey was attempted at this time.
2 Recently, the 2004-06 panel has also been expanded to include data collected during the 2008 federal election.

PART 1

THE NARRATIVE

Point of Departure, 1965

JOHN MEISEL

*It is eminently appropriate that a volume surveying four decades of
election studies should begin with a historical document. What follows
is an extract of a piece that grew out of an after-dinner speech I gave
at a 1990 conference at York University on "Analyzing Democracy in
Canada: The Limits and Possibilities of Election Studies." I subsequently
beefed up and embroidered the piece for publication in the proposed
proceedings under the title "Clio, Psephos and Calculi: Some Historical
and Analytical Perspectives on Election Studies in Canada." For some
reason, the volume never saw the light of day, and my pearls, as well
as those of the other participants, were never enshrined in a volume
emanating from the conference. I intended to recycle most of it for
publication elsewhere but somehow never got around to it. When Mebs
Kanji, Antoine Bilodeau, and Thomas J. Scotto invited me to contribute
a chapter to the present volume, I realized that the perfect venue had
miraculously emerged. What follows is about half of the original paper,
dwelling on how the first Canadian Election Study came into being and
portraying the social and academic context. Although I did some light
manicuring and editing, no attempt was made to update, or otherwise
enrich, the piece – it is left more or less in its pristine form of a genuine
archaeological artifact. Anyone driven by irresistible curiosity to unearth
the removed parts can obtain them from me at meiselj@queensu.ca.*

Why, you may ask, did Canada's first academic survey-based election study take place in 1965? Why did it not happen in 1962 or 1968? Columbia University had started in the 1940s, and the University of Michigan in the 1950s (see, for example, Lazarsfeld, Berelson, and Gaudet 1948; Berelson, Lazarsfeld, and McPhee 1954; Campbell, Gurin, and Miller 1954; Campbell et al. 1960). Plumbing the electorate's mind was in the air. We would have had an election survey about that time in any case, but the fact that 1965 was the precise year is bound up with my own activities and my own intellectual development, as well as my tastes, as you will see.

When I went to the London School of Economics and Political Science (LSE) in 1950 to do a Ph.D., I had intended to undertake a comparative study of the Canadian and British party systems, the hypothesis being that the Canadian party system was "better" than the British system. I was totally wrong, but then I was young and all too ready to pass judgment. I believed that the Canadian party system mediated more effectively between the major contending interests than the British system because it cut across the basic cleavage lines, with the major parties trying to appeal to both French and English voters, whereas the British party system was less effective because it followed the main cleavages in society, which were, of course, class based. The British parties exacerbated class cleavages, whereas our system accommodated the needs of the French and English populations.[1]

To undertake the study, I had to look at surveys and polls and perhaps to conduct some of my own. It turned out that H.R.G. Greaves, my supervisor, whose interests were in political ideas and public administration, did not believe in this kind of research. I would have to change my topic if I were to work with him. I was too timid to ask for a different supervisor. Instead, I decided to return to Canada for a year, from where I could apply for scholarships to American graduate schools. Queen's University offered me a job, and once I was there, under the influence of J.A. Corry, I eventually undertook to study parties and political behaviour in Canada.[2] I was launched on a process that, in the context of election surveys, included a number of steps.

As a first step in 1953 and again in 1955, I conducted constituency studies in Kingston, out of which grew my "Religious Affiliation and Electoral Behaviour: A Case Study" (1956). This piece utilized not only survey data but also a variety of other kinds of observations. In re-reading it recently, I was struck by the considerable rewards accruing from the combination of a number of research techniques – a form of eclecticism that has all but disappeared.

I had twelve assistants – most but not all were students, and none was paid a red sou. My budget was risible, covered by a small grant from Queen's University. Together, we conducted about 450 face-to-face interviews during the 1953 federal election in the Kingston constituency and a slightly larger number after the subsequent provincial vote, held in 1955. Census tracts were used to map demographic and other characteristics and to identify strongly Catholic and Protestant areas. The voting records were then related to the identified characteristics. This work followed the methodology pioneered by André Siegfried (1913). My students and I also attended virtually all political gatherings and generally became non-partisan participant observers. Every evening in my house, and with the help of my wife and Bokar coffee (decaf was unknown then), we discussed the day's interviews, interpretations of our questionnaire, respondents' quirks, and the significance of what we had learned. There was an immediacy of the data to us, and to me – who finally wrote something about it – that one misses under present conditions. Today's marvellous technological assistance creates, I believe, serious barriers between the researcher and his or her field of study. It might be wise to consider how something like the early primitive research practices might be fused with the sophisticated gimmickry now available to us. This might be a particularly worthwhile exercise if, as Scotto, Kanji, and Bilodeau note in their chapter in this volume, we turn to the Internet for delivery of future iterations of the Canadian Election Studies.

An interesting wrinkle, which I have marvelled about ever since, emerged during the construction of this initial questionnaire. I included a question through which I was trying to test the knowledge of the respondents of various provincial and federal political figures. Among the names of the politicians listed, which the respondents were asked to identify, I included a fictitious name. I forget the made-up person's initials, but it was something like "J. Small." When I started recording the answers, I found that about half a dozen people responded by saying, yes, they knew who Small was and then, when asked to identify him, said that he had disappeared or that he had left. It turned out that in inventing a non-person I had unwittingly used the surname of someone who had vanished: Ambrose Small. He was a well-known individual in Ontario who had disappeared some years previously without a trace but to the accompaniment of much media attention. My having used his name provides a nice footnote to the vagaries of scientific inquiry. Survey researchers often question the degree to which respondents display non-rational or irrational behaviour without pausing to reflect that they themselves may sometimes bring less than Cartesian rigour to the tasks at hand and that they too are subject to mental quirks. My subconscious had played a trick on me.

The data-processing method we used is also worth a comment. We are, you will recall, in the mid-1950s. I was then a member of the Canadian Institute of International Affairs, Kingston Branch, where I came to know an actuary employed by the Empire Life Insurance Company, the head office of which was in Kingston at the time. I told him what I was doing and that I had a formidable task of coping with the enormous quantities of collected data – they seemed enormous at the time. He informed me that a device at his office might help and was not used at night. He referred to a counter sorter, a contrivance of which I had heard nothing until then. He made it available to me, as well as his help. All of my data were formatted into the notorious eighty-column cards, and in the evenings and at night we did all of the tabulations in his office building. While, according to present-day standards, it took a very long time and I certainly would not recommend it to anyone now, there is an insight one gets from working in a literally hands-on relationship with the data. We could *see* and *feel* our responses. We did not have recourse to a statistical software package that we could just "plug in." Much thought had to be given to the analytical routines we applied. Again, one cannot and should not go back to these primitive forms, but I wonder whether there are not some ancient means of work that, even now, can be grafted onto the contemporary methodology to the benefit of more subtle insight. Immersion in the real thing, as language students know, can be most salutary.

The second step came a little later when I decided that I needed a Ph.D. I never made it to an American graduate school as planned, and just did a lot of research armed only with a master's degree. C.A. Curtis, the head of my department, called me in one day and asked when I was going to get my doctorate. I had started publishing a bit by then and said: "Never. I don't need a Ph.D." He accepted this as my choice but added that he would not recommend a salary increase or promotion for me until I was properly hooded. Sometime before this delicate encounter, I decided to undertake a country-wide election study and had already begun the fieldwork. I returned to LSE to write my projected book and, prodded by the Curtis ultimatum, also submitted it as my thesis. The result was *The Canadian General Election of 1957* (1962). It was modelled after the early Nuffield studies and, other than Gallup polls, used no survey data (McCallum, Buchanan, and Readman 1947; Butler 1952, 1969; Butler and Rose 1960).

So, deeply aware of this lacuna, I decided to put together *Papers on the 1962 Election* (1964), which would incorporate a variety of methodological approaches, including survey material.[3] This collection, which was the third step on the road to a proper countrywide survey, mobilized a group of scholars who together had a much broader perspective than is now found in election studies. Among those asked to write papers was Bob Alford, who, in fact, published the first election study based on Canadian public opinion surveys. His chapter reanalyzed data from the Canadian Institute for Public Opinion. Morris Davis was another contributor. He was doing fascinating work on the Halifax double-member constituencies and getting a lot of mileage out of that information. Léon Dion, Bill Irvine, Vincent Lemieux, George Perlin, Terry Qualter, Peter Regenstreif, Howard Scarrow, Mildred Schwartz, Dennis Smith, Norman Ward, Walter Young, and I were other authors – something of a smorgasbord. Nevertheless, it was a very interesting collection in terms of the variety of disciplines and approaches, including virtually every type of analysis anyone might have wanted to undertake at that time. But it lacked focus and strength, because it ignored some currently interesting theoretical issues of political behaviour. In that sense, it fell a little below the level of the other studies then coming out of the United States.

It was this recognition that convinced me that we really needed to conduct a countrywide survey, and this is what finally led to the 1965 initiative. It was essential, I believed, that the Canadian survey be done in a manner echoing some of the paths blazed by Angus Campbell, Philip Converse, Warren Miller, and Donald Stokes at the University of Michigan – then the platinum standard in electoral surveys – and that our work should provide material comparative with that generated by Ann Arbor and the various European studies following its general approach.[4] This led to the utilization of what were then the conventional methods of sample design and of interviewing.

At about this time, Peter Regenstreif was doing a good deal of electoral work, mostly on behalf of some newspapers and later for politicians. His approach, while highly imaginative, was considerably looser than that of the major American social scientists. He was inspired by Samuel Lubell's (1952) methods, as reported in *The Future of American Politics*. Peter had interviewed what I considered to have been rather idiosyncratically selected samples in the 1958, 1962, and 1963 elections. His analyses attracted a lot of attention in the popular press as well as on radio and television and led to the publication of *The Diefenbaker Interlude: Parties and Voting in Canada: An Interpretation* (1965). Much as I admired Peter's skill, intelligence, and articulateness, I did not think that his Lubell-inspired approach was suitable for a flagship Canadian electoral study. He was interested in undertaking one, and I thought that it might be better all around if his considerable skill was shared with a more or less conventional group of scholars. In the end, I decided to do what I could to bring together such a group – with his full and enthusiastic support.

Like most people, I am given to procrastination, sometimes gracing this Hamlet-like approach with the words "mature reflection." Had it not been for the perceived necessity of mounting a pre-emptive strike, so to speak, I might well have delayed applying for the needed funds in time for the 1965 election, and we might have had an entirely different kind of history of electoral research in Canada.

In assembling a research team, I was guided primarily by intellectual considerations, but the other usual criteria were not absent because, I believed, they often do affect the intellectual content of what one does. Although we had no formal ties of any sort to Michigan, it seemed to me essential that its experience and high standards should, if possible, be built into our efforts, without merely creating a Canadian clone. I had been involved with the Consortium for Political Research and knew all of the Michigan scholars very well. Phil Converse, who had done electoral research in France (with Georges Dupeux), seemed the ideal "Michigan partner." A Quebecer was essential, and Maurice Pinard was the obvious choice. Mildred Schwartz from Calgary gave us a Western dimension and a strongly focused interest in regional aspects of voting. The fact that she was a woman was, in those days, not of central importance, but it was a welcome enhancement. And Peter Regenstreif brought a lot of experience, enormous energy, and a link to an American university (Rochester) *other* than Michigan. However, as I mentioned, the most important factor around which we cohered was an intellectual compatibility. It was an intellectual, and not a political, imperative that brought us together.

The question of funding posed a major challenge. I applied to the Canada Council for $25,000, but it had never provided a grant as large as that before. I figured my survey would require approximately $50,000 or $60,000, even if it was executed with draconian parsimony. This sum was at the time astronomical in social science research. Although the present costs of surveys dwarf what we needed, the sum I sought then was close to unthinkable. My request for $25,000 caused a near crisis and much serious discussion in the council. Happily, my boss, J.A. Corry, was on the Canada Council, so I had some inkling of what was going on, despite his great discretion. It at first rejected the request, not only because of the money but also because opinion surveying was not seen by some members as a respectable academic activity. The entire Canada Council apparently had a couple of long debates in which this issue was discussed. Finally, by a narrow margin, they decided that it was appropriate to support surveys, and they gave us $25,000, which was, I believe, the largest single grant the council had made until then.

However, I still needed to raise another $25,000 or $35,000. Fortunately, the Barbeau Committee on Election Expenses had recently been created, with Khayyam Paltiel as its research director.[5] I went to Khayyam and said: "How would you like to know what people really think about these things? If you give me $10,000, I'll attach up to twelve questions to my national sample for you," and that is how we got another $10,000.[6] Luckily, our interests converged very nicely. I then approached a number of foundations and finally managed to obtain $5,000 from the Laidlaw Foundation. Again, Alec Corry was most helpful here. Phil Converse closed the gap when he produced $5,000 from the University of Michigan. By this time, we had $45,000, and Queen's University put up the rest in one form or another. To raise the needed funds from that many sources was a very time-consuming activity, since the successful sorties for money were also accompanied by many failed ones, of course. I suppose that things are easier now in some respects, except, as Richard Johnston and André Blais highlight in their chapter in this volume, there are significant challenges that still persist in securing resources for election studies, and you have to be much more rigorous in putting together an application. In the earlier days, there was probably less paperwork, less red tape, and certainly fewer deans and research administrators involved. The idea that one would have to meet certain ethical criteria in research, and satisfy the "watchdogs" enforcing them, had not occurred to a soul.

As for communicating with each other, the five of us were scattered all over the map. There were no fax machines or e-mail, of course, but we were able to make conference calls, and we met once or twice at a motel near what was then called Malton Airport in Toronto. We also used a quaint method of communicating called the mail. It worked perfectly well and promptly. Although we relied on the phone a good deal, it was possible and even easy to communicate by letter.

One of the questions you may have asked yourself, and one that I have certainly contemplated, is why it is that with all these surveys I have been .

involved in I have never really produced the all-embracing, definitive book? My feckless character and excessively Catholic interests no doubt best explain this lapse. I was interested in too many things and am something of an intellectual dilettante. I published papers, some of them unrelated to elections, gave them at conferences, and collected some of them in my *Working Papers on Canadian Politics* (1972, 1973, 1975). One major study – Mildred Schwartz's *Politics and Territory* (1974) – did come out of our survey, but Pinard did not do a book either on the areas in which he was most interested. Also, Phil Converse and I presented a methodological paper to a seminar at the University of Michigan, comparing French, Canadian, and American data. However, this was really Phil's piece, to which I contributed little.

Our little band of sleuths perhaps let the discipline down by not producing the kind of magisterial study for which we certainly had the necessary data. Our coming together was somewhat fortuitous and resulted in our lacking a strongly articulated, lean theoretical focus. As Mildred Schwartz details in the next chapter, we had several foci. In some respects, we were engaging in something of a fishing expedition, at least some of us were. Many fish were, of course, standard variables illuminating voting behaviour. It is well known, and attested to by the impressive list of references in Ronald Lambert's bibliography (1990), that there is a lot of very rich material in both the 1965 and my subsequent 1968 Canadian election survey. What does not leap at once to the eye is the central question, or core of questions, that animated them. The data we gathered and immediately made available to scholars everywhere via the Michigan and York data banks, the National Library, and other data banks provided fodder for a massive volume of secondary work and provided a baseline for innumerable future studies.[7] So although some important books and papers have been written on the basis of our data, it is on the whole fair to say that we have built a lot of cottages but not a cathedral.

Overall, I have no deep feelings of regret about the absence of a major book, but one consequence was most unfortunate. I suspect that the failure to obtain funding for a survey during the important 1972 election was in part caused by what was seen by some as an inadequate follow-up on the earlier fieldwork. Someday, I may say more about this part of our history, which is quite suggestive about Canadian academic politics and our sociology of knowledge, but for now I will leave sleeping dogs lie ...[8]

NOTES

1 The events of the Quiet Revolution during the 1960s and the subsequent rise of Quebec nationalist parties shortly thereafter exposed the limitations of the established parties to deal with linguistic and societal divides between anglophone and francophone Canada. The consequences are discussed at greater length in this volume in the chapters provided by Richard Nadeau and Éric Bélanger and Richard Johnston.

2 The cleavage conundrum kept occupying me, and in the early 1970s I published a short monograph on the topic. Although it dealt primarily with Canada, I first gave it at a meeting of the International Sociological Association in Bulgaria (see Meisel 1974).

3 This book had a cottage industry, informal air about it. To save costs, I had the pages typed in Kingston according to specifications supplied by the press. These pages were then photographed and reproduced in the book – a procedure that, at that time, was exceedingly rare. The cover – cutout silhouettes of the four party leaders – was designed and executed by my wife, Murie.

4 For a deeper understanding of this comparative literature, see the chapters provided by Mildred Schwartz and Lawrence LeDuc in this volume.

5 This committee was set up after the 1964 Speech from the Throne to examine the financing of federal elections in Canada. The committee's recommendations were largely incorporated into the 1974 *Election Expenses Act,* SC 1973-74, c 51, which heavily regulates the financing of elections.

6 See, for example, Meisel and van Loon (1966). Richard van Loon, then a doctoral student at Queen's University, was the principal research assistant and co-ordinator of the 1965 survey. His intellectual rigour and managerial skills contributed enormously to our efforts. He is an unsung hero of the early Canadian academic election surveys.

7 See, for instance, the reference list provided in the appendix of this volume.

8 A fuller, introspective note about the absence of a full-scale book is available in my memoirs, *A Life of Learning and Other Pleasures* (Stirling, ON: Wintergreen Studios Press, forthcoming 2012).

REFERENCES

Berelson, Bernard, Paul Lazarsfeld, and William McPhee. 1954. *Voting: A Study of Opinion Formation in a Presidential Campaign.* Chicago: University of Chicago Press.

Butler, David. 1952. *The British General Election of 1951.* London: Macmillan.

–. 1969. *The British General Election of 1955.* London: Cass.

Butler, David, and Richard Rose. 1960. *The British General Election of 1959.* London: Macmillan.

Campbell, Angus, Gerald Gurin, and Warren Miller. 1954. *The Voter Decides.* Evanston, IL: Row, Peterson and Company.

Campbell, Angus, Philip Converse, Warren Miller, and Donald Stokes. 1960. *The American Voter.* New York: Wiley.

Lambert, Ronald D. 1990. "Publications, Theses, Dissertations and Scholarly Papers Based on the 1965 and 1968 Canadian National Election Studies." Unpublished manuscript, Department of Sociology, University of Waterloo.

Lazarsfeld, Paul Felix, Bernard Berelson, and Hazel Gaudet. 1948. *The People's Choice: How the Voter Makes Up His Mind in a Presidential Campaign.* New York: Columbia University Press.

Lubell, Samuel. 1952. *The Future of American Politics.* New York: Harper.

McCallum, Ronald Buchanan, and Alison Violet Readman. 1947. *The British General Election of 1945.* London: G. Cumberlege.

Meisel, John. 1956. "Religious Affiliation and Electoral Behaviour." *Canadian Journal of Economics and Political Science* 22(4): 481-96.

–. 1962. *The Canadian General Election of 1957.* Toronto: University of Toronto Press.

–. 1964. *Papers on the 1962 Election: Fifteen Papers on the Canadian General Election of 1962.* Toronto: University of Toronto Press.

–. 1972. *Working Papers on Canadian Politics.* Montreal: McGill-Queen's University Press.

–. 1973. *Working Papers on Canadian Politics,* enlarged edition. Montreal: McGill-Queen's University Press.

–. 1974. *Cleavages, Parties and Value in Canada*: Sage Professional Papers in Contemporary Political Sociology, no. 06-003. London: Sage Publications.

–. 1975. *Working Papers on Canadian Politics,* 2nd enlarged edition. Montreal: McGill-Queen's University Press.

Meisel, John, and Richard van Loon. 1966. "Canadian Attitudes to Election Expenses 1965-1966." In Committee on Election Expenses, *Studies in Canadian Party Finance,* report (Ottawa: Queen's Printer).

Regenstreif, Peter. 1965. *The Diefenbaker Interlude: Parties and Voting in Canada; An Interpretation.* Toronto: Longmans Canada.

Schwartz, Mildred A. 1974. *Politics and Territory: The Sociology of Regional Persistence in Canada.* Montreal: McGill-Queen's University Press.

Siegfried, André. 1913. *Tableau politique de la France de l'Ouest sous la Troisième République.* Paris: A. Colin.

2

Theoretical Perspectives in the Canadian Election Studies

MILDRED A. SCHWARTZ

According to Arthur Stinchcombe (1968, 3), good theory consists of ideas with the capacity to create good explanations. Theory has scientific merit when it follows a logical argument for explaining empirical reality. It should then be subject to testing in order to determine whether it is effective in accounting for observed relations. I am convinced that it is important to make overt the theoretical assumptions that underlie empirical research. Theory affects what questions are asked, how data are gathered, and how findings are explained. By understanding theoretical assumptions, we can better understand the critical role of theory in advancing our understanding of the voting public. With this objective in mind, I begin with a review of how theory played a role in the first Canadian Election Study (CES).

Theoretical Underpinnings in the 1965 Election Study

In anticipation of the 1965 CES, I was invited to a meeting in Toronto along with four other people, all of whom I knew relatively well. We were Maurice Pinard of McGill University, Peter Regenstreif from the University of Rochester, John Meisel from Queen's University, Philip Converse from the University of Michigan, and myself, then at the National Opinion Research Center at the University of Chicago. As Meisel has already explained in Chapter 1, our experiences were varied. It is also important to note, however, that not all of us came from the same discipline, which meant that we had different expectations and theoretical motivations. What can be said about the theoretical underpinnings of the 1965 CES is that, for the most part, they were not overt and, to the extent that they were present, they were not clearly articulated. But if we think about the participants and their work up to this point, I believe we can discern a number of theoretical currents. All of them were represented, in a rather uneasy fashion, in the questionnaire we eventually jointly crafted.

As the representative from Michigan, Phil was promoting the funnel concept of causality.[1] At the large end of the funnel were social structural attributes, manifested, for example, in social class. These attributes influenced, at the narrow end, social psychological factors, primarily long-standing emotional attachments to parties and political attitudes mainly about political efficacy and government. The relations between structurally based characteristics and social psychological attitudes then predicted vote choice (Campbell et al. 1960). In other words, Phil brought us theories that were based on a social psychology that saw individual behaviour as the end result of emotional ties originating from group membership. Voters were otherwise politically uninformed and unable to articulate a coherent political philosophy (Converse 1964). To the Michigan researchers, survey research was the ideal instrument for obtaining information about politically relevant attitudes and behaviour.

John and Peter were focused on the election itself and on all of the contingent factors that led to particular electoral outcomes. In their past work, they had examined an election by paying attention to the campaign, the party platforms, the leadership, the role of the media, and the responses of voters (Meisel 1962, 1964; Regenstreif 1965). It was an approach that presumed that voters were interested in political events and able to be persuaded by proximate influences at the same time as they were anchored in a political milieu that provided some historical continuity. For them, survey research was a handle for understanding voters, but it could not substitute for all of the other activities that made up an election campaign. I have never discussed with them what theoretical orientation they brought with them, but I am prepared to surmise that it was one rooted in democratic theory. By that I mean it understood democracy as based on institutions that allowed free elections and offered choices to voters.

Maurice and I shared some similar perspectives, although his had been honed by participation in the exciting political milieu that characterized Quebec's Quiet Revolution. For both of us, the starting point was the social context in which political events and choices took place. This context was made up of both immediate events and past history, generating cultures and institutions that created societal strains and social cleavages. In contrast to Phil, whose sociology was shaped by a specialization in social psychology and oriented more toward the individual, Maurice and I put greater emphasis on social structure and on the constraints and opportunities that stemmed from structure. That is, we were closer to the Columbia school of voting studies that had led to stressing the importance of social cleavages.[2] For us, survey research was a useful instrument for measuring the outcomes of societal strains, and an election was a useful focal event that crystallized the social and political tensions of the time.

Beyond the affinities in sociological outlook that I shared with Maurice, I also came to our collaboration with a not yet fully articulated theory of regionalism. My view was that regions, though based on, or even simultaneously, provinces, are different – provinces are political units, whereas regions are sociological constructs. Regionalism arises from the interaction between economic conditions, demographic patterns, distributions of power, and cultural responses.[3] What I wanted from the survey were questions that would tap voters' perceptions of the territorial makeup of Canada, which I could then relate to the economic and political character of regions themselves. As mentioned at the start of this section, the final questionnaire in 1965 was a compromise between the competing interests of the five participants. The brief history provided in this section should help explain why we asked the questions we did and how we each understood what the responses to those questions could explain about Canadian politics.

Theoretical Assumptions in Later Studies

As outlined in the introductory chapter of this volume, the 1965 CES marked the beginning of a series of studies, yet it was almost totally atypical of what would follow. In 1965, three of the five investigators were not entirely anchored in political science; since that time, with the exception of the 1984 study, only political scientists have been involved. A prime mover in 1965 was an American academic with only a cursory knowledge of Canadian politics; since then only one American academic, Henry Brady, has been involved. The only book produced from the 1965 survey did not even have the election as its focus; subsequently, publications have been plentiful, and the majority of them have been focused on the election studied.[4]

Still, all of the Canadian election surveys share certain characteristics, and this is even true of the 1965 study. They are all premised on a conception of democratic governance based on popular elections held at regular intervals and offering clear choices through competitive parties. This conception of democracy rests on the participation of an informed electorate able to judge the past and/or promised performance of those individuals or parties vying for office. It anticipates that partisan policies and programs are responsive to political problems and accessible to citizen concerns. The primary purpose of these election studies has also been consistent – to determine how voters make decisions about whether or not to vote and whom to vote for.

In terms of theoretical assumptions and analytical approaches, I believe it is fair to say that all of the political scientists engaged in Canadian voting studies have generally contended with two primary competing models of voting behaviour. One, which some have called the "sociological approach," conceives of voters as being subject to long-term forces that serve to socialize them into their social roles, resulting in stable patterns of individual voting behaviour. In this model, change is introduced mainly through new cohorts of voters, and voters are less directly affected by political forces stemming from parties, leaders, campaigns, and issues than they are by the social milieus in which they live and the way in which those milieus mediate distinctly political stimuli. As I have already indicated by contrasting the perspectives that Phil, Maurice, and I brought to the 1965 study, there are, in effect, two variants of the sociological model, one stressing the social psychology of voting choice and the other stressing the social structural basis of divisions in the electorate.

The second model, which we can call the "political model," places greater weight on short-term factors such as current issues and the campaign efforts of political parties. It was virtually inevitable that, as political scientists delved deeper into voting behaviour, they would reject the first model, or at least give it much less prominence in their thinking and in their analysis, given the volatility characterizing the Canadian electorate. Antoine Bilodeau, Thomas Scotto, and Mebs Kanji actually demonstrate in the conclusion of this volume that this shift is indeed what has happened. Over the years, scholars using the CES have started paying progressively more attention to short-term factors.

Volatility in partisan choice at the individual level is evident not only from one election to another but also during a single election. The centrality of volatility first appears in the studies of the 1974, 1979, and 1980 elections, initiated by Harold Clarke, Jane Jenson, Lawrence LeDuc, and Jon Pammett (Clarke et al. 1979; 1991). They attribute voters' fragile attachments to partisan choices to the weakness of the Canadian party system in not providing clear alternative positions on issues. Instead, most issues that come to voters' attention are valence issues, where the parties agree on the import- ance of issues and voters are left to judge which party would be most com- petent in handling them (Clarke et al. 1991, 122), an approach that leans on a theoretical perspective developed by Donald Stokes (Butler and Stokes 1969; Stokes 1992). At the same time, the Clarke team did not totally reject the importance of long-term factors any more than Stokes did, but, of those factors, it was religion and region that were important and not, as in the United States or especially Britain, class (Clarke et al. 1979, 372). Clarke and Allan Kornberg's piece in this volume reiterates the importance of valence issues and adds to it the significance of leader images and flexible partisan attachments to account for voter choices.

When Ronald Lambert and his colleagues at the University of Waterloo directed the 1984 study, they turned for theoretical inspiration to social and cognitive psychology. The Lambert team drew a relation between long- and short-term influences by viewing behaviour as rooted in beliefs and as- sumptions affected by the long-term impact of education and the more im- mediate impact of the media (Lambert et al. 1988). For example, when voters are asked to evaluate political leaders, they do so through schematic thinking – that is, they evaluate new stimuli by calling on knowledge and frameworks developed from past experience. This process means that vot- ers can use schema for judging leaders, including new ones, separately from partisanship or self-interest (Brown et al. 1988). In this respect, the Waterloo group appeared less concerned with election dynamics per se than those researchers either preceding or following them. They maintained, instead, a disciplinary and theoretical bias that favoured psychological processes of decision making, and they then applied them to the electoral setting. This group was also interested in exploring the effects of social class, but as Barry Kay and Andrea Perrella demonstrate in their chapter in this volume, the payoffs with this line of investigation in the Canadian case have been rela- tively modest.

The volatility of the Canadian electorate was once again the central focus in 1988. Richard Johnston, the principal investigator of this study along with André Blais, Henry Brady, and Jean Crête, has told me that in the mid-1980s he had become disillusioned with the sociological model because of its em- phasis on the stability of voters' choices. He was reinforced in his thinking by what he saw commercial polling agencies doing to take account of campaign events. As a result of the heated debate over the Free Trade Agreement and the Liberal party now under the leadership of John Turner, the 1988 election proved to be a critical time for testing his views (Johnston et al. 1992).

The 1988 CES demonstrates with particular clarity how methods are intrinsically linked with theoretical underpinnings. It was this study, as identified in the Introduction and Chapter 4 of this volume, that introduced the rolling cross-sectional method of sample selection and adopted computer-assisted telephone interviewing as a means to quickly obtain and process responses. Both of these innovations in data collection enabled Johnston and his colleagues to design a study that could directly test the impact of the campaign as it was underway (Johnston 2001; Johnston and Brady 2002).

These methodological innovations continued in the studies centred in Montreal, where they were the responsibility of André Blais, Elisabeth Gidengil, Neil Nevitte, and Richard Nadeau in 1997 and 2000. Beginning in 2004, the Montreal team gained Joanna Everitt and Patrick Fournier and lost Nadeau. This team has produced a rich literature that includes a variety of books and numerous published and unpublished articles (Nevitte et al. 2000; Blais et al. 2002; Gidengil et al. 2004). These most recent studies have also had the advantage of working with data that have been accumulated since 1965 and a literature that reveals the myriad possibilities for analyzing election studies.

The result of this accumulated experience is an approach that currently pays attention to a number of theoretical concerns. Most basically, the Montreal team members have reaffirmed a commitment to understanding democratic theory from the perspective of competitive elections and the choice by voters whether or not to participate and, if participating, how to do so. Beyond this overarching theory, they have relied on theories drawn from sociology, psychology, economics, and political science (in the case of political science, often through a reworking of theories adapted from those other disciplines), to explore why voters choose as they do. In their analysis, long-term factors such as regionalism remain important (Gidengil et al. 1999), while age and gender introduce dynamic qualities that are associated with cultural shifts (Blais et al. 2004; Gidengil et al. 2006). Also important are short-term factors associated with particular elections, such as the leadership debate in 2000 (Blais et al. 2003) or the "Liberal sponsorship" scandal in 2004 (Blais et al. 2005). At the same time, the Montreal team has been open to testing the Canadian experience against that of other democratic societies – for example, in party identification (Blais et al. 2001a) or in finding the best model for predicting partisan choice (Blais et al. 2001b).

Using the activities of the Montreal team as a reference point leads to an appreciation of the full range of accomplishments from the CES over the past four decades. However, at this juncture, I believe it is appropriate to discuss how much it matters that the debates between the political science and sociology theories on voting and behaviour remain unresolved. What many, and especially recent, analysts have found is a place for both, along with room for contributions from psychology and economics. As positive as I feel about much that has already been done, I also feel that there is still more to be learned from a greater self-consciousness about theoretical assumptions.

Some Sources of Theories for Election Studies

Since the principal investigators of recent Canadian election surveys have all been housed in political science departments, and since those investigators have become increasingly skilled in what they do, I believe it is now, more than ever, worthwhile to look outside the field of political science for new ideas that could be applied to election studies. Before suggesting psychology as a possible source of stimulation for students of elections, I begin, not surprisingly, by revisiting sociology. I want to urge election researchers to take another look at social cleavages because they are such a fundamental way of viewing individual voters, not as disaggregated units but, rather, as individuals anchored in their social milieus. There are, to be sure, valid criticisms of past research by those who saw the decline of social cleavages, particularly those tied to class, and to their apparent replacement by the rise of the "postmodern" voter, who is more concerned with issues of lifestyle. More recent work, however, has reinvigorated the importance of social cleavages, presented most convincingly by Jeff Manza and Clement Brooks (1999). They do so by locating cleavages within the context of social changes. That is, they recognize that there is fluidity to social existence that makes it important to examine how cleavages are translated into partisan choices by a variety of mechanisms and processes. Mechanisms that are the root of cleavages include economic interests and social-psychological factors that lead to group consciousness and social networks. Processes are grounded in social structure; group identification and conflict; the actions of organized interests, political parties, and social movements; and the feedback that comes from policies (Manza, Brooks, and Sauder 2005, 206-8). This more comprehensive way of viewing the dynamics through which social cleavages are formed and become politically salient leads away from a static view toward one that recognizes the possibility that some cleavages can decline in importance, such as social class, while others can emerge as major divisions, as is true today of religion and gender in the United States.

In the chapter that he has written for this volume, Johnston gives us a brilliant analysis of how the dynamism of social cleavages in Canada is related to the changing nature of the party system. By using the accumulation of data on demographic variables as indicators of social structure, he is able to capture what remains the same and what has changed in Canada's political life.[5] While, at the simplest level, demographic data are a way of tapping into the potential for cleavage formation, they are not likely to be sufficient if we want to more fully understand how cleavages take shape and affect political behaviour. To do so, we then need more information, for example, about social networks, the homogeneity of social milieus, the importance attached to group ties, and relations with organized groups.[6] Gidengil's chapter in this volume also makes an argument that is along similar lines.

Additional insight could come from new ways of sampling and collecting data. Each election provides its own context (Katz and Warshel 2001, 6-7; Curtice 2002, 8;). Some of the election context can be captured through the survey instrument in questions about issues, leaders, and parties. Yet it also requires independent data collection about those latter features as they appear in each election.[7] Treating elections in this way is a strategy that becomes increasingly attractive as we accumulate more election studies.

Context also means the institutional and structural characteristics of the time, both as they remain stable and as they change. For example, there may not be much variation across Canada today in electoral arrangements, but there are gross differences in industrial makeup, overall wealth, economic opportunities, population growth and composition, and governing parties, among others. While we may analyze survey results to partition out the presumed effects of regionalism on political dispositions, we are still left with a different kind of contextual effect. It is one that stems from the actual differences associated with the social, economic, and political institutions present, independently of how they may be perceived by voters. Just how those differences should be incorporated into electoral research is a matter worth debating.

There is much more that sociology still has to offer to election studies, but I will comment on only one additional possibility. It stems from what has been called the "cultural turn" in sociology. It is not my intention to survey this development, which, in its extreme form, rejects much of what electoral research considers a fundamental part of the social scientific enterprise, or even to review its impact on political sociology (see Hicks, Janoski, and Schwartz 2005, 7-11). I want to proceed more selectively, taking from the new cultural studies some themes and ideas that have the potential for enriching our understanding of elections as they have been developed in an essay by James Jasper (2005).

Most generally, culture is a perspective on the political world that, along with history and community, emphasizes the particularities of human experience. To fully understand political behaviour, we need to know the meanings that people attach to their actions. If we assume that "cultural meanings channel political action and aspirations" (Jasper 2005, 130), we can find those meanings in shifting narratives, symbols, identities, and emotional attachments that provide what Ann Swidler (1986, 273) calls a toolkit of strategies for coping with problems. While culture in this sense is a characteristic of a social unit, whether a nation, organization, family, or friendship group, it is neither static nor uniform to all of its individual carriers.

If culture operates at the individual and collective level, where it gives meaning to events by first affecting choices made and then justifying them, how can this be made relevant to election studies? Would the exponents of the cultural turn in sociology be satisfied with studies of civic culture, such as the one by Gabriel Almond and Sidney Verba (1963)?[8] Or would they find the argument for postmodern values in Ronald Inglehart's (1977, 1997) work an affirmation of their perspective? The new culturalists would answer "no" because they find such studies too static, excessively based on an individualistic perspective, and not attuned to the multiple cultures present in any society (Sewell 1999). However, that aside, we know that culture, broadly defined, is important to an understanding of politics, and it remains up to us to find ways of incorporating cultural thinking into our analyses. For example, those interested in media effects on voters should be exploring how to capture the emotional and informational aspects of media messages as they are differentially assimilated into the action frames of voters.

The place of culture as a tool for interpreting elections relates directly to another issue, one more closely associated with psychology and behavioural economics. It is an issue that arises whenever we ask respondents their opinions because, each time we do so, we make assumptions about how they reason, what they remember, and the candour of their responses. One approach to how voters reason, which is especially strong in US political science as popularized by Anthony Downs (1957), is a reliance on rational choice models. Rationality assumes that individuals will vote for the party that provides the most benefits. In a sense, all political scientists who consider voting the primary democratic process for linking citizens with institutions of the state assume some level of rational reasoning, in which past events, personal circumstances, and information about possible choices are weighed in making decisions.[9] Such assumptions also underlie the conceptual connection between the act of voting and the vitality of democracy (Gidengil et al. 2004). But even to the extent that voting choices are rational decisions, we should not be satisfied to end there. There are still unanswered questions about the meaning that voting has for citizens themselves and the stability of the opinions they express in supporting their choices. Here we can look to psychology for further insights.

Contemporary psychology's concern with decision making distinguishes between two kinds of cognitive processes. In System 1, operations are "fast, automatic, effortless, associative, and often emotionally charged: They are also governed by habit, and are therefore difficult to control or modify. The operations of System 2 are slower, serial, effortful, and deliberately controlled; they are also relatively flexible, and potentially rule-governed" (Kahneman 2007). System 2's thinking best resembles the assumptions of rational choice theory. However, that is not the entire extent of this matter. There are also other reasons to suppose that problem solving uses both intuition and reasoning, with the first being more prominent. In addition, emotion plays a central role in intuition. Furthermore, Eldar Shafir (2007, 348) points out how much of choice behaviour is affected by the local context, and, since context is changeable, how it alters the cues that affect choices: "As a result of this malleability, our decisions often violate the most basic consistency requirements, including the requirement of independence of irrelevant alternatives, and of independence from irrelevant descriptive or procedural nuances." In other words, staying exclusively with a consistent and rational perspective on voting misses the true complexity of how thinking takes place.

Just as this cognitive psychology has come to influence behavioural economics, it deserves equal attention in election studies. I see lessons to be drawn that will affect virtually everything we do when we construct a questionnaire, from the wording of questions, the order with which they are presented, and the conclusions we draw about the selection of preferences. It also affects how we construct and interpret scales. Obviously, the potential of cognitive psychology is an enormous topic and one that I cannot do justice to here. But, at the least, I want to join those who remind us that asking voters about their opinions and behaviour is not a straightforward exercise in obtaining information (Sirken et al. 1999)

Although I have long felt at home in political science, and many people, especially in Canada, identify me as a political scientist, it is sociology that provides my theoretical base. This fact makes it easy for me to encourage looking beyond political science for theoretical insights that can enrich election studies. In particular, sociology emphasizes the importance of social structure and of context in general. However, we should not stop there. Sociology and psychology, in different ways, push us to examine the meanings we attribute to voters' responses. The former urges a more comprehensive view of culture, while the latter ensures a more nuanced conception of decision making that recognizes the dominant role of intuition and emotion. Staying alert to theoretical developments in the social sciences, regardless of disciplinary boundaries, is one way that future election studies will remain a rich and reliable source for understanding the Canadian electorate.

NOTES

1 See Lawrence LeDuc's chapter in this volume for more on the University of Michigan approach to the study of voting behaviour.

2 See LeDuc's chapter in this volume for more on the Columbia school's approach to the study of voting.

3 Some of this theory became elaborated in later publications (see, for example, Schwartz 1974). For a summary, see my introduction to a volume edited by Lisa Young and Keith Archer that grew from a 1999 conference to re-examine the contributions of that book (Schwartz 2002, viii-xi).

4 These generalizations apply to studies done from 1974 onward. Canadian Market Opinion Research is listed as the principal investigator for the 1972 study, and I am not aware of who was involved or what was done with the results.

5 Despite Richard Johnston's criticism of the sociological model, cited earlier, he in fact demonstrates a deep appreciation of how social structures operate. This is evident from his paper on the persistence of the religious cleavage in Canadian politics (Johnston 1985), a theme recently elaborated by Paul Bélanger and Munroe Eagles (2006).

6 For example, Amanda Bittner (2007) shows how political information has different effects on social groups.

7 At the same time, Cees van der Eijk (2002) cautions us against over-burdening election studies.

8 In the face of earlier criticism, both Gabriel Almond and Sidney Verba defend the 1963 publication on the grounds that they were constrained by the methods and

thinking of the time. Almond (1989, 16) argues that the rational-activist model of citizenship presented was only one part of what is needed to sustain a democracy, while political culture is treated as both a cause and effect of political structure (ibid., 29). Contemporary cultural sociologists would still object that culture cannot be captured solely, or even primarily, through individual attitudes.

9 It is interesting that a review of rational choice thinking in sociology ignores voting "because we believe the small costs and benefits associated with voting make it beyond the scope of rational choice theory" (Kiser and Bauldry 2005, 174).

REFERENCES

Almond, Gabriel A. 1989. "The Intellectual History of the Civic Culture Concept." In Gabriel A. Almond and Sidney Verba, eds., *The Civic Culture Revisited*, 1-36. Newbury Park, CA: Sage Publications.

Almond, Gabriel A., and Sidney Verba. 1963. *The Civic Culture: Political Attitudes and Democracy in Five Nations.* Princeton, NJ: Princeton University Press.

Bélanger, Paul, and Munroe Eagles. 2006. "The Geography of Class and Religion in Canadian Elections Revisited." *Canadian Journal of Political Science* 39: 591-609.

Bittner, Amanda. 2007. "The Effects of Information and Social Cleavages: Explaining Issue Attitudes and Vote Choice in Canada." *Canadian Journal of Political Science* 40: 935-68.

Blais, André, Joanna Everitt, Patrick Fournier, Elisabeth Gidengil, and Neil Nevitte. 2005. "The Political Psychology of Voters' Reactions to a Corruption Scandal." Paper presented to the Annual Meeting of the American Political Science Association, Washington, DC.

Blais, André, Elisabeth Gidengil, Richard Nadeau, and Neil Nevitte. 2001a. "Measuring Party Identification: Britain, Canada, and the United States. *Political Behavior* 23: 5-22.

–. 2001b. "The Formation of Party Preferences: Testing the Proximity and Directional Models." *European Journal of Political Research* 40: 81-91.

–. 2002. *Anatomy of a Liberal Victory: Making Sense of the Vote in the 2000 Canadian Election.* Peterborough, ON: Broadview Press.

–. 2003. "Campaign Dynamics in the 2000 Canadian Election: How the Leader Debates Salvaged the Conservative Party." *PS: Political Science and Politics* 36: 45-50.

–. 2004. "Where Does Turnout Decline Come From?" *European Journal of Political Research* 43(2): 221-36.

Brown, Steven D., Ronald D. Lambert, Barry J. Kay, and James E. Curtis. 1988. "In the Eye of the Beholder: Leader Images in Canada." *Canadian Journal of Political Science* 21: 729-55.

Butler, D., and D. Stokes. 1969. *Political Change in Britain.* London: Macmillan.

Campbell, Angus, Philip E. Converse, Warren E. Miller, and Donald E. Stokes. 1960. *The American Voter.* New York: Wiley.

Clarke, Harold D., Jane Jenson, Lawrence LeDuc, and Jon H. Pammett. 1979. *Political Choice in Canada.* Toronto: McGraw-Hill Ryerson.

–. 1991. *Absent Mandate: Interpreting Change in Canadian Elections*, 2nd edition. Toronto: Gage Education Publishing Company.

Converse, Philip E. 1964. "The Nature of Belief Systems in Mass Publics." In David A. Apter, ed., *Ideology and Discontent*, 75-169. New York: Free Press.

Curtice, John. 2002. "The State of Election Studies: Mid-life Crisis or New Youth?" In Mark N. Franklin and Christopher Wlezien, eds., *The Future of Election Studies*, 5-12. Amsterdam: Pergamon.

Downs, Anthony. 1957. *An Economic Theory of Democracy*. New York: Harper and Row.

Gidengil, Elisabeth. 2004. *Citizens*. Vancouver: UBC Press.

Gidengil, Elisabeth, André Blais, Neil Nevitte, and Richard Nadeau. 1999. "Making Sense of Regional Voting in the 1997 Federal Election: Liberal and Reform Support Outside Quebec." *Canadian Journal of Political Science* 32: 247-72.

Gidengil, Elisabeth, Joanna Everitt, André Blais, Patrick Fournier, and Neil Nevitte. 2006. "Gender and Vote Choice in the 2006 Canadian Election." Paper presented to the Annual Meeting of the American Political Science Association, Philadelphia, PA.

Hicks, Alexander, Thomas Janoski, and Mildred A. Schwartz. 2005. "Introduction: Political Sociology in the New Millennium." In Thomas Janoski, Robert Alford, Alexander Hicks, and Mildred A. Schwartz, eds., *The Handbook of Political Sociology: States, Civil Societies, and Globalization*, 1-30. New York: Cambridge University Press.

Inglehart, Ronald. 1977. *The Silent Revolution: Changing Values and Political Styles among Western Publics*. Princeton, NJ: Princeton University Press.

–. 1997. *Modernization and Post-Modernization: Cultural, Economic, and Political Change in Forty-Three Societies*. Princeton, NJ: Princeton University Press.

Jasper, James M. 2005. "Culture, Knowledge, Politics." In Thomas Janoski, Robert Alford, Alexander Hicks, and Mildred A. Schwartz, eds., *The Handbook of Political Sociology: States, Civil Societies, and Globalization*, 115-34. New York: Cambridge University Press.

Johnston, Richard. 1985. "The Reproduction of the Religious Cleavage in Canadian Elections." *Canadian Journal of Political Science* 18: 99-113.

–. 2001. "Capturing Campaigns in National Election Studies." In Elihu Katz and Yael Warshel, eds., *Election Studies: What's Their Use?* 149-72. Boulder, CO: Westview Press.

Johnston, Richard, André Blais, Henry Brady, and Jean Crête. 1992. *Letting the People Decide: Dynamics of a Canadian Election*. Stanford, CA: Stanford University Press.

Johnston, Richard, and Henry Brady. 2002. "The Rolling Cross-Section Design." In Mark N. Franklin and Christopher Wlezien, eds., *The Future of Election Studies*, 123-35. Amsterdam: Pergamon.

Kahneman, Daniel. 2007. "Maps of Bounded Rationality: Psychology for Behavioral Economics" [unpublished paper; on file with author].

Katz, Elihu, and Yael Warshel. 2001. "Introduction." In Elihu Katz and Yael Warshel, eds., *Election Studies: What's Their Use?* 1-14. Boulder, CO: Westview Press.

Kiser, Edgar, and Shawn Bauldry. 2005. "Rational-Choice Theories in Political Sociology." In Thomas Janoski, Robert Alford, Alexander Hicks, and Mildred A. Schwartz, eds., *The Handbook of Political Sociology: States, Civil Societies, and Globalization*, 172-86. New York: Cambridge University Press.

Lambert, Ronald D., James E. Curtis, Barry J. Kay, and Steven D. Brown. 1988. "The Social Sources of Political Knowledge." *Canadian Journal of Political Science* 21: 359-74.

Manza, Jeff, and Clement Brooks. 1999. *Social Cleavages and Political Change: Voter Alignments and US Party Coalitions*. New York: Oxford University Press.

Manza, Jeff, Clement Brooks, and Michael Sauder. 2005. "Money, Participation, and Votes: Social Cleavages and Electoral Politics." In Thomas Janoski, Robert Alford, Alexander Hicks, and Mildred A. Schwartz, eds., *The Handbook of Political Sociology: States, Civil Societies, and Globalization*, 201-26. New York: Cambridge University Press.

Meisel, John. 1962. *The Canadian General Election of 1957*. Toronto: University of Toronto Press.

—. 1964. *Papers on the 1962 Election: Fifteen Papers on the Canadian General Election of 1962*. Toronto: University of Toronto Press.

Nevitte, Neil, André Blais, Elisabeth Gidengil, and Richard Nadeau. 2000. *Unsteady State: The 1997 Canadian Federal Election*. Don Mills, ON: Oxford University Press.

Regenstreif, Peter. 1965. *The Diefenbaker Interlude: Parties and Voting in Canada; An Interpretation*. Toronto: Longman's Canada.

Schwartz, Mildred A. 1974. *Politics and Territory: The Sociology of Regional Persistence in Canada*. Montreal: McGill-Queen's University Press.

—. 2002. "Forward: Revisiting Regionalism and Political Parties." In Lisa Young and Keith Archer, eds., *Regionalism and Political Parties*, vii-xiii. Toronto: Oxford University Press.

Sewell, William H., Jr. 1999. "The Concept(s) of Culture." In Victoria E. Bonnell and Lynn Hunt, eds., *Beyond the Cultural Turn: New Directions in the Study of Society and Culture*, 35-61. Berkeley, CA: University of California Press.

Shafir, Eldar. 2007. "Decisions Constructed Locally: Some Fundamental Principles of the Psychology of Decision Making." In A.W. Kruglenski and E.T. Higgins, eds., *Social Psychology: A Handbook of Basic Principles*, 2nd edition, 334-53. New York: Guilford Press.

Sirken, Munroe G., Douglas J. Herrmann, Susan Schechter, Norbert Schwartz, Judith Tanur, and Roger Tourangeau, eds. 1999. *Cognition and Survey Research*. New York: Wiley.

Stinchcombe, Arthur L. 1968. *Constructing Social Theories*. Chicago: University of Chicago Press.

Stokes, Donald. 1992. "Valence Politics." In D. Kavanaugh, ed., *Electoral Politics*, 141-64. Oxford: Clarendon Press.

Swidler, Ann. 1986. "Culture in Action: Symbols and Strategies." *American Sociological Review* 51: 273-86.

Van der Eijk, Cees. 2002. "Design Issues in Electoral Research: Taking Care of (Core) Business." In Mark N. Franklin and Christopher Wlezien, eds., *The Future of Election Studies*, 33-49. Amsterdam: Pergamon.

To Ann Arbor ... and Back
A Comparative Perspective on Election Studies

LAWRENCE LEDUC

Electoral research has become one of the most thoroughly comparative and highly internationalized subfields of political science. Scholars in this area come from an increasingly large number of countries, and they have for years been reading the same literature, employing the same theoretical models, and exchanging data through international archives such as the Inter-University Consortium for Political Research. How did the field develop as a comparative enterprise rather than merely as a collection of national studies, and how has Canadian scholarship in the field been affected by the research traditions growing out of work in the United States, Western Europe, and elsewhere?

To be sure, the work of Angus Campbell, Philip Converse, Warren Miller, and Donald Stokes (1960); Campbell, Gerald Gurin, and Miller (1954); and Bernard Berelson, Paul Lazarsfeld, and William McPhee (1954) has shaped the future of American election studies for years to come. It also has extended their influence to early studies in other countries, sometimes directly through collaboration and replication and, as Mildred Schwartz discusses in Chapter 2, sometimes indirectly by means of conceptual and theoretical influences. Based on surveys conducted during the 1952 and 1956 US presidential elections, Campbell et al.'s publication *The American Voter* (1960) quickly became the key book that had to be read by all researchers in the field, and the "Michigan model" generated hypotheses capable of being tested in a variety of different electoral environments. However, even in this early period, the comparative character of the field was becoming well established.

Before the publication of *The American Voter*, important studies had been conducted in Sweden by Bo Särlvik in 1956, in Norway by Stein Rokkan and Henry Valen in 1957, and in France by Georges Dupeux in 1958. Along with early German studies conducted by Erich Reigrotzki in 1953 and by Rudolf Wildemann and his colleagues in 1961, these provided a strong basis for the development of European research traditions well before the influences of the American work began to be felt.[1]

In an analysis of the 1957 Norwegian data by Rokkan, published in the seminal volume *Party Systems and Voter Alignments* (Lipset and Rokkan 1967), the Ann Arbor work is not cited. A companion article by Juan Linz in the same volume, which utilizes Reigrotzki's 1953 German data, also contains little in the way of American concepts, models, or comparisons. In this important anthology of primarily European work of the late 1950s and early 1960s, the core concept of "cleavage structures" provides the dominant theoretical framework. The social-psychological concepts more prominently associated with the Ann Arbor traditions are nowhere to be found.

It is also worthwhile to note that comparative research interests in almost every instance developed in tandem with national ones. Generally, this development came about in one of three ways – through publication, collaboration, or exchange. The simplest and most widespread of these was publication, in that most practitioners in the field read and were influenced by the same literatures. As noted earlier, a researcher in this field in the early 1960s would certainly have read *The American Voter* and could not fail to have been influenced by the theoretical model of voting behaviour that it advanced or by the methodological debates taking place in the United States. It was only a matter of time, therefore, before work in other countries would begin to reflect some of the social-psychological concerns associated with the Michigan model and before some of the methodological issues arising from it became cross-national.

The flow of communication, however, was not only one-way. The Scandinavians, in particular, wrote extensively in English, and by the mid-1960s a North American student of electoral behaviour would certainly have encountered the work of scholars such as Rokkan, Valen, or Erik Allardt, to mention only a few of the European researchers whose work was well known on this side of the Atlantic at that time.[2]

Alongside this growing literature, comparative research was fostered through collaboration and exchange. Scholars associated with the US-based studies formed relationships with European researchers for the purpose of developing comparative analytical frameworks and exchanging data. Converse's collaboration with Dupeux, for example, produced articles (first published in 1962) comparing partisan attachments in France and the United States as well as the appeal of Eisenhower and de Gaulle as political leaders. Daniel Katz collaborated with Valen on a study of *Political Parties in Norway*, bringing together the Ann Arbor and Bergen traditions in a single project (Valen and Katz 1964). At almost the same time, Stokes began his collaboration with David Butler on the 1963 British pre-election study, linking up the Michigan model of voting research with the non-survey-based Nuffield studies of British elections, which extended back as far as 1945. *Elections and the Political Order*, published in 1966, reflects both the diversity of the research of this period and the blending of these different traditions (Campbell et al. 1966).

The early 1960s also saw the publication of several major comparative projects, organized and financed mainly in the United States. Seymour Martin Lipset (1960) drew upon a diverse array of European and US surveys for his *Political Man*, published at the same time as *The American Voter* in 1960. Robert Alford (1963) utilized a twenty-year pool of public opinion poll data from the 1940s and 1950s to compare class voting in the United States, Britain, Canada, and Australia in *Party and Society*. Gabriel Almond and Sidney Verba (1963) mounted *The Civic Culture* surveys, which, although not specifically oriented toward elections, utilized a common survey instrument to collect data from the United States, Britain, Germany, Italy, and Mexico in 1959-60. Similarly, Hadley Cantril (1965) collected data from fourteen nations between 1957 and 1963 for his work *The Pattern of Human Concerns*.

The point here is to establish that in the development of survey-based electoral research dating back a half-century or more from the present, American models and data did not necessarily set the standard for comparative work. The Scandinavian and German research traditions, in particular, were largely indigenous, and the research centres at the universities of Bergen or Cologne were as important and influential in fostering comparative research as was the University of Michigan in Ann Arbor. Indeed, the concept of "frozen cleavages" advanced by Lipset and Rokkan (1967) had at least as much theoretical currency and staying power in the field as anything associated with the Michigan school. Consequently, by the time that the first Canadian Election Study (CES) was conducted in 1965, the field had already acquired a broadly comparative flavour and focus. Yet in spite of the fact that survey research was rapidly becoming a comparative enterprise, only a handful of studies of national elections outside the United States had yet been conducted. By the mid-1960s, the American studies were well known – the French, German, and Scandinavian ones somewhat less so. There was still plenty of room for pioneers.

The 1965 CES

Through the work of John Meisel and his colleagues, Canada joined this small group of countries conducting full-scale election surveys in 1965. Both Meisel's and Schwartz's chapters in this volume document how Canadian electoral research in this period likewise represented a blending of home grown and imported intellectual interests. However, there is more to the story. Voting studies in Canada did not just begin in 1965 with the arrival of an expeditionary force from Ann Arbor. The first survey-based study conducted in 1965 also was strongly influenced by the work that had been done in other countries, which had coincided with the period when comparative electoral research was beginning to flower, and the CES was also a significant part of that flowering. In fact, within three years, there would also be new studies in Japan (1967), the Netherlands (1967), and Italy (1968). Research in Britain (1964 and 1966), France (1967), Germany (1965), Norway (1965), and Sweden (1964 and 1968) also continued to evolve, sustained or nurtured in many of these instances by Ann Arbor connections.

What did these various pioneering studies have in common, aside from the fact that they were all studies of national elections employing the developing methodology of survey research? There was a surprising amount of common ground. Like the Canadian co-investigators, European researchers were predominantly interested in questions of political sociology and demography – the role of social class, religion, ethnicity, or regionalism in national politics, for example. Whether approached from the perspective of Rokkan's "cleavage structures" or of Converse's "reference groups," the scholars of this period studied many of the same political and social phenomena from slightly different theoretical perspectives. A model of individual voting behaviour in which vote or partisanship was the dependent variable, and class, religion, or ethnicity the independent variables, provided plausible explanations for the observed patterns of political stability and was not inconsistent with changes driven by demography.

American scholars tended to look at these variables in psychological as well as sociological terms and sought to uncover their connection to concepts such as party identification or party images.[3] In a survey of work on

Canadian voting behaviour utilizing the 1965 data, Schwartz (1974) examines the impact of variables such as region, ethnicity, religion, occupation, and education in attempting to better understand the effects of "social structure." She notes that relatively little work had been done on "social-psychological influences" such as partisan attachment or the perception of party differences (ibid.).[4] At the time that Meisel conducted the next survey in 1968, however, the interest of Canadian researchers was already turning toward some of these psychological variables, particularly those that had been prominent in the US studies. Suggesting that the concept of party identification might be of little value in Canada and directing the attention of scholars in the field toward party image variables, Meisel (1972) set a direction for future Canadian research as well as for some of the comparative inquiries that would follow.

The Next Decade

It is of course somewhat arbitrary to divide comparative electoral research into decades. Yet such a division corresponds quite accurately to major developments in the field. Following the pioneering studies of the 1960s, the research trends in Canada in each of the next two decades were likewise influenced by the work done in other countries and by the publication of that work in one or more important books that were widely read by scholars all over the world. Whenever a major study in one country broke important new theoretical or methodological ground, the effects were soon evidenced among researchers elsewhere.

The second CES in 1968 was only one of a rapidly growing number of election studies conducted in the late 1960s and early 1970s. To the list of countries noted earlier were added others such as Australia (1969), Israel (1969), Denmark (1971 and 1973), Austria (1969 and 1972), and Switzerland (1972). Perhaps more important than the increasing number of such studies, however, was their growing theoretical and methodological sophistication. Many of these studies had an explicitly comparative research agenda inspired at least in part by the Ann Arbor work or by the large comparative projects such as Almond and Verba's *The Civic Culture* (1963). The work of Samuel Barnes in Italy, Donald Aitkin in Australia, or Asher Arian in Israel, for example, applied concepts and measures that had become widely accepted elsewhere (see Arian 1974; Aitkin 1977; and Barnes 1977). Replication of research designs facilitated comparative work, and the application of common theoretical concepts and measures gave electoral research a theoretical coherence that would otherwise have been difficult or impossible to obtain in single national studies.

If Campbell et al.'s *The American Voter* (1960) represented the key book of the 1960s, then in many ways Butler and Stokes's *Political Change in Britain* (1969) did so for the 1970s. First published in 1969, *Political Change in Britain* refined and extended the Michigan model but, at the same time, introduced new ideas, theoretical concepts, and methodologies. Utilizing data from panel studies spanning the 1964 and 1966 British elections, Butler and Stokes explored the forces of stability and change in British politics both in these two elections and over much longer periods of time.[5] Some concepts such as party identification or class voting were familiar ones. But Butler and Stokes gave them a different twist in attempting to explain factors such as "the decline of working class Conservatism" or "the aging of the class alignment" (ibid.). This marriage of demographics and survey data provided researchers in Britain and elsewhere with new tools and concepts and with a greatly expanded agenda for their research. Soon, scholars in Canada and other countries would also be writing about age cohorts, social mobility, and the impact of generational change. Subsequent election studies in a number of other countries would be based on a panel design similar to the British one, including those in Germany (1967/69), the Netherlands (1970/73), Denmark (1970/73), the United States (1972/76), and Canada (1974/79).[6] Although a panel design had been employed in one of the earlier Michigan studies (1956/60) and in a few other countries at around the same time as the British studies, notably Norway (1965/69) and Sweden (1964/70), it was not until after the publication of *Political Change in Britain* that the analytical potential of multi-election panels began to be fully realized.[7]

"Change" was an important theme for other scholars as well. Ronald Inglehart (1971, 1977) posited a trend toward "post-materialism" in Europe based on generational differences in value orientation, which he termed a "silent revolution." Others, drawing upon similar themes, explored the emergence of a "new politics" and its possible implications for electoral behaviour – for example, greater volatility, increasing support for new parties, or changing electoral alignments (see, for example, Hildebrandt and Dalton 1978). Norman Nie, Verba, and John Petrocik (1976) analyzed the decline and weakening of partisanship in the United States and the rise of "issue voting" in *The Changing American Voter* – another important book of the 1970s that was widely read by scholars in the field in both Europe and North America. In presenting a detailed argument that the American

politics of the 1970s had changed dramatically from the political world described in *The American Voter*, Nie, Verba, and Petrocik also implicitly
mounted a challenge to the Michigan school on important theoretical
grounds. Echoing V.O. Key's (1966) famous admonition that "voters are not
fools," the authors of *The Changing American Voter* argued forcefully that
issues were an important element in the individual voting calculus:

> One of our major themes is that the electorate *does respond* to stimuli; that
> is, how it votes, how it decides to vote, and how it thinks about political
> matters is a function not merely of some inherent social and psychological
> characteristics but of the issues and candidates that it faces in the real world
> of politics. (ibid., 290)

Throughout the 1970s, a number of US scholars re-conceptualized, re-
examined, and debated the role of issues in American voting behaviour in
what came to be called the "issue voting controversy" (see especially RePass
1971; Brody and Page 1972; Pomper 1972; Jackson 1975; and Page and Jones
1979, for examples of one or more alternative ways of looking at issues in
voting choice). Their research, as well as that reported in *The Changing
American Voter*, was based largely on secondary analyses of the Michigan
studies. This is an important point to emphasize here because the availabil-
ity of data through survey archives and other sources not only opened the
door to new ways of looking at old problems and new methods of analysis,
but it also made it possible for a single researcher to make direct comparisons of findings from different studies. It is not surprising then to discover
that the period when major secondary analyses of the American, British, or
German studies became commonplace is also the period when comparative
research in the field began to develop more rapidly.

One such example of a major comparative project that emphasized data
analysis rather than data collection was the study organized by Richard Rose
(1974). In pulling together analyses of data from twelve countries in individual chapters (in many cases written by principal investigators of studies in
those countries), Rose sought to impose a simple comparative framework
within which the relative weight of "social structure" variables such as occupation, religion, or region could be compared across nations. While the
different traditions of electoral research are clearly reflected in a number of
chapters, the effects of a decade of collaboration and cross-fertilization in
the field were equally evident in the ways that individual researchers handled the concepts and literature as applied to particular countries.[8]

Another such broadly comparative cross-national collaborative project was the re-examination of the party identification concept associated with the Michigan school organized by Ian Budge, Ivor Crewe, and Dennis Farlie in *Party Identification and Beyond* (1976). Inspired partly by Butler and Stokes's (1969) often-cited comparison of party identification in Britain and the United States, scholars in Europe and elsewhere actively debated the utility of the party identification concept in comparative research. Jacques Thomassen (1976), for example, concluded that party identification in the Netherlands was of little value since it was actually found to be more un-stable than the vote across a three-wave panel. Others, however, proposed refinements of the concept and alternative ways of applying it to different types of party systems (see, for example, the chapters by Inglehart and Klingemann, Kaase, and Crewe on France, Germany, and Britain respect-ively in the Budge et al. 1976 volume). In Canada, Meisel (1972) had con-cluded that party identification was "almost inapplicable" because of its tendency to travel with the vote, and Jane Jenson (1975) considered it "a rationally limited allegiance" quite unlike the US concept. Paul Sniderman, H.D. Forbes, and Ian Melzer (1974), however, maintained that partisanship in Canada was not significantly more unstable than in the United States or Britain. In Canada, as in Germany, the debate ranged across matters of con-ceptualization, measurement, and interpretation (see, for instance, Jenson 1975; Norpoth 1978).

Political Choice in Canada

It is easy to discern from this brief synopsis of the major trends in compara-tive electoral research during the early 1970s the kinds of influences that would be felt in the design of the third CES in 1974. Since there had been no new study in 1972, a rather large research agenda had accumulated since Meisel's studies in the 1960s. Canadian politics, like that in other countries, appeared to be undergoing rapid change with the election of Pierre Trudeau in 1968 and his near defeat in 1972. American models and concepts of vot-ing research were being actively questioned and scrutinized by scholars both within and outside the United States. New methods and approaches were being developed and tested in the British, German, and Dutch studies con-ducted by Ivor Crewe and Bo Särlvik at the University of Essex, the For-schungsgruppe Wahlen at the University of Mannheim, and by the teams of researchers at the universities of Amsterdam and Leiden. A new major col-laborative project involving both European and American researchers was underway in the form of an eight-nation study of political participation, later reported in Samuel Barnes and Max Kaase's *Political Action* (1979). In most of the countries where electoral research had become well established over the past decade, a new generation of scholars was beginning to carry on, challenge, or refine the work of the pioneers in the field.[9] *The American Voter* was no longer the dominant theoretical work, and the Canadian research agenda was crowded with questions deriving from both domestic and foreign research.

Any election survey instrument represents a blend of both continuity and innovation, and the 1974 CES provides a variety of examples of both tendencies. Building upon Meisel's work in 1965 and 1968, which in turn built upon the Ann Arbor studies, Harold Clarke and his colleagues replicated many of the items found in previous surveys, in a few instances even where these measures might have been improved (see Clarke et al. 1979). As Thomas Scotto, Mebs Kanji, and Antoine Bilodeau discuss further in the next chapter of this volume, improvements in certain items could have been realized only at the cost of creating discontinuities with previous studies or undermining the potential for comparative analysis.[10] However, Clarke and his colleagues also developed entirely new measures of concepts such as regional consciousness, perceptions of the federal system, and issue proximity, to mention only a few prominent examples. Many of the socio-demographic items familiar from earlier studies were included in standard form, but the investigators also believed that substantial measurement improvements could be made in some items such as occupation and education. These, in turn, were used to construct more sophisticated and objective social class indices.[11] Further, the 1974 team adapted Barnes's measures of political participation, both to encompass a wider range of political activities and to foster comparability with studies in other countries.

Clarke and his colleagues were especially concerned with building a better measure of partisan attachment, reflecting both the theoretical and conceptual concerns of some of the literature cited earlier as well as the realities of the Canadian political environment. The resulting typology, developed in Clarke et al.'s *Political Choice in Canada* (1979) and discussed further in Clarke and Allan Kornberg's chapter in this volume, took into account three distinct aspects of partisan attachment: intensity (as understood in the Michigan studies), stability (reflecting the influences of the British work), and cross-level consistency (because of the particular federal-provincial characteristics of the Canadian party system). The typology of durable and flexible partisanship developed from this study helped to explain individual voting behaviour at that time and interpret later patterns of political change in Canada during the next decade. Similar to work conducted in Western European nations during this period, this work applied a theoretical understanding of the concept of partisanship to a particular partisan environment, which was very different from that of the United States.[12]

Not surprisingly, there are a number of other areas in which the influences of US and European work are apparent, both in the design of the 1974 CES and in the analyses found in *Political Choice in Canada*. Two, in particular, are worthy of mention. I have already noted the importance of the issue-voting controversy in much of the American literature on voting behaviour in the early 1970s (see earlier discussion). The influence of Butler and Stokes is likewise noteworthy here, both in the way that issues were conceptualized and in some aspects of the analysis. Butler and Stokes distinguished clearly between issues that were important merely because they were salient to the individual voter and those that were important in the outcome of an election because of the particular way in which they were linked to political parties. This distinction proved to be of considerable significance in 1974 with respect to issues such as inflation, wage, and price controls and majority government (see Clarke et al. 1979, 257-69 and 375-80). By the time that Edward Carmines and James Stimson (1980) would again take on the topic of issue voting in American politics a few years later, the "issues" in the issue-voting controversy had become much clearer.

A second area in which the British work, in particular, exerted a strong influence was with regard to our conceptualization of processes of political change. Butler and Stokes, together with others such as Norman Nie, Sidney Verba, and John Petrocik (1976), Inglehart (1977), and Warren Miller and Teresa Levitin (1976) had explored the interaction of issues, partisanship, and demography, particularly as manifested in generational differences with respect to one or more of these variables. Crewe, Alt, and Särlvik (1977), in extending Butler and Stokes's work with the 1974 British Election Studies, had already begun to develop an interpretation of the process of partisan decomposition in Britain. Although Canada in 1974 seemed to exhibit aggregate patterns of stability rather than change, Clarke and his colleagues became convinced that the conditions for substantial volatility in Canadian elections were already present. In the conclusion to *Political Choice in Canada*, we wrote,

> The Liberal party has won most of the federal elections held in this century ... The implication of our analysis however is that this pattern of Liberal dominance is more apparent than real. The composition of the

electorate changes substantially at each election with infusions of newly eligible voters and mobilization of different groups of transient voters. In addition, there is a substantial amount of vote switching from one election to the next. Since many of these switchers, transients, and new voters are motivated by the issues, leaders and candidates associated with a particular election, the possibilities for dramatic election reverses such as the Conservative victories in 1957-58 are always present. (Clarke et al. 1979, 390)

The 1974 CES was not a panel study, and because the Liberals regained a majority in 1974, we would have to wait five years before the opportunity arose to explore some of the more compelling questions of stability and change in Canadian politics with data collected from the same respondents over more than a single election. However, in keeping with the design of many other election studies of this period, it was well understood that the 1974 survey was to be the first wave of a longer-term panel study. By the end of the decade, multi-election panels had been conducted in Britain (February/October 1974/1979), the Netherlands (1971/77), Norway (1977/81), Sweden (1973/76), Denmark (1971/81), and the United States (1972/74/76) – many of these including multiple waves of interviews. In the British case, the occurrence of two elections in one year (1974) produced a particularly rich data set consisting of a February/October panel and a 1974/79 panel as well as one involving all three waves. The Dutch panel eventually extended to six waves and resulted in one of the most valuable of the European studies with regard to its potential to address important questions of both long-term and short-term political change.[13] And the Canadian panel study, although delayed by the longevity of the Trudeau government, eventually provided us with a unique opportunity to study the behaviour of the electorate across the two elections of 1979 and 1980 as well as in the 1980 Quebec Referendum. It also opened the door to a genuinely comparative treatment of some of the more compelling research questions of the decade, such as the stability of party identification and the role of issues in voting choice (see, for example, LeDuc 1981; LeDuc et al. 1984; Clarke et al. 1985). As Canadians, together with the citizens of most other Western countries, moved into an era when dramatic changes in government and politics would seem commonplace, the analytical potential of these studies was just beginning to be realized.

The 1980s

Studies oriented toward understanding the politics of volatility, change, and voter discontent were well positioned for the politics of the late 1970s and early 1980s. Changes in government took place in nearly every Western country during this period, in a number of instances laying the foundations of an entirely new political era. Margaret Thatcher came to power in Britain; Ronald Reagan was president of the United States; Helmut Kohl served as chancellor in West Germany; and Joe Clark, and later Brian Mulroney, were selected as prime ministers of Canada. Yet the sources of voter discontent that brought about the triumph of neo-conservative political movements also paved the way for the dramatic return of Trudeau in the 1980 election and brought victory in 1981 to François Mitterand in France and Robert Hawke in Australia. Scholars who sought explanations for such sweeping political change were increasingly pressed to distinguish between simple volatility in the electorate and the establishment of entirely new patterns of thought and behaviour among voters. It is not surprising then to discover that interpreting, rather than merely describing and explaining, these patterns of change became the most important single theme in the comparative electoral research of the 1980s. In Clarke et al.'s *Absent Mandate* volumes (1984, 1991, 1996), which came after the publication of *Political Choice in Canada*, the attention turned to interpreting rather than simply documenting the wide swings in voting behaviour evident in Canada and elsewhere. Following events such as the rapid demise of the Clark government and the Mulroney landslide, it was no longer necessary to argue the case for patterns of voter volatility underlying aggregate stability.[14] The theme of voter discontent and its implications were reflected in the choice of subtitle for the first of the *Absent Mandate* volumes published in 1984 – *The Politics of Discontent in Canada*.

It was clear that the economic problems of the period, and the tendency of citizens to hold government responsible for the performance of the economy, lay behind the fate of many of the parties dismissed from office. In *Retrospective Voting in American National Elections*, Morris Fiorina (1981) provided a framework for understanding the linkages between economic performance and voting choice as well as an interpretation of some of the patterns of change in American politics. His work also continued the party identification debate by re-conceptualizing partisanship in the United States as a "running tally" of individual attitudes toward parties based on performance rather than as an affective or emotional tie. Utilizing similar methods and concepts, other researchers tested prospective and retrospective issue explanations of electoral outcomes (Miller and Shanks 1982; Miller and Wattenberg 1985) and examined the relative effects of economic variables on voting behaviour in the United States and a number of European countries, spawning a broadly comparative literature on "economic voting" (see, for example, Hibbs 1981; Lewis-Beck 1986; or Hibbing 1987).

Changes in economic conditions also made it possible to test a number of hypotheses regarding the interplay of short-term and long-term forces of political change. In "Post-Materialism in an Environment of Insecurity," Inglehart (1981) argued that the growth of post-materialist values among younger cohorts in the electorate represented a genuine long-term generational trend because it had withstood the shorter-term challenge of an unfriendly economic environment. His analytical task was made easier by the fact that the Euro-barometer surveys on which many of his analyses had been based were by then conducted semi-annually across the nine nations of the European Community (EC) and also by the fact that the entire series represented a continuous data collection enterprise spanning over ten years.[15] Inglehart's measures of post-materialist values, which were revised and expanded in the 1973 European Communities Study, were subsequently included in many other national surveys, spawning a variety of cross-national analyses of these items as well as an active debate regarding their interpretation.[16]

Perhaps the most important themes in the voting literature of the 1980s, however, were those of "dealignment" and "realignment." Certainly, these concepts were not new at the time that they first began to pervade the literature of electoral research. Indeed, much of the literature on the evolution of the American party system was couched in terms of historic "alignments" (Burnham 1970; Sundquist 1983). However, the observed partisan decomposition of the 1980s accelerated this discussion and gave it a new shape. If an entrenched party system appeared to be collapsing or "dealigning," would such a process not inevitably lead to the establishment of a new one? The election of Ronald Reagan in the United States appeared to some to signal the consolidation of a new conservative Republican alignment, and the seeming collapse of the Labour party in Britain, coupled with the sudden rise of the Social Democratic party (SDP), shook the foundations of the British party system. American scholars actively debated the existence and/or the nature of a US realignment (Ladd 1985; Norpoth 1987), and Särlvik and Crewe (1983) argued that Britain had undergone a "Decade of

Dealignment." Mark Franklin (1984) posited that the decline of long-term forces such as social class had opened the door to sudden and unpredictable patterns of change. In similar fashion, Dutch scholars took note of the processes of "depillarization" and "deconfessionalization" that were transforming and destabilizing politics in the Netherlands (van der Eijk and Niemoller 1983; Irwin and Dittrich 1984).

One major attempt to explore these themes cross-nationally is found in Russell Dalton, Scott Flanagan, and Paul Allen Beck's *Electoral Change in Advanced Industrial Democracies* (1984). Like Rose ten years earlier, Dalton, Flanagan, and Beck brought together studies from Canada and the United States, most Western European countries, and Japan in an effort to evaluate both the causes and consequences of political change. While the goals of these editors were very similar to those of Rose in the earlier volume, the evolution of the field over this ten-year period would be evident to even the most casual peruser of these two books. While Rose had sought to compare the explanatory power of "social structure" variables across different political systems, Dalton, Flanagan, and Beck argued that

> regardless of how it is conceptualized, a process of value change clearly is oc-curring. Evidence of generational changes in value priorities is available for almost twenty industrial democracies ... The process [of change] begins with the weakening of traditional political alignments. These eroding cleavages mean that many social groups are open to new political appeals and might be mobilized by new issues or new ideologies. If the parties can capture these new issues or ideologies, the widespread partisan mobilization of a realignment may result. (Ibid., 21)

The latter part of the 1980s saw a further flowering of comparative research. In a compendium of national surveys compiled at the end of the decade, major national election studies were found in no fewer than twenty-five countries (de Guchteneire, Niemi, and LeDuc 1991). The rapid growth and accessibility of data archives made these data available to a wider range of secondary analysts. Non-election studies such as general social surveys and major public opinion polls in many countries routinely began to include questions of interest to students of electoral behaviour in their instruments. As the length of some of the series of election studies and other surveys (notably in the United States, Norway, Britain, Germany, and Canada) began to exceed thirty years or more, the opportunity to address longer-term questions of political change presented itself to secondary analysts. Pooling some of the longer series of studies yielded much larger numbers of cases and suggested analytical possibilities that had not been previously considered (Markus 1988; Stimson 1989). Methodologically, a greater diversity of study designs occurring side by side with increased standardization and replication of many key measures began to evolve.[17] A US study experimented with a series of rolling cross-section samples to better track the dynamics of a presidential campaign – a design that was later adapted in the 1988 CES. While panels, both short and longer term, continued to be the design of choice, in many instances these were combined with, or supplemented by, various pre-post waves of interviews. In some countries (for example, Germany, the Netherlands, and Britain), more than one study was undertaken in some elections, producing an even wider range of analytical possibilities.

Letting the People Decide

The 1984 CES, conducted by Ronald Lambert, Steven Brown, James Curtis, Barry Kay, and John Wilson, was a large-N, single-wave, post-election survey similar to those that had gone before but with a much stronger sociological orientation. Among other things (see Schwartz's chapter in this volume), Lambert and his colleagues (1986, 1987) explored in greater depth the elements of social class and ideology in Canadian politics and also the short-term forces that had led to the 1984 Mulroney landslide (Kay et al. 1991). This study was the last of the large-sample, post-election surveys involving face-to-face interviews.

The 1988 CES utilized a completely different design, employing a rolling cross-section survey across the entire duration of the campaign. As Scotto, Kanji, and Bilodeau note in the next chapter, the decision to change the mode of survey delivery from face-to-face to telephone interviewing meant that some items from the previous studies could not be easily replicated. However, the 1988 survey was particularly well suited to study the dynamics of an election campaign, and the 1988 campaign, with its unrelenting focus on the free trade issue, and the intervention of dramatic events such as the leader debates, provided the perfect subject matter. In *Letting the People Decide*, Richard Johnston, André Blais, Henry Brady, and Jean Crête (1992) were able to document the impact of specific campaign events and to demonstrate both the powerful effects of short-term forces in the voting calculus and the uncertainty of election outcomes.

A British study of similar design also contributed to the growing consensus in the field that "campaigns matter," but the 1987 British campaign

featured fewer dramatic events than occurred in Canada during the following year (Miller et al. 1991). The use of different survey designs, combined with multiple studies of the same election, facilitated comparison
both across and within systems. A study of elections in the European Parliament in 1989, which involved all of the (then) twelve member nations of
the EC, provided new opportunities for comparative analysis both between
countries and across levels of the political system within each country
(van der Eijk, Franklin and Marsh 1995; van der Eijk and Franklin 1996).
Concurrent with the 1988 CES, a number of respondents from the 1984
study were re-interviewed, thereby creating a second multi-election panel.[18]
Results of this analysis, together with other findings from the longer-term
Canadian panels, were reported in a second edition of *Absent Mandate* published in 1991. In this volume, Clarke and his colleagues (1991, 152) developed an interpretation of Canadian electoral politics that argued that a
reciprocal relationship existed between the behaviour of voters and political
parties that had significant implications for the formation of public policy:

> Political parties have learned that their electoral coalitions are fragile cre-
> ations ... for their part, voters have learned that they will not be offered clear
> choices ... Their engagement is limited, as they express feelings of cynicism,
> dissatisfaction with politics and politicians, and general negativity about
> the political process.

The politics of the early 1990s confirmed hypotheses about the volatility
of electorates in Canada and elsewhere. The dramatic outcome of the 1993
federal election in Canada raised many new questions regarding the future
of the party system, but it was also consistent with many of the interpretations of elections and voting that had been developed in the earlier surveys. The defeat of President George Bush in the 1992 US election called
into question the "realignment" thesis that had occupied the attention of
American scholars during much of the previous decade and focused attention once again on the erosion of partisan attachments. The "decline of partisanship" became an important theme in both US and European research
during this period, but its longer-term implications for the future of electoral politics remained uncertain (Wattenberg 1986; Mair 1993). A new comparative volume edited by Franklin, Thomas Mackie, and Valen, *Electoral
Change: Responses to Evolving Social and Attitudinal Structures in Western
Countries* (1992), again compared findings from a number of national
studies, emphasizing the theme of value change, which in turn had driven

partisan change in many countries. The formation of new party systems in the emerging democracies of Latin America and Eastern Europe provided new opportunities for comparative research. Thematic approaches to comparative research also complemented those involving direct cross-national comparisons (see, for example LeDuc, Niemi, and Norris 1996).

The third edition of *Absent Mandate*, published in 1996, utilized data from a range of different surveys, including the various panels and the 1988 rolling cross section (Clarke et al. 1996). Organized around a theme of "economic restructuring" and the manner in which such restructuring had been undertaken, the volume explored the electoral implications of the aftermath of the Free Trade Agreement that had dominated the 1988 election as well as the rejection by voters of the Charlottetown constitutional agreement in the 1992 referendum. In spite of the dramatic partisan upheaval of that time, Clarke and his colleagues took a cautious view of the longer-term implications of changes in the party system:

> Parties are not able to call upon loyal electorates, and instead attempt to harness a variety of less predictable short-term forces to achieve victory. It is this predominance of short-term forces that has led us to be skeptical about whether 1993 marks any realignment, despite the dramatic changes and the appearance of new parties. For a party system to be realigned, changes would have to be more than temporary and patterns would have to begin to gel into a stable shape. The specific circumstances of the 1993 election, as well as the history of earlier elections, suggests a cautious assessment. (Ibid., 184)

The five election studies that followed the 1988 CES employed a similar rolling cross-section design, complemented by pre- and post-election interviews of subsets of respondents and, with the exception of the 2006 study, a separate mail-back questionnaire. The 1993 study also incorporated a panel component that was initiated at the time of the 1992 referendum. The referendum component was analyzed in detail by Johnston, Blais, Elisabeth Gidengil, and Neil Nevitte (1996), employing an analytical strategy similar to that of Johnston and his colleagues' study in *Letting the People Decide* (1992). Subsequent studies of the 1997 and 2000 elections were analyzed by Nevitte, Blais, Gidengil, and Nadeau (2000) and by Blais, Nevitte, Gidengil, and Nadeau (2002) respectively. At the same time, Clarke, Kornberg, and Peter Wearing (2000) pulled together data from these and a wide range of other surveys to examine the regionalization and fragmentation of the Canadian political system, which appeared to be in evidence after the 1993 cataclysm.

Comparative work was also flourishing during the latter part of the decade. The establishment of the Comparative Study of Electoral Systems (CSES) in 1996 brought together scholars from some thirty-three countries (including Canada) for the purpose of establishing and maintaining a common module of questions in national election studies. The CSES structure allowed this wealth of survey data to be analyzed within a framework of institutional variation. Other types of comparative projects of relevance to the study of elections also expanded rapidly over the next decade. The 1990 World Values Study, for example, was carried out in forty-four countries, and Nevitte (1996) utilized World Values Study data to compare the process of value change in Canada with that of eleven other countries in his book *The Decline of Deference*.

As we look back at the evolution of the election studies, both in Canada and elsewhere, it is clear that they are, and have always been, a largely comparative enterprise. As Dalton, Flanagan and Beck (1984, xv) noted in their acknowledgments to *Electoral Change in Advanced Industrial Democracies*,

> the work stands as a tribute to the development of a truly international community of Political Scientists. Although we occasionally differ in theoretical interests or in the interpretation of data, we share a common scientific language and method that enables us to discuss and evaluate these theories within a comparative framework.

The increase in the number of countries in which election studies are conducted continues to expand the potential for comparative analysis – well beyond what would have been imagined even twenty years ago. Enterprises such as the CSES make such analysis more systematic and theoretically meaningful as well as more accessible to secondary analysis. As the length of some of the series of election studies and other surveys now exceeds fifty years or more (notably in the United States, Norway, Britain, Germany, and Canada), the opportunity to address truly long-term questions of political change will increasingly begin to attract the attention of scholars in the field.[19] From the beginning, election studies have been a comparative enterprise, in spite of their early origins in national politics. Today, they are by their very nature more comparative than ever before, and the CES is no exception.

NOTES

1 On the evolution of these early election studies, see Thomassen (1994).

2 See Allardt and Littunen (1964).

3 Compare, for example, Stein Rokkan's (1967) examination of geography, religion, and social class in Norway with that of Philip Converse and Henry Valen (1971).

4 The essay referred to here was written in 1970 and published in the volume edited by Richard Rose (1974). Mildred Schwartz's postscript on this point (ibid., 607) makes clear the extent to which changes in the field both in Canada and elsewhere were occurring at this time.

5 The term "panel" here refers to those studies in which the same respondents are interviewed at times coinciding with more than one election – that is, multi-election panels. Studies in which respondents are interviewed more than once during a single election campaign or before and after an election are also "panel" studies, but their analytical potential is quite different, and they are therefore treated as a separate category for the purposes of this discussion.

6 The German panel was conducted by Max Kaase, Uwe Schleth, Wolfgang Adrian, Manfred Berger, and Rudolf Wildemann at the University of Mannheim. Another 1969 German election study of pre-post design was also conducted by Hans Klingemann and Franz Urban Pappi. In the Netherlands, the three-wave panel was conducted by Felix Heunks, M. Kent Jennings, Warren Miller, Philip Stouthard, and Jacques Thomassen (Miller and Stouthard 1975). A 1971 pre-post election study was conducted by Robert Mokken and Frans Roschar, and this study formed the basis for the later series of Dutch panel studies conducted at the University of Amsterdam. Methodological information on the Dutch election studies may be found in van der Eijk and Niemoller, *Electoral Change in The Netherlands* (1983). In Denmark, the 1970/73 study was conducted by Ole Borre and his colleagues at Aarhus University (see Borre et al. 1976). In the United States, the 1972/76 panel study was conducted by the Center for Political Studies at the University of Michigan (see Converse and Markus 1979), and in Canada, the 1974/79/80 panel was conducted by Harold D. Clarke, Jane Jenson, Lawrence LeDuc, and Jon H. Pammett (see Clarke et al. 1984; LeDuc 1984).

7 An analysis of the first American panel may be found in Campbell et al. (1960, 1966), and the Norwegian data are described by Stein Rokkan and Henry Valen (1970) and Rokkan et al. (1970). See also Särlvik (1970) for an analysis of the Swedish study.

8 Compare, for example, Rose's (1974) own chapter on Britain and Särlvik's (1970) on Sweden with Rokkan and Valen's (1970) piece on Norway.

9 One good example of this trend by a principal investigator of the 1974 British studies may be found in Crewe (1974).

10 Political efficacy, which by then had become a "standard" item in most studies, provides one such example (LeDuc 1976). The hard cover edition of *Political Choice in Canada* contains an extensive methodological appendix illustrating many of the items discussed here (Clarke et al. 1979, 397-438). This appendix is not included in the abridged 1980 edition nor are many of the methodological footnotes throughout the book. All references here are to the hard cover edition.

11   For example, see the Blishen socio-economic status index as discussed by Bernard Blishen and Hugh McRoberts (1976).

12   See, for comparison, Borre and Katz (1973), Thomassen (1976), and Norpoth (1978).

13   See van der Eijk and Niemoller (1983).

14   See LeDuc (1984). On this point, see also Bakvis (1988).

15   The Euro-barometers had their origins as the European Communities Study in 1970, conducted by Ronald Inglehart and Jacques-René Rabier. Repeated in 1973 on the then nine nations of the European Community, the series became a semi-annual survey in 1975. Inglehart's analysis in the article cited was based upon the surveys in this series conducted in 1970, 1973, 1976, and 1979.

16   See, among other such examples, Dalton (1977), Flanagan (1982), and Abramson and Inglehart (1986). In Canada, the twelve-item set of these measures was included for the first time in the mail-back wave of the 1988 national election study.

17   For example, see the introduction in this volume for a more specific description of what this meant for the Canadian case.

18   This study was conducted by the Carleton University School of Journalism Survey Centre (see Clarke et al. 1991).

19   See, for example, the treatment of issues in *Dynasties and Interludes* (LeDuc et al. 2010) or the analysis of turnout utilizing a pooled data set (Pammett, Thiessen, and Bilodeau 2001).

REFERENCES

Abramson, Paul, and Ronald Inglehart. 1986. "Generational Replacement and Value Change in Six West European Societies." *American Journal of Political Science* 30: 1-25.

Aitkin, Donald. 1977. *Stability and Change in Australian Politics*. Canberra, Australia: Australian National University Press.

Alford, Robert. 1963. *Party and Society*. Chicago: Rand-McNally.

Allardt, Erik, and Yvan Littunen, eds. 1964. *Cleavages, Ideologies, and Party Systems*. Helsinki: Westermarck Society.

Almond, Gabriel, and Sidney Verba. 1963. *The Civic Culture*. Princeton, NJ: Princeton University Press.

Arian, Asher. 1974. *The Choosing People*. Cleveland, OH: Case Western Reserve Press.

Bakvis, Herman. 1988. "The Canadian Paradox: Party System Stability in the Face of a Weakly Aligned Electorate." In Steven Wolinetz, ed., *Parties and Party Systems in Liberal Democracies*, 245-68. London: Routledge.

Barnes, Samuel. 1977. *Representation in Italy*. Chicago: University of Chicago Press.

Barnes, Samuel, and Max Kaase, eds. 1979. *Political Action*. Beverly Hills, CA: Sage.

Berelson, Bernard, Paul Lazarsfeld, and William McPhee. 1954. *Voting: A Study of Opinion Formation in a Presidential Campaign*. Chicago: University of Chicago Press.

Blais, André, Neil Nevitte, Elisabeth Gidengil, and Richard Nadeau. 2002. *Anatomy of a Liberal Victory*. Toronto: Broadview Press.

Blishen, Bernard, and Hugh McRoberts. 1976. "A Revised Socioeconomic Index for Occupations in Canada." *Canadian Review of Sociology and Anthropology* 12: 71-79.

Borre, Ole, and Daniel Katz. 1973. "Party Identification and Its Motivational Base in a Multiparty System." *Scandinavian Political Studies* 8: 69-111.

Borre, Ole, Hans Nielsen, Steen Saurberg, and Thom Saurberg. 1976. *Vaelgere i 70erne*. Copenhagen: Akademisk Forlag.

Brody, Richard, and Benjamin Page. 1972. "The Assessment of Policy Voting." *American Political Science Review* 66: 450-58.

Budge, Ian, Ivor Crewe, and Dennis Farlie, eds. 1976. *Party Identification and Beyond*. London: Wiley.

Burnham, Walter. 1970. *Critical Elections and the Mainsprings of American Politics*. New York: Norton.

Butler, D., and D. Stokes. 1969. *Political Change in Britain*. London: Macmillan.

Campbell, Angus. 1966. *Elections and the Political Order*. New York: Wiley.

Campbell, Angus, Philip Converse, Warren Miller, and Donald Stokes. 1960. *The American Voter*. New York: Wiley.

Campbell, Angus, Gerald Gurin, and Warren Miller. 1954. *The Voter Decides*. Evanston, IL: Row and Peterson.

Cantril, Hadley. 1965. *The Pattern of Human Concerns*. Piscataway, NJ: Rutgers University Press.

Carmines, Edward, and James Stimson. 1980. "The Two Faces of Issue Voting." *American Political Science Review* 74: 78-91.

Clarke, Harold D. 1984. *Absent Mandate: The Politics of Discontent in Canada*. Toronto: Gage.

–. 1991. *Absent Mandate: Interpreting Change in Canadian Elections*. Toronto: Gage.

–. 1996. *Absent Mandate: Canadian Electoral Politics in an Era of Restructuring*. Toronto: Gage.

Clarke, Harold D., Kai Hildebrandt, Lawrence LeDuc, and Jon H. Pammett. 1985. "Issue Volatility and Partisan Linkages in Canada, Great Britain, the United States, and West Germany." *European Journal of Political Research* 13: 297-63.

Clarke, Harold D., Jane Jenson, Lawrence LeDuc, and Jon H. Pammett. 1979. *Political Choice in Canada*. Toronto: McGraw-Hill Ryerson.

Clarke, Harold D., Allan Kornberg, and Peter Wearing. 2000. *A Polity on the Edge: Canada and the Politics of Fragmentation*. Toronto: Broadview.

Converse, Philip. 1966. "DeGaulle and Eisenhower: The Public Image of the Victorious General." In Angus Campbell et al., eds., *Elections and the Political Order*, 292-345. New York: Wiley.

Converse, Philip, and Georges Dupeux. 1966. "Politicization of the Electorate in France and the United States." In Angus Campbell et al., eds., *Elections and the Political Order*, 269-91. New York: Wiley.

Converse, Philip, and Gregory Markus. 1979. "Plus Ça Change: The New CPS Election Study Panel." *American Political Science Review* 73: 1055-70.

Converse, Philip, and Henry Valen. 1971. "Dimensions of Cleavage and Perceived Party Distances in Norwegian Voting." *Scandinavian Political Studies* 6: 107-52.

Crewe, Ivor. 1974. "Do Butler and Stokes Really Explain Political Change in Britain?" *European Journal of Political Research* 2: 43-100.

–. 1976. "Party Identification Theory and Political Change in Britain." In Ian Budge, Ivor Crewe, and Dennis Farlie, eds., *Party Identification and Beyond*, 33-62. London: Wiley.

Crewe, Ivor, James Alt, and Bo Särlvik. 1977. "Partisan Dealignment in Britain: 1964-74." *British Journal of Political Science* 7: 129-90.

Dalton, Russell. 1977. "Was There a Revolution?" *Comparative Political Studies* 9: 459-73.

Dalton, Russell, Scott Flanagan, and Paul Allen Beck, eds. 1984. *Electoral Change in Advanced Industrial Democracies*. Princeton, NJ: Princeton University Press.

de Guchteneire, Paul, Richard G. Niemi, and Lawrence LeDuc. 1991. "A Compendium of Academic Survey Studies of Elections around the World: Update." *Electoral Studies* 10: 231-43.

Fiorina, Morris. 1981. *Retrospective Voting in American National Elections*. New Haven, CT: Yale University Press.

Flanagan, Scott C. 1982. "Measuring Value Change in Advanced Industrial Society: A Rejoinder to Inglehart." *Comparative Political Studies* 15: 99-128.

Franklin, Mark. 1984. "How the Decline of Class Voting Opened the Way to Radical Change in British Politics." *British Journal of Political Science* 14: 483-508.

Franklin, Mark, Thomas Mackie, and Henry Valen. 1992. *Electoral Change: Responses to Evolving Social and Attitudinal Structures in Western Countries*. New York: Cambridge University Press.

Hibbing, John. 1987. "On the Issues Surrounding Economic Voting: Looking to the British Case for Answers." *Comparative Political Studies* 20: 3-33.

Hibbs, Douglas. 1981. "Economics and Politics in France." *European Journal of Political Research* 9: 133-45.

Hildebrandt, Kai, and Russell Dalton. 1978. "The New Politics: Political Change or Sunshine Politics?" In Max Kaase and Klaus von Beyme, eds., *Elections and Parties*, 171-90. London: Sage.

Inglehart, Ronald. 1971. "The Silent Revolution in Europe: Intergenerational Change in Post-Industrial Societies." *American Political Science Review* 65: 991-1017.

–. 1977. *The Silent Revolution*. Princeton, NJ: Princeton University Press.

–. 1981. "Post-Materialism in an Environment of Insecurity." *American Political Science Review* 75: 880-900.

Inglehart, Ronald, and Hans-Dieter Klingemann. 1976. "Party Identification, Ideological Preference and the Left-Right Dimension among Western Mass Publics." In Ian Budge, Ivor Crewe, and Dennis Farlie, eds., *Party Identification and Beyond*, 243-73. London: Wiley.

Irwin, Galen, and Karl Dittrich. 1984. "And the Walls Came Tumbling Down: Party Dealignment in The Netherlands." In Russell Dalton et al., eds., *Electoral Change in Advanced Industrial Democracies*, 267-97. Princeton, NJ: Princeton University Press.

Jackson, John E. 1975. "Issues, Party Choices and Presidential Votes." *American Political Science Review* 69: 161-85.

Jenson, Jane. 1975. "Party Loyalty in Canada: The Question of Party Identification." *Canadian Journal of Political Science* 8: 543-53.

Johnston Richard, André Blais, Henry E. Brady, and Jean Crête. 1992. *Letting the People Decide: Dynamics of a Canadian Election*. Montreal: McGill-Queen's University Press.

Johnston Richard, André Blais, Elisabeth Gidengil, and Neil Nevitte. 1996. *The Challenge of Direct Democracy*. Montreal: McGill-Queen's University Press.

Kasse, Max. 1976. "Party Identification and Voting Behaviour in the West German Election of 1969." In Ian Budge, Ivor Crewe, and Dennis Farlie, eds., *Party Identification and Beyond*, 81-102. London: Wiley.

Kay, Barry J., Steven D. Brown, James E. Curtis, Ronald D. Lambert, and John M. Wilson. 1991. "The Character of Electoral Change: A Preliminary Report from the 1984 Election Study." In Joseph Wearing, ed., *The Ballot and Its Message: Voting in Canada*, 283-314. Toronto: Copp Clark Pitman.

Key, V.O. 1966. *The Responsible Electorate*. Cambridge, MA: Harvard University Press.

Ladd, Everett C. 1985. "As the Realignment Turns: A Drama in Many Acts." *Public Opinion* 7: 2-10.

Lambert, Ronald D., James E. Curtis, Steven D. Brown, and Barry J. Kay. 1986. "In Search of Left/Right Beliefs in the Canadian Electorate." *Canadian Journal of Political Science* 19: 542-63.

–. 1987. "Social Class, Left/Right Political Orientations and Subjective Class Voting in Provincial and Federal Elections." *Canadian Review of Sociology and Anthropology* 24: 526-49.

LeDuc, Lawrence. 1976. "Measuring the Sense of Political Efficacy in Canada." *Comparative Political Studies* 8: 490-500.

–. 1981. "The Dynamic Properties of Party Identification: A Four Nation Comparison." *European Journal of Political Research* 9: 257-68.

–. 1984. "Canada: The Politics of Stable Dealignment." In Russell Dalton et al., eds., *Electoral Change in Advanced Industrial Democracies*, 402-24. Princeton, NJ: Princeton University Press.

–. 1985. "Partisan Change and Dealignment in Canada, Great Britain, and the United States." *Comparative Politics* 17: 379-98.

LeDuc, Lawrence, Harold D. Clarke, Jane Jenson, and Jon H. Pammett. 1984. "Partisan Instability in Canada: Evidence from a New Panel Study." *American Political Science Review* 78: 470-84.

LeDuc, Lawrence, Richard G. Niemi, and Pippa Norris, eds. 1996. *Comparing Democracies: Elections and Voting in Global Perspective*. Beverly Hills, CA: Sage.

LeDuc, Lawrence, Jon H. Pammett, Judith I. McKenzie, and André Turcotte. 2010. *Dynasties and Interludes: Past and Present in Canadian Electoral Politics*. Toronto: Dundurn.

Lewis-Beck, Michael. 1986. "Comparative Economic Voting: Britain, France, Germany, Italy." *American Journal of Political Science* 30: 315-46.

Lipset, Seymour M. 1960. *Political Man*. New York: Doubleday.

Lipset, Seymour M., and Stein Rokkan, eds. 1967. *Party Systems and Voter Alignments.* New York: Free Press.

Mair, Peter. 1993. "Myths of Electoral Change and the Survival of Traditional Parties." *European Journal of Political Research* 24: 121-33.

Markus, Gregory. 1988. "The Impact of Personal and National Economic Conditions on the Presidential Vote: A Pooled Cross-Sectional Analysis." *American Journal of Political Science* 32: 137-54.

Meisel, John. 1972. *Working Papers in Canadian Politics.* Montreal: McGill-Queen's University Press.

Miller, Arthur, and Martin Wattenberg. 1985. "Throwing the Rascals Out: Policy and Performance Evaluations of Presidential Candidates: 1952-1980." *American Political Science Review* 79: 359-72.

Miller, Warren, and Teresa Levitin. 1976. *Leadership and Change.* Cambridge, MA: Winthrop.

Miller, Warren, and Merrill Shanks. 1982. "Policy Directions and Presidential Leadership: Alternative Interpretations of the 1980 Presidential Election." *British Journal of Political Science* 12: 299-356.

Miller, Warren, and Philip Stouthard. 1975. "Confessional Attachment and Electoral Behaviour in the Netherlands." *European Journal of Political Research* 3: 219-58.

Miller, William, Harold Clarke, Martin Harrop, Lawrence LeDuc, and Paul Whiteley. 1991. *How Voters Change: The 1987 British Election Campaign in Perspective.* Oxford: Oxford University Press.

Nevitte, Neil. 1996. *The Decline of Deference: Canadian Value Change in Cross-National Perspective.* Toronto: Broadview.

Nevitte, Neil, André Blais, Elisabeth Gidengil, and Richard Nadeau. 2000. *Unsteady State: The 1997 Canadian Federal Election.* Toronto: Broadview.

Nie, Norman, Sidney Verba, and John Petrocik. 1976. *The Changing American Voter.* Cambridge, MA: Harvard University Press.

Norpoth, Helmut. 1978. "Party Identification in West Germany: Tracing an Elusive Concept." *Comparative Political Studies* 11: 36-59.

—. 1987. "Under Way and Here to Stay: Party Realignment in the 1980's." *Public Opinion Quarterly* 51: 376-91.

Page, Benjamin, and Charles Jones. 1979. "Reciprocal Effects of Policy Preferences, Party Loyalties and the Vote." *American Political Science Review* 66: 979-85.

Pammett, Jon H., Erin Thiessen, and Antoine Bilodeau. 2001. *Canadian Voting Turnout in Comparative Perspective.* Ottawa: Elections Canada.

Pomper, Gerald. 1972. "From Confusion to Clarity: Issues and American Voters: 1956-68." *American Political Science Review* 66: 415-28.

Repass, David. 1971. "Issue Salience and Party Choice." *American Political Science Review* 65: 389-400.

Rokkan, Stein. 1967. "Geography, Religion and Social Class: Crosscutting Cleavages in Norwegian Politics." In Seymour M. Lipset and Stein Rokkan, eds., *Party Systems and Voter Alignments,* 367-444. New York: Free Press.

Rokkan, Stein, Angus Campbell, Per Torsvik, and Henry Valen. 1970. *Citizens, Elections, Parties.* Oslo: Universitetsforlaget.

Rokkan, Stein, and Henry Valen. 1970. "The Election to the Norwegian Storting in September 1969." *Scandinavian Political Studies* 5: 287-300.

Rose, Richard, ed. 1974. *Electoral Behavior: A Comparative Handbook.* New York: Free Press.

Särlvik, Bo. 1970. *Electoral Behavior in the Swedish Multiparty System.* Gothenburg, Sweden: University of Gothenburg, Statsvetenskapliga Institutionen.

Särlvik, Bo, and Ivor Crewe. 1983. *Decade of Dealignment.* Cambridge: Cambridge University Press.

Schwartz, Mildred. 1974. "Canadian Voting Behavior." In Richard Rose, ed., *Electoral Behavior: A Comparative Handbook,* 543-61. New York: Free Press.

Sniderman, Paul, H.D. Forbes, and Ian Melzer. 1974. "Party Loyalty and Electoral Volatility." *Canadian Journal of Political Science* 7: 268-88.

Stimson, James. 1989. "Perceptions of Politics and Economic Policy: A Macroanalysis." In Harold D. Clarke et al., eds., *Economic Decline and Political Change: Canada, Great Britain, the United States.* Pittsburgh, PA: University of Pittsburgh Press.

Sundquist, James. 1983. *Dynamics of the Party System.* Washington, DC: Brookings.

Thomassen, Jacques. 1976. "Party Identification as a Cross-National Concept: Its Meaning in The Netherlands." In Ian Budge et al., eds., *Party Identification and Beyond,* 63-79. London: Wiley.

–, ed. 1994. "The Intellectual History of Election Studies." *European Journal of Political Research,* special issue, 25(3).

Valen, Henry, and Daniel Katz. 1964. *Political Parties in Norway.* Oslo: Universitetsforlaget.

van der Eijk, Cees, and Mark Franklin. 1996. *Choosing Europe: The European Electorate and National Politics in the Face of Union.* Ann Arbor, MI: University of Michigan Press.

van der Eijk, Cees, Mark Franklin, and Michael Marsh. 1995. "What Voters Teach Us about Europe-Wide Elections: What Europe-Wide Elections Teach Us about Voters." *Electoral Studies* 14: 149-66.

van der Eijk, Cees, and Broer Niemoller. 1983. *Electoral Change in the Netherlands.* Amsterdam: CT Press.

Wattenberg, Martin. 1986. *The Decline of American Political Parties: 1952-1984.* Cambridge, MA: Harvard University Press.

Advancements in Methodology
A Recurring Process

THOMAS J. SCOTTO, MEBS KANJI,
AND ANTOINE BILODEAU

As mentioned briefly in the previous chapters, the first Canadian Election Studies (CES) were designed as basic cross-sectional post-election surveys and administered through face-to-face interviews. The first panel series and referendum study were introduced during the 1970s and in 1980 respectively. Multi-wave, short-term panel surveys, utilizing a rolling cross-sectional (RCS) design and computer-assisted telephone interviewing (CATI), were launched in 1988. In this chapter, we present a more detailed overview of how the methodology behind the CES has evolved since the mid-1960s. The bulk of our discussion centres on changes in study design and survey content, but we also highlight how such transformations have contributed to our understanding of voting behaviour. We then conclude with a brief discussion of whether further design innovations and modern advances such as the Internet might benefit the project in the years to come.

Cross-Sectional, Post-Election Studies

As John Meisel suggests in Chapter 1 of this volume, many questions pertinent to understanding the political behaviour of Canadians emerged during the mid-1960s, which could only be answered via the analysis of data from large-scale surveys that covered a wider set of topics and allowed researchers to make inferences about the Canadian population. Getting these studies off the ground was not easy, in part because the process was expensive and funding sources were difficult to come by. Telephone interviewing was in its nascent stages and could not cover all of the Canadian population. Such realities had practical implications, which meant that the earliest CES conducted in 1965 and 1968, and even the 1984 survey, were administered as stand-alone cross-sectional projects, and the data were collected through face-to-face interviews that were conducted after each respective election.

The 1965 and 1968 surveys had suitable sample sizes (2,118 and 2,767 respectively), and respondents were randomly chosen through multi-stage, stratified cluster sampling. However, to ensure that representative samples were drawn, certain additional precautions were taken. For example, controls for urban and rural regions were built into the randomization process, and representation of political minorities was obtained by stratifying the sample to control for the vote obtained by the Liberal party (or the Social Credit party in rural Quebec) (Meisel and van Loon 1966, 143-45). In addition, in order to meet the theoretically motivated goal of comparing Canadians across regions, less populated regions of the country were oversampled (see Schwartz 1974; and the chapter by Mildred Schwartz in this volume).[1]

Slightly more respondents were interviewed in 1984 (n = 3,377), but the sampling technique remained essentially the same. In this instance, the first stage of the sampling procedure segmented the population according to the degree of urbanization before utilizing census enumeration areas as sampling units. The next two stages involved randomly selecting households and individuals from within those dwellings. Also similar to the 1960s, oversampling was done to ensure that researchers could compare regions as well as urban and rural populations. Furthermore, weights were created in order to account for the over-representation of certain regions and to bring the sample in line with the population's age and sex distribution. Moreover, provincial weights were developed to make inferences about the distribution of beliefs within the individual provinces.

In terms of questionnaire design and content, many of the questions asked in the 1965 and 1968 studies were close-ended and built around ordinal response categories, which helped to streamline the interviewing process. Considerable survey time was given to tapping respondents' attitudes toward their own and other Canadian provinces. For example, certain questions probed whether survey participants would be willing to live in other provinces, and others asked about how connected they thought national party leaders were to their province. In addition, these studies asked whether respondents would rather be governed at the provincial or federal level and which level of government they thought to be most important to their daily lives.

The analyses of responses from these questions were instrumental in driving the conclusions of scholarly work that conceptualized regions and provinces as viable units where political subcultures developed. For example, Mildred Schwartz's (1974, 313) pioneering work documented that respondents in Atlantic Canada, Quebec, Ontario, the Prairies, and British Columbia pictured their own locales differently from other regions in Canada. Moreover, her conclusion that "regionalism is not a declining force in a country that otherwise bears all of the characteristics of a modern state" became particularly prescient during the constitutional debates of the 1980s and 1990s. Also, these studies helped to detect the differences between political choice in Quebec and the rest of Canada (ROC) – a theme that re-emerges in several chapters in this volume.[2]

Another notable feature of these two early studies was an array of questions designed to gauge perceptions of ideal traits for political parties and how existing Canadian parties measured up in the eyes of the interviewees. It was the instability in answers to these questions from one election study to the next that formed the basis for Meisel's (1975) assertion that party images mattered greatly in Canada, even more so than the vaunted theoretical concept of partisan identification that dominated American models of voter choice at that time (for example, Campbell et al. 1960; see also Jenson 1976 and the chapter by LeDuc in this volume). In fact, there is evidence to suggest that Meisel's early finding of fleeting support and opposition to Canada's major political parties applies even today (Clarke, Kornberg, and Scotto 2009).

It is interesting to note, however, that Meisel's original batteries on party images no longer appear on the CES and that the consistency of these follow-up findings has been verified using different measures. CES investigators face difficult trade-offs when contemplating changes and innovation in survey design and content. What this means, unfortunately, is that even good questions, which may have yielded meaningful insights in the past, are not immune from being removed or altered in future surveys. Such adjustments can happen for a host of reasons, including incompatibilities in the research interests of investigators or changes in the methods of survey delivery rendering questions or question formats unviable.

The opposite is also true. There are certain questions that appear on nearly all of the CES, although the question wordings sometimes vary slightly across election studies. Consequently, it is now possible to conduct longitudinal investigations of Canadians' political efficacy, their economic evaluations, and their willingness to partake in various forms of political participation. Likewise, since 1968, the CES have included feeling thermometers for candidates, parties, and groups as well as questions tapping respondents' locations on positional issues and their perceptions of which parties are furthest and closest to them on such issues. In addition, views on the relationship between Quebec and the ROC, political trust, tolerance, divorce, gay rights, and the death penalty were initially probed in 1968, and questions of a similar nature continue to appear in more recent studies.

In 1984, a major research objective was to look more closely at the effects of different sociological forces on the vote. Consequently, respondents were asked about the political behaviours of their family members. They were asked to interpret the meaning of social class and to provide their perceptions of how political parties responded to those in different classes. Interviewees were presented with an extended battery of feeling thermometer questions that probed their feelings toward various social- and membership-based groups in Canadian society, and were asked about their views on the degree of power held by certain groups and institutions within Canadian society. Questions of this sort were considered valuable for probing deeper into the relevance of class divides in Canada, a debate that Barry Kay and Andrea Perrella revisit later in this volume. However, similar to Meisel's earlier party trait batteries, not all of these indicators have found their way onto more recent CES.

The First Panel Series and Referendum Study

The cross-sectional post-election studies described above provided us with many insights about the Canadian voter. Investigations of this sort resulted largely in a static understanding derived entirely from one-time interviews and respondents' post-electoral recollections. The first election study conducted during the 1970s was in many ways similar to its predecessors from the mid-1960s in that it too was a cross-sectional post-election survey that sampled over two thousand respondents (n = 2,562). However, as LeDuc points out in the preceding chapter, five years later, approximately half of the respondents in the 1974 federal election study were re-interviewed after the 1979 election. Thus, not only did the 1979 election study result in another cross-sectional, post-election sample of the target population (consisting of a total of 2,744 respondents), but it also yielded longitudinal panel data, which were the first of their kind to emerge from the CES. Moreover, this initial panel study was extended one year later when 1,748 of the respondents who had been sampled in the 1970s were re-interviewed during the 1980 post-election study, which was the first survey in the CES collection to be administered over the phone. The end result of these three election studies, therefore, was the development of a multi-election panel series, inclusive of 812 Canadian respondents who had been interviewed and re-interviewed over more than two consecutive waves of post-election studies.

These surveys enabled researchers to delve deeper into the attitudes and behaviours of individual Canadians and to examine issues of change and continuity within Canadian elections. In addition, because more than three hundred Quebec respondents were re-interviewed a few months after the 1980 election, either shortly before or after the May 1980 Quebec Referendum, this particular series of CES also opened up new possibilities for investigating voting behaviour in different electoral contexts and for conducting cross-contextual comparisons.

In terms of sampling, the procedures employed during these years were not all that different from those used in 1965, 1968, and 1984. Respondents for both the 1974 and 1979 studies were also selected through a process of multi-stage, stratified cluster sampling. Accessible constituencies, divided by province, constituted the first sampling unit. Polling divisions within constituencies were then randomly selected as clusters proportionate to their size to constitute the second sampling unit. And between five and ten random respondents residing within a selected poll were sampled in each year's post-election survey (LeDuc et al. 1974).[3] Respondents for the 1980 post-election study and the 1980 referendum study were then drawn from these preceding samples.

Content wise, there was a clear effort made to maintain some continuity and comparability with earlier cross-sectional, post-election surveys. For example, the 1974 survey included several questions designed to tap regional identities. It also probed the level of government (federal, provincial, or local) that people thought affected them the most and which level of government (provincial or federal) they felt was more important in handling issues such as foreign affairs and education. In addition, the "fairness" of federalism in Canada was measured through a question asking respondents if they thought their province received more or less than its rightful share of government benefits. Various follow-up questions elicited the names of "have" and "have not" provinces as well as tapped views on bilingualism, renewed federalism, the energy program, and inflation. Analyses of variables such as these allowed Harold Clarke and his colleagues (1979; and Clarke and Kornberg's chapter in this volume) to extend Schwartz's earlier line of theorizing and analysis. They concluded that sectionalism in Canadian politics was alive and well because of the presence of regional, but not necessarily provincial, loyalties among the young and educated.

In other ways, the 1974, 1979, and 1980 CES were also notably distinct from earlier surveys in that they experimented with new approaches to data collection and sought to draw out supplemental information for further analysis. Certain questions in this collection of surveys were posed to only half of the respondents sampled, which made it easier to balance the trade-off between escalating data collection costs and incorporating more variables theorized to be close to respondents' voting decisions. This split format also allowed for an increase in the number of open-ended questions. One consequence of this shift was an increase in the depth of the information that was collected. For instance, when respondents were asked to provide evaluations of party leaders and their positions on key issues, the content, articulation, and intensity of their answers was carefully noted. Moreover, when it came to tapping partisanship, these studies looked in detail at partisan identification at different levels of government.

The combination of this expansion in content and the incorporation of a panel component made it possible for the principal investigators of these studies to highlight the considerable volatility that existed among the Canadian electorate during the 1970s. For example, Clarke and his team (1984) verified that the basis for party support among the same voters was far from stable. A voter who was most concerned with inflation in 1974 and voted for the party she thought best able to tackle the issue was, by 1980, voting for a different party because it had the strongest leader who had the best position on the energy program. Moreover, these investigations demonstrated that in such environments successful parties were those whose candidates and leaders exhibited a set of traits that voters found desirable (for example, effectiveness, confidence, and intelligence) and parties that were capable of adapting to problems that had suddenly arisen rather than simply abiding by a rigid ideology.[4]

It is important to mention, however, that absent from these studies were questions measuring respondents' locations on traditional Left-Right positional issues and their perceptions of party positions on such issues. In fact, such questions have continued to have less than full coverage in subsequent election studies. Consequently, it could be argued that in some instances the CES may be stacked in favour of particular models of voter choice. To counter this criticism, investigators of future iterations of the CES need to ensure that the surveys they design contain as many of the variables necessary to test rival explanations. In other words, election studies must go beyond gathering data to generate preferred models and aim instead to obtain citizen beliefs on competing groups of explanatory variables (Clarke et al. 2004, 2009).

Lastly, the extended panel component for Quebec voters, which stretched across four time points, was equally instrumental in highlighting the volatility of Quebecers' attitudes, both prior to and shortly after the 1980 referendum campaign. For example, one surprising finding showed that attitudes toward a variety of constitutional options (for example, "special status" for Quebec) were subject to change over a short time (Pammett et al. 1983). Part of this flexibility was a function of voters' fuzzy comprehension of fairly complex matters. But a principal factor contributing to this variation involved the distinct positions that parties and leaders took on the question of Quebec's independence. Analyses of the 1980 Quebec Referendum study, along with other referendum studies of the 1970s (for example, Särlvik et al. 1976), established an interrelationship between attitudes toward referendum questions, community support, and short-term political forces. Furthermore, this finding has remained intact as shown in subsequent analyses of referendum voting both in Canada and abroad (for example, Butler and Raney 1994; LeDuc and Pammett 1995; Johnston et al. 1996).

Multi-Wave, Short-Term Panel Surveys, RCS Design, and CATI

Since 1988, the design of the CES has changed significantly. They are now best described as multi-wave, short-term panel surveys that are administered both during and after campaigns. The most immediate effect of this shift in design has been to increase the number and types of surveys that are fielded with each election campaign. This change in methodology has considerably expanded the number of opportunities available for interviewing respondents. The standard approach, as outlined in more detail in the introduction of this volume, has been to conduct up to three rounds of surveys with each consecutive election. The first – the campaign period survey – is administered daily throughout the course of a campaign. The second – the post-election survey – is conducted, similar to its predecessors, once an election has been contested. And the third – the mail-back survey – is administered usually after the post-campaign surveys have been completed. Between 1988 and 2006, the only two exceptions to this basic mix were the 1992 Charlottetown Accord Referendum study and the 2006 federal election study – both of which included a campaign and post-campaign component but no mail-back surveys.

Other major adjustments that have taken place since 1988 are as follows. First, rather than the conventional face-to-face method of interviewing, the majority of surveys are now conducted over the telephone. Recall that telephone interviewing was experimented with initially in 1980. The main advancement since 1988 has been the implementation of CATI, which adds to the cost-effectiveness and convenience of telephone interviewing.

Of course, this is not to suggest that everything about the new computer-facilitated technique of telephone interviewing and data collection is necessarily better. For instance, the carefully structured and guided approach of face-to-face interviewing leaves very little room for confusion, whereas respondents may have greater difficulty visualizing multiple response categories over the telephone. As a consequence, questionnaires administered via CATI frequently use branching formats, whereby respondents are first asked if they agree or disagree with a question and then asked a follow-up question about the intensity of their feelings. Of course, changing question formats may have consequences in that they can affect response distributions and complicate comparing older CES with newer ones (Fogarty, Kelly, and Kilburn 2005).

Still, there are many advantages that have been gained through the implementation of CATI. For example, prior to CATI, survey questionnaires were made to be highly uniform, and care was taken to minimize "skips" (for example, if the respondent answers "yes" to question "x," do not ask the next question but skip to question "z") because face-to-face interviewers were more likely to induce survey error by making mistakes with complex questionnaires (Groves and Mathiowetz 1984). CATI technology has made it possible to administer complex questionnaires that can be flexible to survey responses without being as prone to human error, and it also makes it possible to randomize the arrangement of questions and answer choices to reduce ordering effects.

Another advantage of CATI is the greater ease with which experiments can be added to questionnaires and administered to respondents randomly selected for control and treatment conditions (Brady 2000). In fact, it was a CATI experiment that helped to bring about a substantive change in the wording of the traditional party identification question in 1988. During the

1970s, the party identification question asked on the CES was similar in form to the standard Michigan-type question ("Generally speaking, in federal politics, do you consider yourself to be ... or what?"). In the late 1980s, Johnston (1992) posited that the "or what" ending to this conventional question format "loaded the dice" in favour of partisanship. More specifically, his analyses of a 1987 CATI-based survey of Canadian attitudes to civil liberties showed that switching the ending of the standard Michigan-type question from "or what" to "none of these" significantly reduced the numbers of respondents who identified with the Progressive Conservatives or the Liberals, while the number of non-identifiers soared. Moreover, unlike its predecessor, answers to the new variant of the question were not a function of its location on the survey. As a result of these findings, the 1988 election study marked the debut of the version of the partisan identification question with the "none of these" option.

Another important adjustment that was initiated in 1988 was the incorporation of the rolling cross-section design (RCS). Together with the introduction of the campaign period survey, these two changes made it possible to use the CES to investigate the day-to-day dynamics of election and referendum campaigns. The RCS design splits pre-campaign samples into random cross-sections or "replicates," which are equivalent to the number of days in a campaign. Since an individual's probability of inclusion in a day's replicate is random, it becomes possible to derive unbiased estimates of daily opinion throughout a campaign.[5] Furthermore, two of the principal investigators from the 1988 and 1993 CES, Henry Brady and Richard Johnston (2006), have developed a method that "smooths" average daily responses to questions that are asked on campaign period surveys. This helps to produce even better pictures of the relevant campaign trends.[6]

As far as sampling is concerned, the major change in 1988 was to replace multi-stage, stratified cluster sampling with two-stage probability sampling. The first stage of this new approach involves utilizing a computer application known as random-digit dialing to select a random sample of household telephone numbers. The second stage then randomly selects a single respondent from each household sampled, based on criteria such as age, citizenship, and birth date. In terms of sample size, the main point to note is that there has been an inconsistent but nonetheless gradual increase in the number of respondents that the CES have surveyed since the mid-1960s. Recall that the first survey conducted in 1965 sampled slightly more than two thousand respondents. Since 1988, the number of respondents who have participated in campaign period surveys has ranged from more than three thousand in the late 1980s and early 1990s to over four thousand in 2004 and 2006.[7]

It is important to keep in mind, however, that the number of respondents who participate in multi-wave, short-term panel surveys inevitably declines over the duration of any project. The reason is that not all respondents who participate in the campaign period surveys always agree to participate in the post-campaign surveys. On average, attrition for the post-campaign telephone surveys has been approximately 20 percent. Moreover, only 53 percent of the post-campaign samples in 2000 and 2004 completed the mail-back questionnaire, which was a sharp decline from the 80 percent that did so in 1988 (Northrup 2003; Johnston 2008).

Still, every election study that has been conducted since 1988 includes a fairly sizeable short-term panel component that extends from the campaign period to after a campaign is complete. In addition, there are also various longitudinal panels. For example, over 50 percent of the 2,530 respondents who were interviewed as part of the 1992 Charlottetown Accord Referendum study were re-interviewed as part of the 1993 election study. Likewise, 1,500 respondents from the 2004 election study were re-interviewed during the 2006 election study.[8] Since the 1970s, therefore, the number and variety of panel studies conducted has expanded and diversified.

With respect to questionnaire content, a significant amount of attention has been given to maintaining some consistency with the previous CES. However, it is not surprising to find that scholars have also used the multi-wave, short-term panel design in ways that advance their research pursuits and deal more readily with lingering questions. Foremost in this regard has been the link between campaigns and attitudinal/behavioural change. The pre-campaign waves of recent CES have been constructed to leverage the ability of the RCS design to reveal campaign dynamics almost as instantly as they have developed. One line of questioning deals with evaluating the performance of leaders in the debates as well as with the ramifications of this campaign event on voter choice (Fournier et al. 2003). The evidence to date has been quite revealing. For instance, findings suggest that leader debates were consequential to the 1988 election outcome, advantaging the Liberal party and hurting the Progressive Conservative party (see also Blais and Boyer 1996). In addition, André Blais and his colleagues (1999, 2003) found that parties of the Right (namely the Progressive Conservatives and Reform) benefited from the English language debate in 1997, and leadership debates were relevant in 2000 as they helped to improve the standing of Progressive Conservative leader Joe Clark.

The role of the media in influencing campaign outcomes has been another prominent topic of interest. Johnston and his colleagues (1992), for example, have demonstrated that improved ratings for Liberal leader John Turner were linked to the favourable media coverage he received throughout the 1988 election campaign. Likewise, LeDuc and Jon Pammett's (1995) analysis of the 1992 Charlottetown Referendum campaign showed considerable campaign dynamics and voters responding to cues from parties and politicians when making a pro/con decision on the accord (see also Johnston et al. 1996). Many of these messages were conveyed and received through the media and various types of advertising campaigns.

Campaign period surveys also ask respondents to assess the probabilities of each of the major parties winning in their ridings and forming a majority in Parliament. These indicators have been used to measure and document the widespread variation in respondents' predictions of election outcomes over the course of a campaign (Blais et al. 2002; Turgeon 2004; Bodet 2006). In addition, questions designed to measure strategic voting have yielded rich insights on the number of Canadians who, in a majoritarian system, vote for a party that is not their most favourite (Bowler and Lanoue 1992; Blais and Nadeau 1996; Blais et al. 2001; Blais 2002; Justice and Lanoue 2005).

In many ways, the post-campaign surveys are where much of the attention to continuity and long-term comparability gets paid. Since 1988, these surveys have in large measure been extensions of the cross-sectional, post-election studies of the 1960s and 1970s. For instance, these surveys probe attitudes toward provincial politics and political efficacy. They also examine various recurring reasons for voting and party choice, and they have sections devoted to tapping attitudes concerning contentious issues such as gay marriage, sovereignty for Quebec, government spending, and many of the topics have had coverage in past surveys. That said, post-campaign surveys have also been used to conduct various new lines of analyses. For instance, the 1993 post-election survey, which was conducted after the failure of the Charlottetown Accord Referendum in 1992, asked respondents to decide whether future decisions concerning the Constitution should be made by government officials or the people. In addition, post-campaign surveys repeat many of the same questions that were asked initially in the campaign period surveys, which allow researchers to compare survey responses to similar questions both during and after a campaign. These advances in turn have led to many new insights, some of which suggest that during campaigns certain voters acquire more information than others and that it is the media that helps to create this knowledge gap. Moreover, the evidence suggests that information gains during a campaign have an important effect on the vote (Nadeau et al. 2008).

The primary purpose of the mail-back surveys that have been administered from 1988 to 2004 has been to accommodate broader research agendas by providing a more cost-effective means of collecting additional survey data by mail. For example, these surveys tap value orientations, respondents' confidence in political institutions, support for free markets, and attitudes toward feminism. They also contain questions designed to get at interviewees' evaluations of the trade-off between safety and civil liberties, and they include questions on electoral reform, the fairness of elections, the appropriateness of using referendums, and the current and proper influence of groups in the party system.

A major advantage of the mail-back survey is that it is not distracting to the primary objective at hand, which is to study voting behaviour during campaigns. The format is also more conducive for the purposes of eliciting respondents' attitudes toward sensitive topics such as race or immigration because it minimizes the problems of social desirability bias or interviewer effects (Tourangeau and Smith 1996). This is not to say, however, that mail-back surveys are entirely problem-free. Drawbacks include low response rates and the possibility that in multi-member households, the survey may not be completed by the intended respondent. Such error can cause major complications when it comes to analyzing respondents across different waves of a short-term panel.

Still, there are numerous examples of innovative analyses that have emerged out of the data provided by the mail-back surveys. For instance, Elisabeth Gidengil and her colleagues (2001) utilized the 1997 data to study the correlates and consequences of anti-partyism. Donald Blake (2003) used the 1997 and 2000 studies to examine how local context influences the attitudes of white Canadians toward minorities and immigrants. Cameron Anderson and Elisabeth Goodyear-Grant (2005) have found that Canadians' views toward direct democracy and "delegate-versus-trustee" forms of representation were partially a function of political knowledge and ideological individualism. And more recently, Gidengil, Allison Harell, and Bonnie Erickson (2007) have employed the social networks portion of the 2000 mail-back questionnaire to explain female support for the New Democratic party. This is an interesting new area of research that Gidengil elaborates on further in her chapter in this volume.

Conclusion: Toward an Internet-Based Design?

Over the past four decades and more, changes to the design and content of the CES have helped to expand and develop our understanding of why Canadians vote the way they do. The transition from a basic cross-sectional, post-election survey design to the introduction of multi-wave, short-term panel surveys, incorporating the RCS design and CATI in 1988, has made it possible to conduct more dynamic and campaign-centric analyses. It has also made it possible to compare and contrast data from across different political and electoral contexts and has allowed researchers to explore alternative investigative opportunities through survey experimentation and the use of more cost-effective modes of data collection, such as the mail-back surveys.

But even with all of these advances, there are still many limitations on the types of analyses that we can conduct with the data that we currently possess. For example, the accumulation of longitudinal evidence has made it possible to identify change; however, it is still difficult to pinpoint the time at which changes have taken place, in large part because we have very little evidence as to what goes on in the minds of voters in the interim between election campaigns or referendums. Even with the implementation of CATI and mail-back surveys, cost considerations continue to limit the number of surveys we can administer, the number of questions we can ask, and the types of samples we can collect. These factors too place constraints on the breadth and depth of the analyses we conduct. In addition, cost considerations continue to constrain our current ability to fully maximize the RCS design because they limit a given day's "replicate" or sample size to fewer than one hundred individuals. This limitation detracts from our ability to decipher whether campaign dynamics are specific to subgroups or homogeneous, which is a major problem in a country with various deep-rooted socio-political cleavages.

Building on our understanding of the considerable heterogeneity that exists among the Canadian electorate with respect to voting behaviour and any other related curiosities that might currently exist or emerge in the future will almost certainly require more data and a steadier stream of funding. Johnston and Blais attempt to tackle the latter issue in the next chapter. However, in addition to contemplating new funding strategies, we also need to be continuously thinking about, and experimenting with, ways to more feasibly conduct longer panels, collect larger sample sizes, and administer more frequent surveys with broader mandates, even between campaigns. One suggestion in this regard might be to start looking more seriously at the other cost-effective options of collecting data, such as Internet surveys.

Other countries have already begun to experiment with this possibility. For example, Johnston recently co-developed a five-wave Internet survey design for the 2007-09 Annenberg study of American political behaviour. Each wave of this study included an RCS design and sampled approximately ten thousand respondents, which means that the average day's replicate within each wave was far greater than one hundred.[9] In addition, building on the preliminary work they conducted in 2001, the principal investigators of the 2005 British Election Studies simultaneously conducted an Internet study of separate respondents, together with a conventional face-to-face survey of a representative sample of Britons.[10] This study also incorporated an RCS design into its pre-election survey, and it included a post-election survey that re-interviewed over eight thousand respondents. As LeDuc makes clear in the preceding chapter, the study of elections and voting behaviour has always been a very comparative enterprise. The sharing of theories, methodologies, and findings has benefited us in the past, and there is no reason to suppose that this particular lead would be any different as long as we proceed with a healthy degree of caution.

The main concern with Internet surveys is that it is not yet entirely clear whether they produce reliable and valid information about political attitudes and behaviour. Viewpoints on this matter are mixed, and the evidence is still inconclusive. For example, David Sanders and his colleagues (2007) caution that success with Internet surveys in Britain may not necessarily translate into automatic success in other nations. In all countries, there exists the potential for "coverage error" because the demographics of Internet users (and those who are selected into online panels) do not yet mirror those of the population. Further, a weakness in reaching respondents over the Internet is that unlike telephone and face-to-face studies, it requires a high school level of literacy, and this factor could potentially bias samples toward an over-representation of educated people (Johnston 2008).

Be that as it may, evidence shows that by 2005 Internet usage in Canada had approached 70 percent, and there is very little reason to expect that this figure will not continue to increase in the future. As Herbert Weisberg (2005, 31) notes, "in many ways, the status of Web surveys in the years between 1998 and 2005 resembles the status of telephone surveys in the mid-1970s, when procedures for quality phone surveys were still being tested and perfected." In the twenty-first century, the Internet will quite likely come to surpass the telephone's ability to obtain samples that are representative of target populations as area codes no longer tie respondents to specific locations and cellular telephones make people difficult to reach over this medium.

Still, there is the additional concern that survey responses that have been collected via different modes such as the telephone and the Internet may not be compatible. There were similar concerns about switching from conducting face-to-face surveys to administering telephone interviews, and the preliminary evidence on this issue does not appear insurmountable. For instance, Sanders et al. (2007) found that multivariate models of voter choice and turnout, incorporating both Internet and face-to-face respondents, tend to accord well with one another. However, results from simple distributions have been known to vary, and this deviation could create a problem for those wishing to compare data pertaining to common questions asked across time. Consequently, any proposed switch to the Internet may involve some re-tailoring of survey questions. For an obvious example, 100-point candidate and feeling thermometers that are often used on telephone or face-to-face surveys work better as ten-point scales on the Internet because answer choices of more than a dozen categories do not fit easily on a computer screen.

Some other potential benefits and drawbacks to take into consideration are as follows. Internet survey firms usually offer incentives for respondents to stay in panels and devote substantial resources to panel maintenance. As a result, we would expect that attrition may be lower in such surveys, but this practice might also induce conditioning effects, which could have implications for the quality of the information received.[11] Conversely, Walter Borges and Harold Clarke (2008) demonstrate how easily survey experiments can be incorporated into Internet surveys. While this benefit may not currently constitute a priority, it could certainly prove more useful down the road once the integrity of this methodology becomes less of an issue. For example, it is conceivable that in the future the multiple partisan-identification questions that have been used over time could each be asked to a random subset of Internet survey respondents for the purposes of better understanding the true nature of the theoretical concept.

Internet surveys may provide a cost-effective opportunity for acquiring more survey data pertaining to a variety of relevant issues, collected on a more frequent basis. This is not to suggest that Internet surveys are a panacea for answering all of the unanswered questions that still remain about the Canadian electorate. However, just as previous improvements to the methodology and survey design of the CES have helped to advance our substantive understanding about political life in Canada, it might be that adding an online component to the CES is the "next way forward" on this front.

NOTES

1 Even then, approximately 7 percent of the Canadian electorate was deemed too costly to reach. Consequently, coverage of the target population – eligible Canadian voters – was not fully obtained in the 1965 study. More recent studies have made some significant inroads in tackling this problem but only to be faced with new challenges. The nature of these newer challenges will become more evident toward the latter part of this chapter.

2 See, for example, Richard Nadeau and Éric Bélanger's chapter in this volume.

3 To ensure political minorities were adequately represented in the sample, constituencies were selected only after controls for the party finishing second in a province were added to the randomization process. The 1979 study also contained an over-sample of younger voters. Weights were developed to analyze regions and panel waves separately. In addition, Lawrence LeDuc and his colleagues (1974) provided formulas to correct for downward bias in the sampling variance that occurred due to the clustering.

4 For a summary of this narrative, see the trenchant review of *Absent Mandate* by Barry Cooper (1985).

5 As noted by David Northrup and Anne Oram (1989, 9-11) and Richard Johnston and Henry Brady (2002, 284-86), it is the day of the campaign, not the replicate, that is the proper unit of analysis for analyzing campaign dynamics because it often takes a number of days to contact a respondent. Analyzing respondents from replicates will bias results because people who are contacted after one phone call have fundamentally different attitudes from those who need to be phoned multiple times before they answer a survey (Sebold 1988). Consequently, results from the first few days of a rolling cross-section study will feature fewer respondents and are often biased, but if the time to completion is constant throughout the period the survey is in the field, this type of bias disappears after an initial "burn-in" period of about one week. Furthermore, response rates to the pre-campaign components of the Canadian Election Studies (CES) show (aside from responses obtained from the replicates released in the closing days of the campaign) fairly even daily response rates to be the norm (see Northrup and Oram 1989).

6 See Johnston and Brady (2002) and Brady and Johnston (2006).

7 The one exception is the Charlottetown Accord Referendum survey of 1992. Similar to studies conducted during the mid-1960s, the sample size in this case was slightly more than 2,500 (see Table 2 in the introduction of this volume).

8 Many of these respondents were again re-interviewed as part of the 2008 CES, making this the second CES panel that covers the span of three federal elections.

9 For a full exposition of the study design, see Johnston (2008).

10 Full details of the design of the 2005 British Election Studies can be found in the following online presentation: 2005-06 British Election Study, http://www.essex.ac.uk/bes/2005/Introductory%20files/presentation2004.PPT#1.

11 This fear is being mitigated by the fact that online survey firms that conduct political polling are increasingly called upon by private enterprise for commercial-marketing purposes, making it unlikely that members of a panel will receive only politically oriented surveys.

REFERENCES

Anderson, Cameron D., and Elisabeth Goodyear-Grant. 2005. "Conceptions of Political Representation in Canada: An Explanation of Public Opinion." *Canadian Journal of Political Science* 38(4): 1029-58.

Blais, André. 2002. "Why Is There So Little Strategic Voting in Canadian Plurality Rule Elections?" *Political Studies* 50(3): 445-54.

Blais, André, and Marc André Bodet. 2006. "How Do Voters Form Expectations about Parties' Chances of Winning Elections?" *Social Science Quarterly* 87(3): 477-93.

Blais, André, and M. Martin Boyer. 1996. "Assessing the Impact of Televised Debates: The Case of the 1988 Canadian Election." *British Journal of Political Science* 26(2): 143-64.

Blais, André, Elisabeth Gidengil, Richard Nadeau, and Neil Nevitte. 2003. "Campaign Dynamics in the 2000 Canadian Election: How the Leader Debates Salvaged the Conservative Party." *PS: Political Science and Politics* 36(1): 45-50.

Blais, André, and Richard Nadeau. 1996. "Measuring Strategic Voting: A Two-Step Procedure." *Electoral Studies* 15(1): 39-52.

Blais, André, Richard Nadeau, Elisabeth Gidengil, and Neil Nevitte. 1999. "Campaign Dynamics in the 1997 Canadian Election." *Canadian Public Policy* 25(2): 197-205.

–. 2001. "Measuring Strategic Voting in Multiparty Plurality Elections." *Electoral Studies* 20(3): 343-52.

Blais, André, and Mathieu Turgeon. 2004. "How Good Are Voters at Sorting Out the Weakest Candidate in Their Constituency." *Electoral Studies* 23(3): 455-61.

Blake, Donald E. 2003. "Environmental Determinants of Racial Attitudes among White Canadians." *Canadian Journal of Political Science* 36(3): 491-509.

Borges, Walter, and Harold D. Clarke. 2008. "Cues in Context: Analyzing the Heuristics of Referendum Voting with an Internet Survey Experiment." *Journal of Elections, Public Opinion, and Parties* 18(4): 433-48.

Bowler, Sean, and David J. Lanoue. 1992. "Strategic and Protest Voting for Third Parties: The Case of the Canadian NDP." *Political Research Quarterly* 45(2): 485-99.

Brady, Henry E. 2000. "Contributions of Survey Research to Political Science." *PS: Political Science and Politics* 33(1): 47-57.

Brady, Henry E., and Richard Johnston. 2006. "The Rolling Cross-Section and Causal Attribution." In H. Brady and R. Johnston, eds., *Capturing Campaign Effects*, 164-95. Ann Arbor: University of Michigan Press.

Butler, David, and Austin Ranney. 1994. *Referendums around the World: The Growing Use of Direct Democracy*. Washington, DC: AEI Press.

Campbell, Angus, Philip E. Converse, Warren E. Miller, and Donald E. Stokes. 1960. *The American Voter*. New York: Wiley.

Clarke, Harold D. 1984. *Absent Mandate: The Politics of Discontent in Canada*. Toronto: Gage.

Clarke, Harold D., Allan Kornberg, and Thomas J. Scotto. 2009. *Making Political Choices: Canada and the United States*. Toronto: University of Toronto Press.

Clarke, Harold D., Lawrence LeDuc, Jane Jenson, and Jon H. Pammett. 1979. *Political Choice in Canada*. New York: McGraw-Hill Ryerson.

Clarke, Harold D., David Sanders, Marianne Stewart, and Paul Whiteley. 2004. *Political Choice in Britain*. Oxford: Oxford University Press.

Cooper, Barry. 1985. "Review: Absent Mandate: The Politics of Discontent in Canada by Harold Clarke et al." *American Political Science Review* 79(3): 866-67.

Fogarty, Brian J., Nathan J. Kelly, and H. Whitt Kilburn. 2005. "Issue Attitudes and Survey Continuity across Interview Mode in the 2000 NES." *Political Analysis* 13(1): 95-108.

Fournier, Patrick, André Blais, Richard Nadeau, Elisabeth Gidengil, and Neil Nevitte. 2003. "Issue Importance and Performance Voting." *Political Behavior* 25(1): 51-67.

Gidengil, Elisabeth, André Blais, Neil Nevitte, and Richard Nadeau. 2001. "The Correlates and Consequences of Anti-Partyism in the 1997 Canadian Election." *Party Politics* 7(4): 491-513.

Gidengil, Elisabeth, Allison Harell, and Bonnie H. Erickson. 2007. "Network Diversity and Vote Choice: Women's Social Ties and Left Voting in Canada." *Politics and Gender* 3(2): 151-77.

Groves, Robert M., and Nancy A. Mathiowetz. 1984. "Computer Assisted Telephone Interviewing: Effects on Interviewers and Respondents." *Public Opinion Quarterly* 48(1): 356-69.

Jenson, Jane. 1976. "Party Strategy and Party Identification: Some Patterns of Partisan Allegiance." *Canadian Journal of Political Science* 9(1): 27-48.

Johnston, Richard. 1992. "Party Identification Measures in the Anglo-American Democracies: A National Survey Experiment." *American Journal of Political Science* 36(2): 542-59.

–. 2008. "Modeling Campaign Dynamics on the Web in the 2008 National Annenberg Election Study." *Journal of Elections, Public Opinion, and Parties* 18(4): 401-12.

Johnston, Richard, André Blais, Henry E. Brady, and Jean Crête. 1992. *Letting the People Decide: Dynamics of a Canadian Election*. Montreal: McGill-Queen's University Press.

Johnston, Richard, André Blais, Elisabeth Gidengil, and Neil Nevitte. 1996. *The Challenge of Direct Democracy: The 1992 Canadian Referendum*. Montreal: McGill-Queen's University Press.

Johnston, Richard, and Henry E. Brady. 2002. "The Rolling Cross-Section Design." *Electoral Studies* 21(2): 283-95.

Justice, James W., and David J. Lanoue. 2005. "Strategic and Sincere Voting in a One-Sided Election: The Canadian Federal Election of 1997." *Social Science Quarterly* 86(1): 129-46.

LeDuc, Lawrence, Harold Clarke, Jane Jenson, and Jon Pammett. 1974. "A National Sample Design." *Canadian Journal of Political Science* 7(4): 701-8.

LeDuc, Lawrence, and Jon H. Pammett. 1995. "Referendum Voting: Attitudes and Behaviour in the 1992 Constitutional Referendum." *Canadian Journal of Political Science* 28(1): 3-33.

Meisel, John. 1975. *Working Papers on Canadian Politics*, 2nd edition. Montreal: McGill-Queen's University Press.

Meisel, John, and Richard van Loon. 1966. "Canadian Attitudes to Election Expenses, 1965-1966." In Committee on Election Expenses, *Report of the Committee on Election Expenses*, 23-146. Ottawa: Queen's Printer.

Nadeau, Richard, Neil Nevitte, Elisabeth Gidengil, and André Blais. 2008. "Election Campaigns as Information Campaigns: Who Learns What and Does It Matter?" *Political Communication* 25(3): 229-48.

Northrup, David. 2003. *The 2000 Canadian Election Study: Technical Documentation*. Toronto: Institute for Social Research, York University.

Northrup, David, and Anne Oram. 1989. *The 1988 National Election Study: Technical Documentation*. Toronto: Institute for Social Research, York University.

Pammett, Jon H., Harold D. Clarke, Jane Jenson, and Lawrence LeDuc. 1983. "Political Support and Voting Behavior in the Quebec Referendum." In A. Kornberg and H.D. Clarke, eds., *Political Support in Canada: The Crisis Years, Essays in Honor of Richard A. Preston*, 323-52. Durham, NC: Duke University Press.

Sanders, David, Harold D. Clarke, Marianne C. Stewart, and Paul Whiteley. 2007. "Does Mode Matter for Modeling Political Choice? Evidence from the 2005 British Election Study." *Political Analysis* 15(3): 257-85.

Särlvik, Bo, Ivor Crewe, James Alt, and Anthony Fox. 1976. "Britain's Membership of the EEC: A Profile of Electoral Opinions in the Spring of 1974 – With a Postscript on the Referendum." *European Journal of Political Research* 4(1): 83-113.

Schwartz, Mildred A. 1974. *Politics and Territory: The Sociology of Regional Persistence in Canada*. Montreal: McGill-Queen's University Press.

Sebold, Janice. 1988. "Survey Period Length, Unanswered Numbers, and Nonresponse in Telephone Surveys." In R.M. Groves, P.B. Biemer, L.E. Lyberg, J.T. Massey, W.L. Nicholls II, and J. Waksberg, eds., *Telephone Survey Methodology*, 247-56. New York: John Wiley and Sons.

Tourangeau, Roger, and Tom W. Smith. 1996. "Asking Sensitive Questions: The Impact of Data Collection Mode, Question Format, and Question Context." *Public Opinion Quarterly* 60(2): 275-304.

Weisberg, Herbert F. 2005. *The Total Survey Error Approach: A Guide to the New Science of Survey Research*. Chicago: University of Chicago Press.

5

The Relevance and Future of the Canadian Election Studies

RICHARD JOHNSTON AND ANDRÉ BLAIS

Elections are crucial in a democracy. Although there are many other instances of democratic practice in Canada, elections are the one instrument available to all eligible citizens and one that operates with a credible accounting system. The Canadian Election Studies (CES), similar to other election studies around the world, serve to provide a better understanding of this important democratic process. From this critical perspective alone, the CES are a flagship project of Canadian social science. Moreover, as the preceding chapters have outlined, the CES are among the world's oldest academically based election studies, with an almost unbroken record of fieldwork dating back to 1965. They have also served as a major site for methodological innovation. Their broad scope, their continuity in content, their impact on various research and policy communities as well as their accessibility and utility have made the CES a pivotal data source in Canada over the last four decades.

As mentioned in the first two chapters in this volume, over most of their history, the CES have been supported by, in turn, the Canada Council and the Social Sciences and Humanities Research Council (SSHRC). At the time of writing, however, the CES are at a turning point. At the same time that major cross-national comparisons of national election studies are being developed and expanded (as described in Lawrence LeDuc's chapter in this volume), the CES have yet to secure funding over the long haul, even though recent developments are a positive step toward resolving this issue. The purpose of this chapter is first to elaborate on the relevance of the CES and the various players involved and, second, to grapple with this immediate and pressing concern by outlining in more detail the problem at hand and tabling some options for funding and organizational reform.

The Relevance

For those who work with the CES on an ongoing basis, their relevance is probably self-evident. For those who do not, however, there is likely a greater need to explain. Deriving a deep understanding of electoral dynamics and electoral choice requires scientific evidence, which cannot be achieved simply by gathering together scattered commercial polls. In fact, by the time commercial polls became ubiquitous, the CES were already nearly twenty years old. Moreover, the machine-readable files from the early commercial polls are rarely available, in contrast to the lavish documentation and careful preparation of even the very earliest CES. Economic considerations make the process by which commercial samples are framed and cleared opaque and limit the length and depth of questionnaires. The CES, in contrast, are an open book. For the CES, the principal constraint is often the patience of respondents.

Consequently, the CES are generally broader in scope than commercial polls.[1] In addition to being a "go to" data source for analysis and debate about electoral dynamics and electoral choice, the CES are also an important data source for opinions and perceptions in the realm of Canadian Charter of Rights and Freedoms values, multiculturalism, language relations, and the "national question," not to mention opinions on virtually the entire policy agenda and much more.[2] Although Jon Pammett suggests in his chapter in this volume that other social science data sets provide more depth in specific areas, no other study covers as wide a field or as long a time period. Certainly, no other study can gauge the impact of such a diversity of questions on the electoral process.

The CES also offer continuity in their content. An interpretation of a single election cannot be complete unless it is understood in the context of earlier and, eventually later, ones. Accumulation of comparable evidence across several elections opens up research frontiers beyond the specific event. However, as alluded to in the preceding chapter, maintaining continuity is both a requisite and a challenge. Only a study attuned to the academic research community can deliver a delicate balance of continuity and change. Awareness of what has gone before and consciousness of scrutiny by colleagues makes investigators attentive to the long-run value of these data. A major element in that value lies in the maintenance of certain indicators, some of them going back more than forty years.

Another sign of relevance is impact, and it is clear that the CES have had a broad influence. Since 1988, the CES have been arguably a leader on the study of campaign dynamics and media effects, thanks to the incorporation of the campaign period survey and the implementation of the "rolling cross-section" design.[3] The university-based national election studies in New Zealand and Great Britain have come to be modeled on the Canadian approach, as was a component of the 2005 German Election Study. The US National Election Study modeled its 1998 pilot study on the Canadian pattern, and the massive National Annenberg Election Study at the University of Pennsylvania explicitly follows the Canadian design.

It is important to acknowledge that some of this impact reflects the dedicated efforts of individual members of Canadian survey teams. Richard Johnston, for example, has served on advisory boards for the US National Election Study and was closely involved in the design of the 1996 New Zealand study. André Blais and Johnston both currently serve on the Advisory Board for the British Election Study. Blais participated in the 2003 re-evaluation of the US study. Johnston designed the 2000 National Annenberg Election Study and, in 2006, resumed his role as research director for that survey. Harold Clarke of the 1974/1979/1980 CES research team is now co-director of the current British Election Study team, and Blais, along with counterparts from the US, Australian, and German election studies, was a founding member of the Comparative Study of Electoral Systems (CSES) and currently sits as the chair of the planning committee.

In addition, research that stems from the CES contributes to an increasingly global conversation about core analytic concerns in elections, comprising the impact of institutional context (including federalism – which implies the coexistence of two or more electoral arenas – and the constraining force of the single-member plurality electoral system) on a multiparty landscape; the social psychology of partisanship as a potentially dynamic and directive force; and the quality of opinion, its informational base, its stability, and its coherence. Many claims in these debates can be substantiated only by linking corresponding studies of elections in more than one country, and the CES play a central role in that process. In fact, the CES were an early site for the placement of a questionnaire module developed by the CSES.[4]

Through the CSES and other collaborative ventures, and through the energy of various individual scholars, the CES have become a vital element in expanding and consolidating international efforts.[5] They have helped to create analytic possibilities that were unimaginable even twenty years ago, and the juxtaposition of data from other countries leverages the already-considerable power of the Canadian data themselves. Lastly, another worthwhile point to note is that the CES are widely accessible and frequently utilized. Current practice is to make these data publicly available without charge one year after the election in question has taken place. Machine-readable CES data files are accessible at various sites. The Inter-University Consortium for Political and Social Research makes data sets originating from 1965 until today accessible as downloads. The Institute for Social Research at York University does the same back to 1984. The CES's new home site at http://ces-eec.org/ does so for studies back to 1965 via the Canadian Opinion Research Archive. Additionally, the CES are downloadable without charge within the relevant community from virtually every university that maintains its own data archive. As mentioned earlier, data from these studies are also available as part of multi-country data sets, such as those circulated by the CSES.

However, accessibility matters only to the extent that these data are actually used. Examples of multiple books, articles, and chapters in which CES data are employed as primary sources are listed in a reference appendix to this volume. The sheer size of this list speaks for itself. Figure 5.1 summarizes usage in two ways. One captures the publication or presentation date of papers using these data.[6] The other captures references to individual elections, singly or as part of a series of elections. Note that the annual publication rate has grown dramatically, with a sharp acceleration in the mid-1990s. One thing that this figure shows is that the CES have created their own clientele.

In 1965, John Meisel and Maurice Pinard were the only two Canadian-based co-investigators, although two of their US-based colleagues, Peter Regenstreif and Mildred Schwartz, were Canadians.[7] There simply was not the requisite human capital on the Canadian scene to fully exploit the early potential of these data. During the 1970s, scholars with the necessary skills gradually appeared on the scene, usually with American doctorate degrees. Growth remained slow, as new hiring in universities slowed down dramatically after 1977 and as Canadians who entered graduate programs in the later 1970s and 1980s seemed more interested in non-empirical work. The pendulum started to swing back in the late 1980s, as universities slowly started to replace the older members of the 1960s hiring cohort and as Canadian graduate programs with quantitative content matured. They did so to some

FIGURE 5.1

Publications from the Canadian Election Studies

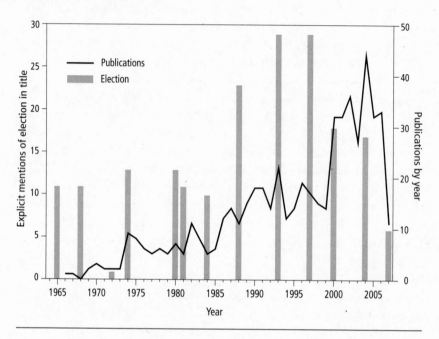

extent because the CES gave them a distinctive analytic base – distinctive from other Canadian preoccupations in being quantitative and cumulative, and distinctive from election studies elsewhere in being Canadian.[8]

Merely by existing, the CES started to make new kinds of social and political research possible. The emergence of such avenues of research is illustrated by the vertical bars in Figure 5.1. These indicate each time an election in a given year is explicitly mentioned in the title of a publication. These calculations do not capture all of the times that data from that year were used, only the number of times it made sense to authors to mention an election year by name.[9] Often the use of the year indicates that the paper accounts for some facet of that particular election as an event in history. Increasingly, however, individual elections figure as points in analyses of trends and processes. Much of this information, of course, reflects the growing analytic capacity of the research community. The apparent drop-off for 2000 and 2004 also indicates that time needs to pass for studies of any given election and for new projects looking back at the long term to be launched.

In addition to the usages just described, there is also evidence to show that the utility of the CES extends beyond political science and the academic community. For example, in litigation, the CES have been applied to assess innumerable issues, including the appropriateness of limitations on third-party advertising (*Somerville v. Attorney General for Canada* 1996; *Pacific Press v. Attorney-General for British Columbia* 1999; *Harper v. Attorney General for Canada* 2004); the regulation of the publication of polls (*Pacific Press v. Attorney-General for British Columbia* 1999); and the regulation of election night broadcasting (*R v. Canadian Broadcasting Corporation* 1990; *R v. Bryan* 2007). All of these cases have had important Charter implications.

The Future? Organizational and Funding Challenges

Despite all of their achievements and growing relevance, the CES may be at a fork in the road. Over most of their history, the CES have been subject to the same third-party assessment as other Canadian research projects in political science. The difficulty, however, has been that fieldwork costs alone for the CES, as currently conceived – a telephone survey with about four thousand respondents contacted just before and just after each federal election – exceed the ceiling for standard research grants. At the same time, even an elaborate research program built around this fieldwork is relatively modest compared to the funding expectations attached to the SSHRC's major collaborative research initiatives (MCRI). Other aspects of the CES also fit awkwardly with the MCRI mould. For one thing, the CES are of primary benefit to a single discipline, notwithstanding their utility to others. For another, where the MCRI program stresses innovation, a key feature of the CES is continuity. At a minimum, then, the long-term survival of the CES requires the SSHRC to adopt a more flexible approach to research support or to recognize projects and programs of intermediate size.

Recently, a significant step was taken to provide some short-term relief. In 2009, together with Elections Canada, the SSHRC launched a special one-time call for proposals seeking to study the forty-first and forty-second Canadian federal elections. This initiative, however, is, as we speak, only a one-time funding opportunity, and, therefore, there is no guarantee that it will secure the long-term financial survival of the CES. What other options are available? The most ideal scenario would be for the SSHRC to recognize that the CES are a *de facto* research resource and give them such status *de jure*. Election studies are already recognized as strategic resources in at least five countries. In the United States, the election study, which dates back to

1952, was designated as a research resource in 1977. In the United Kingdom, the British Election Study (BES) was designated in time for the 2001 election, although competitions for money designated in advance for the BES took place in earlier years as well. Sweden funds its election survey as an expense in gathering election statistics. Switzerland treats the study as a permanent grant to the University of Geneva. Norway has never formally designated its election study as a resource, but the chain is unbroken and fieldwork is always carried out by Statistics Norway.

Designating the CES as a research resource would bring many advantages, including assistance with deliberate planning. The old pattern of support from the SSHRC requires teams to apply in the year before an expected election. The lead time between announcement and fieldwork is often short. In 2000, the election was over *before* the award was made, and the 2000 data set was correspondingly compromised by the need to make instrument shortcuts as a cost-cutting hedge against uncertainty. Even for a single election, then, a multiple-year window and some kind of conditional guarantee would improve matters. Ideally, the window should span two or more elections.

A designated resource would also make it possible to attract supporting proposals in other SSHRC competitions. Even now, most of the analysis of CES data is funded by standard research grants to persons outside the current research team – the longevity and accumulation of data sets make this process possible. To date, however, grant applicants not on the CES team must take the data as given. In the context of an ongoing research resource, one could imagine applications that are forward looking, for example, if the applicant hopes to affect sample or instrumentation choices for the next study. Similarly, ongoing support for the CES could serve as a basis of co-ordination for researchers employing non-survey or parallel-survey data. An obvious example would be researchers proposing a survey of candidates. Another would be students of campaign finance, expecting to work with Elections Canada data. Such researchers would have a beneficial interest in CES instrumentation, certainly not only for geographical codes but also for other variables that pertain to campaigns (media-use batteries, for example).

Commitment by the SSHRC could also create a co-ordination point for other financial supporters. To an extent, this has happened in the past. Support from Elections Canada goes back to 1997, and the Institute for Research on Public Policy was a supporter in 1988 and 2000. For supporters such as Elections Canada, however, the central attribute of the CES is the *credibility* it derives from third-party assessment. Therefore, a properly constituted CES program should also supply the very refereeing – or a layer of refereeing – that is so critical to the study's credibility. The question is where in the process does the major burden of refereeing fall – before the fact or along the way – and this perspective leads us to consider various possible models. In the current climate, three models appear neither attractive nor feasible:

1 An uncoordinated competition model, which has no pre-set budget limit and, critically, no pre-set floor. This was the Canadian model before 1997. In principle, there could be more than one "national" study – or none at all.
2 A self-organized consortium model, which is employed in the Netherlands. Several universities participate and rotate responsibility for co-ordination. It helps that the total number of participating universities is small (and all, of course, are physically close to each other). There are obvious risks in the expectation of quasi-automatic rotation, and the model does not appear to deliver any kind of third-party review.
3 The civil-service model, which is the Scandinavian model. A single principal investigator (PI) is typically named for a long period. As an academic, this person enjoys some insulation from short-term political pressure. Although the model makes it likely that the PI will care for the long-term health of the study, it short-circuits the third-party refereeing that is critical to the study's credibility, and it diminishes the potential for "buy-in" from the research community at large.

In the realms of feasibility and desirability, two models currently dominate the field:

1 The consortium model is essentially the American model. One or two persons are designated as PIs. Although these PIs make the proposal to the funding agency, they present themselves as chairpersons rather than as team leaders. The board they chair is relatively compact, so that it can make real decisions (although the final say, in the event of disagreement, rests with the chairs). The board could include members of other disciplines as necessary. The current US "Board of Overseers" includes psychologists, sociologists, and economists, for example. The task of the non-political scientists is not to direct the substantive objectives of the study but, rather, to bring methodological expertise from their

respective disciplines to the table (for example, from cognitive psychology for questionnaire design). Ideally, the board also includes international members, and it has the responsibility for adjudicating the competing claims of new proposals and of core, continuing content. Commonly, it seeks new proposals in the form of research memoranda. Sometimes it oversees pilot studies to test proposed innovations. The current US National Election Studies runs periodic "online commons" on design topics (blogs, in effect).

In the consortium model, the PIs and the board typically receive a budget for data collection only. Data collection can be defined to include pilot studies for methodological development, but analysis of pilot study data is usually at someone else's expense. (It should be noted, however, that this model also generally presupposes a formularized overhead system, which enables the home university to support the PIs' research by another route.) In this model, data are released as soon as practicable. Depending on the mode of collection, beta versions of data can be posted in a matter of weeks.

2   The team model is the model for the British studies. Here the PI may be the real leader. In any case, the team is compact, no more than four or five members. Third-party review occurs through the assessments of funding proposals and links to the larger community via an advisory board. Teams commonly agree to deliver publications as well as the data set. Among these might be a book focused on the election in question. To this end, and to make the effort worthwhile for persons of ambition, teams usually get budgets to exploit the data. Teams may get more support than consortia from home universities, and they may seek a head start by holding back the data for a year or so, although early release can be mandated.[10] The CES have always been the product of teams, as opposed to consortia. The difference with the British model is that Canadian teams have never been privileged to compete for a targeted program. Not only can a team fail to be funded, but so too can the CES.

Each model has its strengths and weaknesses. Teams are motivated to exploit the data quickly, and this action registers at the publication bottom line. Moreover, they probably can deliver more innovation or a given innovation more quickly than consortia. The price of the team, however, is the risk of insulation from the scholarly community. Advisory boards that meet occasionally and at their own pleasure provide only a limited connection to the larger community. By virtue of its very representativeness, a consortium may be slower to respond to calls for innovation. The number of board members may indicate the number of veto players, and so the system can be very conservative. However, the range of membership can also have the opposite effect and can open up multiple conduits for fresh ideas. Cost considerations may be a wash – the team would require a smaller budget for travel and subsistence, but it might require a larger analysis budget. As we have seen in the preceding chapter, both models seem capable of innovation, as the American and British groups have pioneered movement toward web-based fieldwork.

Conclusion

Just as the existence of older CES data sets increases the power of recent ones, so too does the continuing existence of the CES maintain the relevance of the older data sets. Just as the CES are a vital component of the CSES modules and of comparative electoral survey research more generally, so too do the cross-national data sets enhance the power of the CES. However, if the CES disappear, the international sets will cease to shed light on the Canadian case. The vibrant community of young electoral researchers that the CES helped create would be deprived of the one thing that brings them all together and that leverages their separate talents.

NOTES

This is a greatly modified version of a report to the Social Sciences and Humanities Research Council of Canada on the future of the Canadian Election Studies. We are grateful to the Council for financial assistance for that report and for moral support from Janet Halliwell, Patricia Dunne, and Gisèle Yasmeen. Amanda Bittner was the indispensable research assistant. In preparing the report, we tried the patience of key actors in the national election studies from many countries. We are grateful for their candor. Responsibility for the content remains solely with the authors.

1 See the Introduction and Chapter 4 in this volume for some additional examples.
2 Canadian Charter of Rights and Freedoms, Part I of the Constitution Act, 1982, being Schedule B to the Canada Act 1982 (UK), 1982, c 11.
3 See the preceding chapter by Thomas Scotto, Mebs Kanji, and Antoine Bilodeau for more details.
4 The Comparative Study of Electoral Systems (CSES) agenda (http://www.cses.org/) is very ambitious: "Participating countries include a common module of survey questions in their post-election studies. The resulting data are deposited along with voting, demographic, district and macro variables. The studies are then merged into a single, free, public dataset for use in comparative study and cross-level analysis." Not surprisingly, the themes pursued in these data sets are highly general, such as (again, taken from the CSES website): "The impact of electoral institutions on citizens' political cognition and behavior (parliamentary versus presidential systems of

government, the electoral rules that govern the casting and counting of ballots; and political parties); the nature of political and social cleavages and alignments; and the evaluation of democratic institutions and processes." The modules currently available include individual-level data on demographics, participation, and persuasion, vote histories, perceptions of governmental performance, satisfaction with democratic processes, and perceptions of each party system's Left-Right landscape. These are often linked to data about each respondent's electoral district and to characteristics of each country's party and electoral systems. At present, fifty countries participate in this venture.

5 See Lawrence LeDuc's chapter in this volume for a detailed description of how this effort has developed over time.

6 Note that Figure 5.1 is based on a preliminary appendix compiled by Richard Johnston and Amanda Bittner in 2007. Many papers originated as conference presentations and subsequently appeared in refereed journals. Where this happens, only the journal appearance is counted to avoid double counting. The last two points, 2006 and 2007, are less well documented than are all earlier years.

7 See Chapters 1 and 2 in this volume for more details.

8 See the concluding chapter in this volume for a similar but more elaborate variant of this argument.

9 Mention by name also includes mention by implication. For example, 1965-74 is taken to imply that each of the 1965, 1968, and 1974 elections has been analyzed.

10 Indeed, the British Election Studies makes data available immediately following an election.

REFERENCES

Harper v. Attorney General for Canada, 2004 SCC 33, [2004] 1 SCR 827 (Supreme Court of Canada).

Pacific Press v. Attorney General of British Columbia, 2000 BCSC 0248, 73 BCLR (3d) 264 (British Columbia Supreme Court).

R v. Bryan, 2007 SCC 12, [2007] 1 SCR 527 (Supreme Court of Canada).

Somerville v. Attorney General for Canada (1996), 184 AR 241 (Alberta Court of Appeal).

PART 2

TAKING STOCK

An Overview of the Social Dimension of Vote Choice

ELISABETH GIDENGIL

One piece of conventional wisdom that emerged from the early Canadian Election Studies (CES) is that social background characteristics are only weakly related to vote choice in Canada. The cross-time comparative evidence examined by Richard Johnston in his chapter in this volume indicates that Canada may not be all that unique in this respect. However, research based on more recent CES suggests that we cannot account for individual vote choice or electoral outcomes unless we consider the social bases of voting (Nevitte et al. 2000; Blais et al. 2002; Gidengil et al. 2006). This is not to say that social background characteristics can correctly predict a person's vote choice, but prediction is not the primary goal of voting behaviour research. Our distant ancestors could predict the ebb and flow of the tide, but they could not account for it. Modern-day students of voting behaviour risk finding themselves in a similar situation if they rely too heavily on factors that are proximate to vote choice, such as party identification or candidate evaluations. If the objective is to explain vote choice and not simply to predict it, we need to understand why people identify with one party rather than another and why they prefer one candidate to another. Achieving this goal requires better incorporating the social dimensions of political life into our accounts of voting behaviour.

In this chapter, I provide an overview of key things that we have learned about the social bases of vote choice in Canada. Then I go on to address the

criticism that survey-based research, as typically practised, cannot do justice to the social nature of voting. Almost forty years ago, Allen Barton
(1968, 1) likened surveys to "a sociological meatgrinder, tearing the individual from his social context and guaranteeing that nobody in the study inter-
acts with anyone else in it. It is a little like a biologist putting his experimental
animals through a hamburger machine and looking at every hundredth cell
through a microscope; anatomy and physiology get lost, structure and function disappear, and one is left with cell biology." As Barton notes, it is not
inherent in the survey method that everything be reduced to the micro level
(ibid., 8). In fact, the classic American studies of voting behaviour undertaken by Paul Lazarsfeld and his colleagues in the 1940s took the social
context of voting very seriously. Consequently, the sociological model of
vote choice, which they pioneered, warrants revisiting, and some misunder-
standings regarding this approach necessitate clarification. In addition, future research needs to consider ways of counteracting the meat grinder
effect, and, toward the end of this chapter, I highlight some efforts at incorporating contextual variables into models of vote choice and discuss their
limitations. I also present some newer examples of research that attempt to
incorporate measures of voters' social networks and describe their preliminary results.

Puzzles and Paradoxes

The role of societal cleavages in structuring vote choice and party preference has long puzzled students of Canadian voting behaviour. As John
Meisel (1975, 253) observed in his pioneering analyses of the 1965 and 1968
CES, Canada offers "a cornucopia of intriguing anomalies." Analyses of the
data provided by the CES have resulted in many insights, however.

Social Class: A Case of "Pure Non-Class Voting"?

First, there is the "class-voting conundrum" (Gidengil 2002). Over forty
years ago, Robert Alford (1963, x-xi) characterized Canada as a case of
"pure non-class voting." He measured class voting by subtracting the percentage of white-collar voters voting for Left-wing parties from the percentage of blue-collar voters voting for Left-wing parties. Canada registered the
lowest level of class voting among the four Anglo-American democracies.
Even the United States, hardly known as a bastion of class politics, ranked
higher than Canada on his class-voting index.

This low level of class voting was seen as a paradox because a relationship
between class position and vote choice traditionally was viewed as almost a

given in Western democracies. It is eminently plausible that people's material circumstances should influence their choice of party. After all, according to Harold Lasswell's (1936) famous definition, politics is about "who gets what." Political parties are conventionally differentiated in Left-Right terms according to the position that they take on the role of the state and the extent to which market forces should be given free rein. Following on from these basic ideological differences are parallel differences on the issues of the day, be they welfare spending, tax policies, or managing the economy. Yet, social class seems to make little difference to Canadians' choice of party.

In fact, as Barry Kay and Andrea Perrella demonstrate in the next chapter of this volume, the finding of weak class voting has remained remarkably consistent across time. It has also remained remarkably resistant to attempts at refutation. Critics have taken aim at the method that Alford used to assess class voting, criticizing his measure of voters' class positions and his classification of Canada's parties along the Left-Right scale (see Gidengil 2002). However, whether social class is measured objectively in terms of occupation, income, or education or subjectively in terms of voters' self-identification, the finding holds. And regardless of which political parties are considered to be on the left or right of the ideological spectrum, the result is the same.

Accordingly, research has shifted from simply trying to uncover a straightforward statistical relationship between social class and voting to other directions, such as understanding the conditions under which class voting can occur. Criticizing the "atomized view of politics" that is implicit in much of the research on class and voting in Canada, sociologists have argued that we need to incorporate contextual variables into our models of class voting (Brym, Gillespie, and Lenton 1989, 39). These scholars focus on class mobilization. Their key point is that class voting is contingent on the distribution of power resources among classes. The usual indicator of working-class resources is the strength of unions and/or co-operatives – where these organizations are strong, the New Democratic party (NDP) fares better (Brym, Gillespie, and Lenton 1989; Nakhie 1992; Nakhie and Arnold 1996). The party's electoral viability, in turn, encourages greater support.

However, even on this point, certain scholars such as Reza Nakhaie and Robert Arnold (1996, 201) concede that "if class voting is taken to mean voting on the basis of one's objective class position, we must concur with previous writers who have suggested that it is not of major importance." They argue that the conclusion changes if class voting is instead taken to mean voting on the basis of class ideology. The problem, from the point of view of conventional understandings, is that there is only a loose connection in Canada between objective class position and class ideology. Working-class voters do not necessarily think of themselves as working class, nor can they be counted upon to support the union movement or to subscribe to egalitarian beliefs, something Nakhaie and Arnold attribute to the failure of both the unions and the NDP to promote a working-class ideology.

Religion: The Unwelcome Guest?

The persistence of a strong religious cleavage proved just as puzzling as the lack of a strong class cleavage. In this case, evidence from the CES indicates that Catholics were traditionally much more likely than Protestants to vote Liberal. Indeed, the support of Catholics was one of the keys, if not *the* key, to the Liberal party's electoral dominance for much of the post-war period (Blais 2005). However, the persistence of the religious cleavage defies an easy explanation. It seems anachronistic. Religious issues have not figured on the political agenda in living memory, and religious practice has declined. The anomalous nature of the religious cleavage led William Irvine (1974, 85) to liken it to "a moderately interesting, but strikingly peculiar, houseguest who has overstayed his welcome."

Irvine thought that he had succeeded in sending the unwanted guest packing. His solution to the puzzle was ingenious. He argued that the religious cleavage was a legacy of the past, perpetuated through socialization within the family. Parents pass on both their religious affiliation and their party preference to their children without necessarily making any connection between the two. This explanation seemed to resolve one of the most perplexing aspects of the religious cleavage – when people were asked to explain their vote, they did not mention their religion.

Irvine's success proved short lived, however. Richard Johnston (1985, 107) showed that the explanation had a logical flaw: group differences in party vote shares can only persist across generations if the rate of transmission of party loyalties between generations differs across groups. He concluded that "Liberal [parents] are more successful at transmitting their party loyalty not because they are peculiarly dominant models but because they are more likely to have their influence reinforced by factors outside the home." As Johnston went on to observe, analysis of the religious cleavage "begs for contextual variables and analyses" (ibid., 102). He took up the challenge by using data from the 1979 election study to explore the impact of the religious context on individual vote choice. He argued that voters in heavily

Catholic provinces are more likely to divide along religious lines because a strong Catholic presence serves to mute other potential social divisions in vote choice: "Where Catholics are numerous, class, or union/non-union, differences are suppressed. But where Catholics are few, class differences, at least in NDP voting, can flourish" (Johnston 1991, 128). He found that the religious cleavage was indeed more salient in provinces where Catholics predominated, while the class cleavage became more salient where Catholics were sparse. In Johnston's account, the underlying causal mechanism was strategic voting. However, this explanation does not jibe very well with the more recent finding that only a very small proportion of voters appear to vote strategically (see Blais et al. 2002).

Jon Pammett's (1991) contextual analysis points to social influence as another possible causal mechanism. The purpose of Pammett's research was not to explain the vote but, rather, to consider the role of social context in explaining deviations from strong, stable, and consistent (between the federal and provincial levels) partisanship. Using data from the 1974, 1979, and 1980 CES, he found that people who had initially been partisans of other parties tended to move toward the Liberals when they lived in constituencies with large numbers of Catholics. The presence of a large number of university graduates had a similar effect on NDP partisanship.

More recently, Paul Bélanger and Munroe Eagles (2006) have retested Johnston's hypotheses about the geography of class and religion using data from the 2000 election study. Their findings confirm the role of social context in perpetuating the religious cleavage in vote choice. The individual-level relationship between being Catholic and voting Liberal is strongest in constituencies with high proportions of Catholics. However, they find little support for the notion that a strong Catholic presence induces union members to vote Liberal: "Religion appears to trump class as a determinant of vote choice, regardless of the religious composition of the voter's context" (ibid., 607). Accordingly, they reject Johnston's tactical voting hypothesis in favour of what they term a conventional contextual effect. In other words, individual voters are seen as being embedded in "networks of association, tradition and affiliation" that encourage conformity with group norms (ibid., 594).

Regions: Empty Containers?

Highlighted in the next two chapters of this volume is the finding that regional cleavages run deep in Canada. These cleavages are complex with different regions of the country backing different parties to varying extents at different moments in history. However, next to social class and religion, this variable has received only intermittent attention since Mildred Schwartz's (1974) pioneering work, based on the 1965 election study.[1] As described already by Thomas Scotto and his colleagues in their chapter in this volume, Schwartz's preliminary findings inspired the 1974/1979/1980 election study team to follow up on this line of analysis (Clarke et al. 1979, 1984). However, finding that residents of every province disagreed about the definition of their region, the team concluded that regions were little more than analytical constructs, lacking real meaning to their inhabitants. In a similar vein, Donald Blake's (1978, 293) significant work in this area concluded that "much of what lies behind apparent regional variation in party support consists of relatively more theoretically-tractable environmental factors." His study was one of the first to examine the impact of constituency contexts on vote choice in Canada. Whether he did succeed, in fact, in dispelling "some of the mystery associated with the perennial question of regionalism" is open to question (ibid., 302). For example, one of the key explanatory variables was the degree of political competitiveness, but it left unexplained why some constituencies are more competitive than others.[2] Blake's study is notable for its recognition that variables such as the ethnic or religious composition of a constituency are "undoubtedly surrogates for patterns of interaction among individuals" (ibid., 301). Thus, similar to Johnston, Pammett, Bélanger, and Eagles, he predicted that Catholics living in heavily Catholic ridings would be more likely to vote Liberal because they are more likely to interact with their co-religionists and to be aware of the communal voting norm.

More recently, the 1997 CES team revisited the subject of regional voting patterns and concluded that regions are not simply empty "containers" (Simeon and Elkins 1974, 399; Gidengil et al. 1999). Our analysis reveals that the variations in party vote shares across the country reflect "true" regional differences. In other words, they cannot be explained away by variations in the social makeup of the regions – voters sharing the same social background characteristics vote differently from one region to another. Perhaps the most striking finding of this research was the extent to which regional populations differ in their basic political priorities.

The Neglected Social Bases of Voting

Relative to region, other potential social bases of voting have received even less attention. For instance, evidence shows that the type of community also matters, and, as Kay and Perrella argue in the next chapter, there is a need for deeper analysis of this sort (Blais et al. 2002; Gidengil et al. 2006). One notable exception to the absence of analysis in this area is Martin Turcotte's (2001) examination of the ability of geographical mobility to eradicate differences that have historically existed between urban and rural Canada. Using data from the 1997 election study, he finds that big city residents hold less traditional views on questions of gender roles, sexual mores, and lifestyles. He attributes this finding to the fact that it is easier for unconventional subcultures to form in big cities because social networks provide ready access to like-minded people. Contrary to the rural stereotype, though, people who live in villages and rural areas are no more traditional in their views than residents of towns, medium-size cities, or big city suburbs. Likewise, Fred Cutler and Richard Jenkins's (2001, 385) analysis of data from the 1993 election study reached a similar conclusion: "The intolerant rural hick is a straw man."

What these few studies suggest is that the traditional urban-rural cleavage may well be giving way to a modern inner city–suburban cleavage. In fact, R. Alan Walks's (2004) analysis of data from the 1965, 1984, and 2000 CES shows growing differences in both party preferences and political values between suburban residents and their inner city counterparts. Suburban Canadians – especially those residing in the "outer" suburbs – are clearly to the right of other Canadians, while inner city residents are to the left.

Perhaps the most neglected bases of voting behaviour are ethnicity and country of birth. Canadians of non-European ancestry have stood out more than Catholics in terms of their Liberal voting tendencies, but why this has been so awaits a convincing explanation (Nevitte et al. 2000; Blais et al. 2002; Gidengil et al. 2006). André Blais (2005, 832) examined a number of possibilities, but none have withstood empirical scrutiny: "The bottom line is that we still do not have a good understanding why non-European Canadians so strongly support the Liberals." Research is hampered by the small numbers that show up in Canada-wide samples, but this constraint will diminish as the number of Canadians of non-European ancestry grows and as samples diversify. In addition, as Scotto and his colleagues suggest in their chapter in this volume, there are other methodological changes that might be considered in order to more quickly and cost-effectively acquire larger samples that capture respondents from racial and ethnic minority groups.

Another social background characteristic that deserves much more study is age or generation. It was not until fairly recently, as Pammett reminds us in his chapter in this volume, that we uncovered the fact that young

Canadians are much less likely to vote than their parents or grandparents were at the same age (see, for example, Blais et al. 2002). However, there has been little attention paid to their political attitudes and party preference. Kay and Perrella's analysis in the next chapter suggests some patterns in the relationship between age categories and the vote, but their findings are not immediately consistent with theoretical expectations. This discrepancy points to the need for more research and greater understanding of the trends in this area.

Using data from the 2004 election study, the 2004 CES team found significant generational divides on questions relating to defence spending, gender roles, same-sex marriage, and race (Gidengil et al. 2005). However, there are few other issues that clearly seem to divide Canadians along generational lines since young Canadians prove to have surprisingly similar issue priorities to older Canadians. In other words, the differences between young Canadians and their elders tend to be differences of degree rather than of deep divisions. Analyses based on data from other time points would help to further develop this line of understanding.

Despite this and other gaps in our knowledge that still remain, there can be little doubt that we have learned a good deal about the social bases of vote choice and political preference over the past four decades. Much of this research, though, has treated voters as atomized individuals rather than as social beings who are embedded in networks of social interaction. Few studies have incorporated the social context into their models of voting and policy attitudes. From this perspective, it is worth briefly revisiting the classic American studies to see exactly how they have conceptualized the social dimension of vote choice and attitude formation and to determine if they provide any additional guidance on this matter.

The Columbia School and the Sociological Model

As it turns out, Paul Lazarsfeld, Bernard Berelson, and Hazel Gaudet (1968) took the social context of voting very seriously, but unfortunately their approach is often equated with a crude sociological analysis. Richard Niemi and Herbert Weisberg's (1993, 8) characterization in *Classics of Voting Behavior* is typical: "The Columbia researchers explained the 1940 election with a sociological model, relating voters' socioeconomic status ... religion, and place of residence ... to their vote." True, Lazarsfeld, Berelson, and Gaudet (1968, 27) did claim that "a simple combination of three primary personal characteristics goes a long way in 'explaining' political preferences

... a person thinks, politically, as he is, socially. Social characteristics determine political preference." However, there was much more to their approach than simply finding the best combination of social background characteristics for predicting vote choice.

According to the Columbia researchers, "voting is essentially a group experience. People who work or live or play together are likely to vote for the same candidate" (Lazarsfeld, Berelson, and Gaudet 1968, 137). This is why knowing someone's socio-economic status, religious affiliation, and place of residence is important. It gives us an idea about the company they are likely to keep – their friends and family and their neighbours and workmates – and the sorts of matters they may prioritize, discuss, or vote on. From this perspective, social groups are not mere social categories; they represent live social forces. Vote choice is a social process that is influenced by people's social networks.

Critics have charged that a sociological model cannot explain electoral dynamics, but Lazarsfeld, Berelson, and Gaudet did not see group voting as unchanging across time. On the contrary, social group interactions could help to explain the dynamics of vote choice as people react to changing issues and personalities through the lens of shared group experiences. Moreover, some people are cross-pressured; they have a variety of social affiliations that are not necessarily mutually reinforcing. Their religious affiliation pushes them in one direction, but their socio-economic status pulls them in the opposite direction. Some cross-pressured voters will simply abstain, but those who do vote are likely to switch parties from election to election. In their 1948 study, Berelson, Lazarsfeld, and William McPhee (1954) identified a "breakage effect" – when a voter is cross-pressured, the dominant partisan climate in the community will tend to break through and the voter will vote with the majority. They also developed the idea that contact breeds consensus – the more people interact with a group, the more likely they are to share its dominant partisanship. These are all indications that the model implies more than a crude social analysis that simply relates social background characteristics to vote choice.

Countering the Meat Grinder Effect

Barton (1968, 1) is right: "If our aim is to understand people's behavior ... we want to know about primary groups, neighborhoods, organizations, social circles, and communities." So how do we counter the meat grinder phenomenon and expand the scope of our sociological analysis of electoral choice?

First, at the theoretical level, we need to stop thinking of social background characteristics as being only long-term forces.[3] For instance, the fact that social background characteristics are either fixed or relatively stable does not mean that they cannot have dynamic effects. Nor does it mean that they are necessarily distant from the vote. People's "values" on these variables are typically highly stable and are determined long before the election, but their political effects may well be determined by the campaign itself. Fred Cutler (2002), for example, has shown how the party leaders' social background characteristics can influence vote choice. This finding suggests that the campaign can cue social identities. Second, at the empirical level, we need to find better ways of incorporating social structure into our survey designs and data analysis. Thus far, the standard approach has been to turn to a contextual analysis of some sort using data from the census.

Contextual Analyses

Contextual models treat individual vote choice as a function of both individual characteristics and the characteristics of other people in the same social context: "The distinguishing irreducible element of a contextual analysis is that ... the political behaviour of individuals is characterized as contingent on the environment" (Huckfeldt and Sprague 1993, 281; see also Wellhofer 1991). Salient features of that environment are represented by contextual measures, which as mentioned earlier are usually drawn from information collected through a census. The 1984 election study, for example, includes a variety of constituency characteristics, such as ethnolinguistic composition, country of birth, religious composition, median income, level of education, and labour force participation as well as information on candidates and party vote shares. The 2000 election study also includes a wide range of constituency characteristics. The addition of these variables to the data sets makes it easier to conduct contextual analyses and examine the relationships between constituency characteristics and individual attitudes and behaviour.

Blake's (1978) study of the impact of constituency contexts in the 1968 federal election is an early example of research that combines individual-level election study data with constituency-level data. He employed a hierarchical decomposition technique. First, he estimated the individual-level relationship between social background characteristics (religion, education, and income) and the tendency to vote for the Liberal party. Then he calculated the expected Liberal vote in each constituency, based on its social composition. Finally, he examined the impact of contextual variables on the difference between the actual Liberal vote and the expected Liberal vote. As Blake notes, one drawback of this procedure is that it assumes that the individual-level relationship is the same in every constituency.

The same is true of the type of contextual analysis undertaken by Pammett (1991). In this approach, the contextual variables are disaggregated to the individual level and then included along with the individual-level variables in a single model. For example, if the contextual variable was the proportion of Catholics living in each constituency, every respondent who lived there would receive the same value on this variable. Simply adding contextual variables to an individual-level model can be problematic because it assumes that the independent variables have similar effects regardless of constituency-level characteristics. This is why Johnston (1991) analyzed the impact of the proportion of Catholics separately for Catholics and non-Catholics and for union members and non-union members. An alternative approach is to add interactions between the individual-level variables and the contextual variables to an individual-level model to test whether contextual characteristics condition the impact of individual characteristics on people's attitudes and behaviours.

Even then, however, the approaches considered so far share a common problem – they violate the statistical assumption of independence. If context does indeed matter, people living in the same locale are going to be subject to the same influences. Thus, investigating individual and contextual characteristics within the same model will inflate estimates of statistical significance, thus heightening the risk of inferring relationships that may simply reflect sampling error. In addition, a conventional contextual model entails the unrealistic assumption that aggregated factors can fully account for contextual variation (see Steenbergen and Jones 2002).

When Bélanger and Eagles (2006) revisited Johnston's study, they were able to take advantage of a newer method that enables researchers to avoid these statistical difficulties. They used a three-level model that included variables at the individual, constituency, and provincial level. Multi-level modeling offers a superior approach to combining individual-level survey data with contextual data because it deals with the non-independence of cases within contexts (see Steenbergen and Jones 2002). This technique allows us to directly test hypotheses within and across two or more levels of analysis (individuals and contexts) within a single encompassing model. It recognizes that individual survey responses and contextual characteristics need to be modeled as distinct sources of variation. Most importantly, for our purposes, it allows for the testing of cross-level interactions. In other words, we can determine whether the impact of a given social background characteristic is conditioned by contextual characteristics, and we can do so without the risk of over-estimating the statistical reliability of our findings.

That said, however, multi-level modeling raises sampling issues: "To obtain reliable estimates of both within and between-context variation, we require *many* individuals from *many* places. The former allows a precise assessment of within-context relations, the latter a precise assessment of between-context relations, and the two together allow one to be distinguished from the other" (Duncan, Jones, and Moon 1998, 113). In constituency-based analyses, we will usually have enough places, but they may be represented by very few individuals in a typical national sample. Again, this situation may be something that future advances in data collection methodology can help to address.

Nevertheless, contextual analyses have enabled us to gain an appreciation of the importance of the local context on voting and party preference and have advanced our understanding of the role of individual-level social background characteristics. However, there are certain other limitations, such as the operationalization of a social context with which we still need to contend (see Duncan, Jones, and Moon 1998). As Pammett (1991, 411) himself observes, "it is one thing to be able to demonstrate ... that persons situated in constituencies containing substantial numbers of a similar occupational type or religion behave differently from those in constituencies with a more heterogeneous composition. It is quite another thing to have the means to investigate empirically the reasons for such behaviour patterns." Contextual analyses provide insight into "structural or spatial commonalities," but they cannot tell us about "experienced commonalities" (Scarbrough 1991, 370-71). For such an inquiry, we need data on people's social networks and we need to figure out how best to collect these data.

Blake's (2003) study of the impact of the socio-economic and racial composition of neighbourhoods on the racial attitudes of white Canadians and Fred Cutler's (2007) analysis of contextual influences on issue attitudes are rare exceptions to the typical tendency to define contexts in terms of constituencies (Blake 1978; Pammett 1991), provinces (Brym, Gillespie, and Lenton 1989; Johnston 1991), or both (Bélanger and Eagles 2006).[4] The latter choices are easy to justify when the contextual variables are political, such as competitiveness, incumbency, and partisanship. However, if we are interested in looking at contexts as indicators of patterns of social interaction, provinces are simply too large and so are rural constituencies that cover huge swathes of territory. The boundaries of urban constituencies will not necessarily define meaningful social contexts either. Social interaction occurs in a variety of contexts, including in neighbourhoods, workplaces, and community organizations. Moreover, these social contexts may – or may not – overlap; they rarely coincide with one another or with administrative boundaries. All of these factors need to be kept in mind.

Measuring Social Networks

As Robert Huckfeldt and John Sprague (1993, 289) observe, "contexts are not the same as networks at a conceptual level. And at that level of measurement, it is a mistake to think of contexts as simply an easy measure of networks, obtained on the cheap." So how do we tap social networks in a way that narrows in on the type of social interaction that we are after? In the past, Lazarsfeld, Berelson, and Gaudet (1968) asked their US respondents about the party affiliation of their family members, their three closest friends, their three co-workers, and some of the groups to which they belonged. The problem with this type of approach, however, is that people's reports may not accurately reflect the partisan preferences and political attitudes of their friends and acquaintances. People may fail to perceive other people's preferences correctly, and the people with whom they interact may fail to express their true preferences (Huckfeldt and Sprague 1987). Moreover, people do not necessarily need to be aware of these preferences and attitudes in order to be influenced by them.

Others who study social networks have simply asked respondents to name people with whom they discuss politics and to specify whether these people are relatives, close friends, or acquaintances. This name-generator approach has two drawbacks. First, it is typically only able to tap a small number of ties. Second, the first names to come to respondents' minds will typically be those of people with whom they have close relationships, such as family members and close friends (Lin, Fu, and Hsung 2001). This tendency to name close friends and family is problematic given Mark Granovetter's (1973) "strength of weak ties" argument. His point is simple but powerful. Casual acquaintances (weak ties) can serve as bridges to social circles beyond our own and bring us into contact with ideas and information we might not otherwise encounter within our immediate circle of close friends and relatives (strong ties). Huckfeldt and his colleagues (1995, 1028) have shown that casual interactions can be a more important source of political influence than discussions with close friends and intimates: "If political communication only occurs through close friends, the social reach of political information is likely to be quite limited. Alternatively, the casual acquaintances of my casual acquaintances are not so likely to be my associates, and thus information conveyed through such patterns of interaction is likely to travel farther."

Nan Lin and Mary Dumin (1986) have developed an approach to measuring social networks that is designed to deal with these weaknesses as well as to elicit weak ties. Their position generator is intended to measure the resources that are available to people through their social networks. Respondents are presented with a list of occupations and asked to indicate whether they know anyone in each of the listed positions. If knowing one person in a given occupation is good, knowing five people might seem even better since it would increase the chances of being exposed to new information. However, it is doubtful that respondents could report reliably on just how many people they know in a given occupational category. In any case, the position generator is not designed to measure the *size* of people's social networks but, rather, the *types* of people they know. This is why the occupations are chosen to reflect the range of occupational status or prestige within a given society. In effect, the generator represents a sample of the sorts of people known, and, as such, it "casts a wide net over a range of relationships" (Lin, Fu, and Hsung 2001, 63).

At the request of Bonnie Erickson, a sociologist, the 2000, 2004, and 2008 CES included a position generator in the self-administered mail-back questionnaire. Rather than simply asking whether respondents knew anyone in a given occupation, we asked whether they knew a man, a woman, or both. The occupations were differentiated in terms of gender dominance and spanned the occupational hierarchy to include higher professionals, middle managers, other professionals, skilled trades, lower-level service workers, semi-skilled trades, and the unskilled. At each level, one of the most male-dominated and one of the most female-dominated occupations was selected. To ensure that respondents would have a reasonable chance of knowing someone in each of the occupations, only occupations with at least twenty thousand people were included. The occupations also had to have easily understood job titles. Farmers were included to ensure that rural and agricultural occupations were represented.

So what sorts of things can this measure tell us? I, Allison Harell, and Bonnie Erickson (2007) have used the 2000 election study position generator to examine the role of network diversity in explaining the modern gender gap.[5] In Canada, the traditional gender gap had disappeared by the time of the 1979 federal election, and it was 1997 before the modern gender gap emerged, with women voting NDP in greater numbers than men. Building on Granovetter's (1973) concept of "weak ties," we argue that diverse social networks can provide women with information and psychological resources that enhance their propensity to vote for the Left. First, women with more diverse ties to other women are more likely to encounter women who are voting NDP and to recognize their shared interest in voting similarly. Second, women who might otherwise lack the autonomy to express their gender-related interests in their choice of party are more likely to vote NDP if their social networks include a range of women who do enjoy such autonomy. Susan Carroll (1988) has argued that married women are less likely than single women to enjoy the requisite political autonomy. We argue that ties with higher-status women are a source of psychological resources that can enhance the autonomy of women who are economically dependent on their spouse or partner. This hypothesis was confirmed: married women's odds of voting NDP increase significantly when they know higher-status women. Knowing women in all six higher-status occupations included in the position generator increases a married woman's probability of voting NDP by almost twenty percentage points, compared with a married woman who knows no one in these occupations.

Bonnie Erickson (2006), meanwhile, has used the same data to examine how the composition of women's social networks affects their views on a variety of issues. She finds that knowing women in a wide range of occupations tends to shift women toward the side preferred by other women on a number of issues that divide women and men. Interestingly, though, she finds that this pattern does not hold for issues having to do with gender equity. In fact, women who know women in a wide range of occupations are less likely to agree with the prevailing views of women on these issues. Erickson attributes this result to the fact that these women are getting an unrealistic picture of equality between the sexes because they know women in fields that are traditionally male dominated, such as law and computer science.

Finally, Côté and Erickson (2009) have shown how diverse ties with middle-class people make for more tolerant views toward minorities, whereas diverse ties with working-class people are associated with lower levels of tolerance for out-groups. They attribute this finding to the fact that working-class people are more likely to be in competition for jobs. People who are educated, older, and live in larger communities and people who are themselves minorities are more tolerant. However, the network effects hold even after controlling for these characteristics.

It is impossible to gain a complete picture of people's social networks in an election study. We can only sample egocentric ties – ties that respondents tell us about – and these may not adequately represent their complete social networks (see Luke 2005). In addition, analyses of social networks have to be careful to guard against omitted variable bias – the same factors that explain characteristics of people's social networks may also explain their attitudes and behaviours. Still, incorporating social context and, specifically, measures of people's social networks can help to mitigate the meat grinder effect. What we need to do now is to theorize which characteristics of social networks matter under what circumstances.

Future Directions

Since the mid-1960s, the CES have contributed to our understanding of the social bases of voting, but, in order to maximize that contribution, we must look beyond the simple statistical associations between social background characteristics and vote choice. If the criterion is the percentage of variance explained by social background characteristics, it might seem that our efforts would be better directed toward more proximate factors such as issue attitudes, leader evaluations, and party identification – an approach that is discussed by Harold Clarke and Allan Kornberg in their chapter in this volume. However, we should beware of the "fetish of R^2" (Brym, Gillespie, and Lenton 1989, 31). Variables that are closer to the vote will certainly do a better job of explaining it in the statistical sense. However, how much do we really understand when we say that people tend to vote for the party they identify with, the party they think will do the best job of handling key issues, or the party with the most likeable leader? These variables can certainly provide important insights into electoral dynamics and fluctuations in party fortunes, but they beg a number of questions. Why do people identify with one party rather than another? Why do people take differing stands on the issues of the day, and why do they like some leaders and dislike others? Answering these questions requires that we continue to take the social bases of voting seriously.

Also, we should hardly be surprised that the relationships between social background characteristics and vote choice are often rather weak. After all, we do not have a single social identity. We are not just residents of a particular region or adherents – or not – of a particular religion. We are not solely defined by our occupations or our ancestry. Instead, we have multiple social identities, each jostling for attention. Political parties and the media play an important role in influencing which social identities become salient over the course of an election campaign. This notion brings us back to the central theme of this chapter. Voters need to be understood not as atomized individuals but, rather, as social beings who are embedded in social networks. People form their impressions of the parties and their leaders and figure out where they stand on the issues as they interact with their friends and family, their colleagues, and their casual acquaintances. If we want to develop a fuller understanding of their vote choices and political preferences, we need to work on developing contextual models and better measures of voters' social networks. The old adage "it's not what you know but who you know" may also well apply to electoral behaviour.

NOTES

1 See Mildred Schwartz's chapter in this volume for a first-hand summary of how Schwartz approached this line of research.

2 Competitiveness was measured using J.A.A. Lovink's (1973) "safety index," which takes account of both the margin of victory and the frequency of turnover between political parties.

3 See the chapters provided by Schwartz and Harold Clarke and Allan Kornberg in this volume for more details on the distinction between long- and short-term forces.

4 Donald Blake (1978) and Fred Cutler (2002) both used "forward sortation areas" (FSAs) as surrogates for neighbourhoods. FSAs are determined by the first three characters of respondents' postal codes.

5 According to Ronald Inglehart and Pippa Norris (2003), a process of gender realignment has been underway in Western democracies. Where men were once more likely than women to vote for parties of the Left (the "traditional gender gap"), now it is women who are more likely than men to vote for the Left (the "modern gender gap").

REFERENCES

Alford, Robert R. 1963. *Party and Society: The Anglo-American Democracies.* Chicago: Rand McNally.

Barton, Allen H. 1968. "Bringing Society Back In: Survey Research and Macro-Methodology." *American Behavioral Scientist* 12: 1-12.

Bélanger, Paul, and Munroe Eagles. 2006. "The Geography of Class and Religion in Canadian Elections Revisited." *Canadian Journal of Political Science* 39: 591-609.

Berelson, Bernard, Paul F. Lazarsfeld, and William N. McPhee. 1954. *Voting.* Chicago: Chicago University Press.

Blais, André. 2005. "Accounting for the Electoral Success of the Liberal Party in Canada." *Canadian Journal of Political Science* 38: 821-40.

Blais, André, Elisabeth Gidengil, Richard Nadeau, and Neil Nevitte. 2002. *Anatomy of a Liberal Victory: Making Sense of the 2000 Canadian Election.* Peterborough, ON: Broadview Press.

Blake, Donald E. 1978. "Constituency Context and Canadian Elections: An Exploratory Study." *Canadian Journal of Political Science* 11(2): 279-305.

–. 2003. "Environmental Determinants of Racial Attitudes among White Canadians." *Canadian Journal of Political Science* 36: 491-509.

Brym, Robert J., Michael W. Gillespie, and Rhonda L. Lenton. 1989. "Class Power, Class Mobilization, and Class Voting: The Canadian Case." *Canadian Journal of Sociology* 14: 25-44.

Carroll, Susan J. 1988. "Women's Autonomy and the Gender Gap: 1980 and 1982." In Carol M. Mueller, ed., *The Politics of the Gender Gap: The Social Construction of Political Influence,* 236-57. Beverly Hills, CA: Sage.

Clarke, Harold D., Jane Jenson, Lawrence LeDuc, and Jon H. Pammett. 1984. *Absent Mandate: The Politics of Discontent in Canada.* Toronto: Gage.

Clarke, Harold D., Lawrence LeDuc, Jane Jenson, and Jon H. Pammett. 1979. *Political Choice in Canada.* Toronto: McGraw-Hill Ryerson.

Côté, Rochelle R., and Bonnie H. Erickson. 2009. "Untangling the Roots of Tolerance: How Forms of Social Capital Shape Attitudes toward Ethnic Minorities and Immigrants." *American Behavioral Scientist* 52(12): 1664-89.

Cutler, Fred. 2002. "The Simplest Shortcut of All: Socio-Demographic Characteristics and Electoral Choice." *Journal of Politics* 64: 466-90.

–. 2007. "Context and Attitude Formation: Social Interaction, Default Information, or Local Interests?" *Political Geography* 26: 575-600.

Cutler, Fred, and Richard Jenkins. 2001. "Where One Lives and What One Thinks: Implications of Rural-Urban Opinion Cleavages for Canadian Federalism." In Hamish Telford and Harvey Lazar, eds., *Canada: The State of the Federation 2001: Canadian Political Culture(s) in Transition,* 367-90. Montreal: McGill-Queen's University Press for the Institute for Intergovernmental Relations, Queen's University.

Duncan, Craig, Kelvyn Jones, and Graham Moon. 1998. "Context, Composition and Heterogeneity: Using Multilevel Models in Health Research." *Social Science and Medicine* 46: 97-117.

Erickson, Bonnie H. 2006. "Persuasion and Perception: Two Different Roles for Social Capital in Forming Political Views on Gendered Issues." In Brenda O'Neill and Elisabeth Gidengil, eds., *Gender and Social Capital,* 293-322. New York: Routledge.

Gidengil, Elisabeth. 2002. "The Class Voting Conundrum." In Douglas Baer, ed., *Political Sociology: Canadian Perspectives,* 274-87. Don Mills, ON: Oxford University Press.

Gidengil, Elisabeth, André Blais, Joanna Everitt, Patrick Fournier, and Neil Nevitte. 2005. "Missing the Message: Young Adults and the Election Issues." *Electoral Insight* 7(1): 6-11.

–. 2006. "Back to the Future? Making Sense of the 2004 Canadian Election outside Quebec." *Canadian Journal of Political Science* 39: 1-25.

Gidengil, Elisabeth, André Blais, Neil Nevitte, and Richard Nadeau. 1999. "Making Sense of Regional Voting in the 1997 Federal Election: Liberal and Reform Support Outside Quebec." *Canadian Journal of Political Science* 32(2): 247-72.

Gidengil, Elisabeth, Allison Harell, and Bonnie Erickson. 2007. "Network Diversity and Vote Choice: Women's Social Ties and Left Voting in Canada." *Politics and Gender* 3(2): 151-77.

Granovetter, Mark. 1973. "The Strength of Weak Ties." *American Journal of Sociology* 78 (May): 1360-80.

Huckfeldt, Robert, Paul Allen Beck, Russell J. Dalton, and Jeffrey Levine. 1995. "Political Environments, Cohesive Social Groups, and the Communication of Public Opinion." *American Journal of Political Science* 39: 1025-54.

Huckfeldt, Robert, and John Sprague. 1987. "Networks in Context: The Social Flow of Political Information." *American Political Science Review* 81 (December): 1197-1216.

–. 1993. "Citizens, Contexts, and Politics." In Ada W. Finifter, ed., *Political Science: The State of the Discipline*, 281-303. Washington, DC: American Political Science Association.

Inglehart, Ronald, and Pippa Norris. 2003. *Rising Tide: Gender Equality and Cultural Change around the World.* New York: Cambridge University Press.

Irvine, William P. 1974. "Explaining the Religious Basis of the Canadian Partisan Identity: Success on the Third Try." *Canadian Journal of Political Science* 7: 560-63.

Johnston, Richard. 1985. "The Reproduction of the Religious Cleavage in Canadian Elections." *Canadian Journal of Political Science* 18: 99-113.

–. 1991. "The Geography of Class and Religion in Canadian Elections." In Joseph Wearing, ed., *The Ballot and Its Message*, 108-35. Toronto: Copp-Clark Pitman.

Lasswell, Harold D. 1936. *Politics: Who Gets What, When, How.* New York: McGraw-Hill.

Lazarsfeld, Paul, Bernard Berelson, and Hazel Gaudet. 1968. *The People's Choice: How the Voter Makes Up His Mind in a Presidential Campaign*, 4th edition. New York: Columbia University Press.

Lin, Nan, and Mary Dumin. 1986. "Access to Occupations through Social Ties." *Social Networks* 8 (December): 365-85.

Lin, Nan, Yang-chih Fu, and Ray-May Hsung. 2001. "The Position Generator: Measurement Techniques for Social Capital." In Nan Lin, Karen Cook, and Ronald S. Burt, eds., *Social Capital: Theory and Research*, 57-84. New York: Aldine De Gruyter.

Lovink, J.A.A. 1973. "Is Canadian Politics Too Competitive?" *Canadian Journal of Political Science* 6(3): 343-79.

Luke, Douglas A. 2005. "Getting the Big Picture in Community Science: Methods That Capture Context." *American Journal of Community Psychology* 35: 185-200.

Meisel, John. 1975. *Working Papers on Canadian Politics*, 2nd enlarged edition. Montreal: McGill-Queen's University Press.

Nakhaie, M. Reza. 1992. "Class and Voting Consistency in Canada: Analyses Bearing on the Mobilization Thesis." *Canadian Journal of Sociology* 17: 275-99.

Nakhaie, M. Reza, and Robert Arnold. 1996. "Class Position, Class Ideology and Class Voting: Mobilization of Support for the New Democratic Party in the Canadian Election of 1984." *Canadian Review of Sociology and Anthropology* 33: 181-212.

Nevitte, Neil, André Blais, Elisabeth Gidengil, and Richard Nadeau. 2000. *Unsteady State*. Don Mills, ON: Oxford University Press.

Niemi, Richard G., and Herbert F. Weisberg. 1993. *Classics of Voting Behavior*. Washington, DC: CQ Press.

Pammett, Jon H. 1991. "The Effects of Individual and Contextual Variables on Partisanship in Canada." *European Journal of Political Research* 19: 399-412.

Scarbrough, Elinor. 1991. "Micro and Macro Analysis of Elections." *European Journal of Political Research* 19: 361-74.

Schwartz, Mildred A. 1974. *Politics and Territory: The Sociology of Regional Persistence in Canada*. Montreal: McGill-Queen's University Press.

Simeon, Richard, and David J. Elkins. 1974. "Regional Political Cultures in Canada." *Canadian Journal of Political Science* 7: 397-437.

Steenbergen, Marco R., and Bradford S. Jones. 2002. "Modeling Multilevel Data Structures." *American Journal of Political Science* 46: 218-37.

Turcotte, Martin. 2001. "L'opposition rural/urbain a-t-elle fait son temps? Le cas du traditionalisme moral." *Canadian Journal of Sociology* 26(1): 1-29.

Walks, R. Alan. 2004. "Place of Residence, Party Preferences, and Political Attitudes in Canadian Cities and Suburbs." *Journal of Urban Affairs* 26: 269-95.

Wellhofer, E. Spencer. 1991. "Confounding Sources of Variance in the Macro-Analysis of Electoral Data." *European Journal of Political Research* 19: 425-39.

Eclipse of Class
A Review of Demographic Variables, 1974-2006

BARRY J. KAY AND ANDREA M.L. PERRELLA

Whether it is a reflection of the romantic ideals of their youth, or the impact of the European experience with class-based voting (see Lawrence LeDuc's chapter in this volume), Canadian researchers have frequently turned to class-oriented analyses when examining electoral choice in Canada. This was apparent in the early work of such figures as C.B. Macpherson (1953) and John Wilson (1968). For instance, Macpherson's view of the rise of the Social Credit party in Alberta's "quasi-colonial economy" was reflective of "classist" hostility toward the federal Progressive Conservatives, who were seen at the time as the party of economic elites and Bay Street. This perspective, of course, precedes the establishment of the Canadian Election Studies (CES), but it nonetheless reflects some of the early investment of Canadian political scientists in this line of analysis.

Subsequent attempts to demonstrate a direct empirical link between class and electoral choice have been less encouraging. As described in the previous chapter, scholars such as Robert Alford (1963) and Gerhard Lenski and Jean Lenski (1978) have found that the Canadian electorate is less inclined than electorates in other countries to vote in a manner defined by class concerns. Similarly, Alfred Hunter (1982) has argued that in Canada, class-related measures such as income, education, and occupation cannot be used interchangeably and that none of these measures consistently show a pattern of influence on voting across time. On separate occasions researchers have failed to demonstrate a robust association between objective indicators of class and voting, even when focusing on the only truly "class-based" party in Canada, the New Democratic party (NDP) (see Archer 1985; Gidengil et al. 2006).

The point of raising such observations, however, is not to preclude the potential value of a class-based voter analysis because, as Elisabeth Gidengil (2002) points out, it is entirely possible that when political choices are presented to voters in a context of class conflict, class voting may increase in salience. In addition, regional interactions may exist. For instance, John Wilson (1974) suggested that class voting varies with the cultural development and political maturity of the different provinces, with maturity defined as a party system that reflects class divisions. Furthermore, in the past, certain research has suggested that class effects may work in subjective ways. And although the preceding chapter suggests that the supporting evidence for this proposition has not always been strong, this debate has been effectively suspended for the time being due to the disappearance of subjective measures of class from the CES (Ogmundson 1975; Lambert and Hunter 1979).[1] Still, none of these possibilities can deny the fact that various attempts to relate comparable objective measures of class with distinctive party voting have tended to end in meagre results. And what this evidence seems to suggest is that in Canada class may not be a very relevant variable when it comes to explaining electoral choice.

Our aims in this chapter are twofold. The first is to use the evidence from the CES to systematically assess the cross-time empirical link between class and vote. The second is to investigate how class effects on the vote compare to the effects of various other demographic variables in order to evaluate whether the former are truly less relevant. These are not straightforward questions to answer, as one must take into account the possibility that virtually any factor's influence on the vote is likely to vary depending on the election year and how it is measured. This is why in this investigation we compare data from ten CES conducted from 1974 to 2006 and measure class consistently, as many of our predecessors have in the past, through objective variables such as income and education.[2] For comparative purposes, we also evaluate the effects of a sample of other demographic factors such as age, gender, religion, and region, all of which have been referred to in the preceding chapter as being politically relevant in varying ways.

Our exploratory tools include three basic tables containing election-by-election comparisons of how individuals in different socio-demographic groups voted in relation to Canadians as a whole. More precisely, the values in these tables correspond to vote differentials, which represent the difference between the percentage of respondents of a particular demographic group that voted for a specific party and the average proportion of Canadians who supported that party.[3] A positive differential suggests individuals within the respective demographic group display above-average support for the party being examined, while negative differentials indicate below-average support.

Class

Beginning with the evidence relating to class, the cross-time findings are mixed. There is evidence to suggest that people at different income levels resort systematically to different parties. However, the trends are not always what one would expect. For example, the Liberals typically attract above-average support from low-income earners (+2.3 points; see Table 7.1) and below-average support from other income categories. The NDP, on the other hand – the party that one might theoretically assume would rally above-average support from low-income earners – is usually most supported by those in the middle-income bracket (+1.7 points; see Table 7.3). The Conservatives typically receive above-average support from high-income earners (+2.7 points; see Table 7.2), as opposed to low-income earners (−1.6 points). Note also that in most cases the vote differentials are fairly small, which is consistent with the claim that in Canada the mobilizing effect of class on vote is typically weak.

It is possible, of course, that income may not be the best survey indicator with which to objectively measure class effects as one's placement in income categories can vary depending on the average income of a sample of respondents, which may fluctuate from one election to the next. By comparison, education may be a more stable measure. However, the evidence indicates that average vote differentials at different education levels are often weaker, and the results from different time points are not as consistent. For example, the least-educated group's 1974-97 average vote differential for the Liberals was +2.1 points and much less for the Conservatives (−1.1 points). During the 2000s, however, this trend reversed, and it is now the Conservatives who benefit from above-average support from the least-educated individuals. Furthermore, when we examine the cross-time association between education and NDP support, we find the same sort of weak and inconsistent results.

Overall, therefore, regardless of the data set that we examine, the average findings suggest that the effect that income and education have on the

TABLE 7.1

Vote differentials for the Liberal party (percentages)

		1974	1979	1980	1984	1988	1993	1997	2000	2004	2006	Average
Income	Low	1.6	.3	5.1	.1	3.2	4.0	-.5	5.0	2.0	2.0	2.3
	Mid	-2.4	2.3	-5.2	.1	-.5	-1.4	-1.1	-3.2	-4.4	-4.2	-2.0
	High	1.2	-1.9	-5.1	-.6	-4.0	-1.3	2.4	-.3	4.0	3.6	-.2
Education	Low	1.4	1.9	4.6	3.3	1.3	2.2	-.2	3.7	.3	-2.3	1.6
	Mid	-4.3	1.1	-.9	-1.8	-1.6	2.1	.3	2.6	-1.8	-1.8	-.6
	High	0	-3.0	-4.1	-2.3	.1	-2.1	0	-2.1	.5	1.1	-1.2
Religion	Catholic	13.6	15.1	17.5	8.9	5.8	.9	4.5	3.9	4.7	.8	7.6
	Protestant	-11.1	-13.0	-14.1	-6.2	-4.1	-.6	-4.7	-6.2	-2.9	-.8	-6.4
	Other	27.8	12.7	11.5	6.4	5.3	11.0	3.1	9.0	37.5	42.3	16.7
	None	-9.2	-16.3	-12.7	-11.8	-12.6	-4.8	-1.9	-3.7	-5.6	-2.8	-8.1
Region	Atlantic	2.3	2.9	6.1	6.0	16.3	23.9	-5.3	2.6	13.5	12.1	8.0
	Quebec	18.0	24.5	26.3	7.1	-2.5	-10.9	-.3	-1.1	-1.1	-8.8	5.1
	Ontario	-2.7	-5.4	-5.1	3.8	7.6	13.0	15.5	10.6	8.6	7.9	5.4
	Prairies	-15.0	-22.5	-24.1	-10.8	-9.8	-7.8	-10.4	-14.2	-12.8	-7.6	-13.5
	BC	-12.8	-19.4	-23.5	-9.7	-13.5	-9.6	-6.0	-5.9	-8.1	-.4	-10.9
Gender	Male	-3.2	-.24	-3.4	-1.9	-3.6	-1.8	-1.0	-1.7	-.4	-1.8	-2.1
	Female	2.8	2.2	3.3	1.6	3.7	2.0	1.0	1.8	.4	1.8	2.0
Age	18–34	-2.5	-1.6	1.6	-2.8	-.4	-3.5	1.1	-2.0	-6.0	-4.2	-2.0
	35–59	2.9	2.0	0	-.8	-2.8	-.9	-.5	-.2	-.8	-1.8	-.3
	60+	-2.9	-1.2	-2.7	5.6	7.2	8.7	-.2	2.2	5.5	4.9	2.7

Source: 1974–2006 Canadian Election Studies.

TABLE 7.2

Vote differentials for the Progressive Conservative party (percentages)

		1974	1979	1980	1984	1988	1993	1997	2000	2004	2006	Average
Income	Low	-2.0	0	-3.6	-.5	-4.3	-3.5	1.2	-1.1	-1.5	-.8	-1.6
	Mid	.7	-4.1	0	-.2	-2.5	0	-2.2	0	1.2	.2	-.7
	High	1.1	2.7	5.0	2.1	8.6	2.7	2.7	.6	.4	.6	2.7
Education	Low	-1.1	-.5	-.9	-1.9	-1.7	-2.4	.8	-3.3	3.0	13.7	.6
	Mid	1.9	-.5	-.7	2.7	-.3	.6	-.5	-1.0	2.3	3.4	.8
	High	.8	1.0	1.2	.3	1.2	.8	-.1	1.4	-1.5	-4.0	.1
Religion	Catholic	-14.5	-16.5	-16.6	-4.8	-.5	-2.3	.3	-3.9	-11.8	-4.6	-7.5
	Protestant	12.4	16.3	14.7	5.9	3.0	3.4	2.3	6.2	14.7	12.2	9.1
	Other	-14.1	-14.1	-11.9	-22.6	-10.6	-5.2	-1.3	.2	-17.0	-29.3	-12.6
	None	-2.6	-2.7	-2.2	-3.5	-3.2	.2	-6.3	-1.5	-3.5	-11.8	-3.7
Region	Atlantic	4.8	5.0	2.1	3.6	-1.6	4.5	17.8	18.8	-3.7	-.2	5.1
	Quebec	-22.7	-25.5	-23.7	.2	10.7	-2.6	2.8	-7.0	-24.2	-14.4	-10.6
	Ontario	2.5	5.9	3.6	-4.1	-3.5	1.6	-1.6	2.0	.9	2.0	.9
	Prairies	14.5	23.0	19.6	5.3	.2	.4	-3.8	-1.1	19.8	15.4	9.3
	BC	5.7	4.9	12.9	-5.1	-10.1	-2.8	-11.3	-6.0	6.8	1.1	-.4
Gender	Male	.9	2.1	3.5	1.1	4.1	-1.0	-.1	-.8	.9	4.3	1.5
	Female	-.8	-1.9	-3.4	-.9	-4.1	1.1	.1	.9	-.8	-4.1	-1.4
Age	18–34	-3.3	-5.9	-6.7	-1.1	-2.6	-.6	-.4	-4.0	-4.8	-8.0	-3.7
	35–59	-.9	.6	1.2	2.3	2.8	.4	-1.0	1.0	-1.6	-1.1	.4
	60+	8.0	8.0	8.7	-2.6	-1.3	-.1	3.0	1.2	6.2	5.2	3.6

Source: 1974–2006 Canadian Election Studies.

TABLE 7.3

Vote differentials for the New Democratic party (percentages)

		1974	1979	1980	1984	1988	1993	1997	2000	2004	2006	Average
Income	Low	-1.1	-.5	-1.2	.6	1.2	2.9	-.2	-.6	1.1	-.8	.1
	Mid	2.1	2.6	5.2	.4	3.0	-1.0	1.1	1.4	.5	1.8	1.7
	High	-1.3	-1.2	-.3	-2.9	-4.8	-1.0	-1.7	-.8	-2.4	-1.7	-1.8
Education	Low	-1.7	-1.2	-3.0	-.8	.9	1.3	-3.6	-1.4	1.4	-5.9	-1.4
	Mid	3.4	-.3	2.3	-.2	1.2	-1.4	-1.2	-1.2	-1.5	-1.7	0
	High	1.0	1.7	1.8	.9	-1.2	.1	1.7	.9	.2	1.8	.9
Religion	Catholic	-2.7	-2.7	-2.9	-4.3	-3.1	-2.6	-3.9	-3.5	-5.2	-6.5	-3.7
	Protestant	1.5	.1	1.3	.5	-.4	2.2	1.4	-.2	-1.2	-1.4	.4
	Other	-10.4	3.6	-.8	11.6	3.7	-.9	3.0	-1.6	-4.4	-3.2	.1
	None	12.9	20.5	13.7	16.0	12.5	2.3	6.6	12.6	11.3	15.1	12.4
Region	Atlantic	-4.6	-3.8	-6.1	-7.3	-10.7	.3	13.7	7.0	1.7	.2	-1.0
	Quebec	-4.8	-.9	-7.2	-8.3	-5.9	-5.6	-8.4	-6.1	-11.3	-8.1	-7.5
	Ontario	3.6	3.2	2.9	1.2	-1.2	-1.4	-.2	-.2	.4	.6	.9
	Prairies	2.1	2.8	5.6	3.7	2.9	2.9	1.7	2.4	1.6	2.5	2.8
	BC	9.4	17.3	12.1	15.7	20.9	8.4	3.3	6.2	11.3	8.7	11.3
Gender	Male	2.5	.3	0	.2	-1.0	-.7	-3.1	-1.0	-1.1	-1.0	-.5
	Female	-2.2	-.3	0	-.2	1.0	.7	3.1	1.1	1.0	.9	.5
Age	18–34	3.9	4.4	2.9	2.7	2.9	-.2	-.6	1.4	5.9	4.1	2.7
	35–59	-1.4	-.9	0	-1.5	-.1	0	1.2	-.2	.5	1.4	-.1
	60+	-3.3	-5.1	-5.0	-1.1	-5.5	.3	-2.1	-.8	-4.9	-4.1	-3.2

Source: 1974-2006 Canadian Election Studies.

vote is not very powerful, and different objective measures reveal different results. But how atypical are these findings, and how do they compare with the results for other demographic variables? To continue this investigation, we now turn to examine the cross-time evidence relating to other demographic factors and their effects on the vote.

Religion

In the preceding chapter, Gidengil suggests that the robust effect of religious denomination on electoral choice, as defined by the traditional Roman Catholic/Protestant distinction, has been an ongoing mystery for Canadian election researchers. Instead of searching for evidence to support a theory, scholars have in this case been left searching for a theoretical explanation to account for forty years of evidence indicating that Catholics are typically more inclined to vote Liberal than Protestants. However, in empirical terms, how does the mobilizing effect of religious denomination on voting compare to the class effect? The Catholic-Liberal associations presented in Table 7.1 indicate an approximate 15.4-point advantage for Liberals among Catholics prior to the Mulroney sweep in 1984 and the subsequent rise of the Bloc Québécois in Quebec. After this point, there was a precipitous decline in the Catholic-Liberal link in Quebec, but outside of Quebec the relationship hardly appears to change. Conversely, the cross-time evidence shows that Protestants tend to provide above-average support for the Conservatives (+9.1 points; Table 7.2).

Observe as well that there are some additional findings reported here that typically do not receive as much attention. The first is that people in other religious denominations also provide above-average support for the Liberals (+16.7 points; Table 7.1). In fact, in some years, the magnitude of these results is extraordinary, but these figures need to be interpreted cautiously due to the smaller sample sizes. Second, there is an above-average tendency among non-religious people to vote NDP (+12.4 points; Table 7.3). This is perhaps one of the strongest demographic correlates for supporters of that party, and it is not surprising given that the NDP is normally hostile to the perceived conservatism and hierarchical elitism of established religions. Each of these findings contributes to the enigma relating to the relevance of the religion variable in Canada, and what they suggest is that the secular-religious divide (in its various forms) is much more strongly associated with vote than are the class-related variables found to be important in other countries (see, for example, Butler and Stokes 1974).

Region

Relative to most European nations or the United States, regional variation in Canada ranks as an important determinant of voting. For example, since 1974, the absolute deviation for Canadian parties by region averages twice that of American parties. To illustrate, in 2004, the Conservative vote proportion in Alberta was almost 62 percent as compared to nearly 9 percent in Quebec, a difference of fifty-three percentage points, and in 2006 the difference was just short of forty percentage points. By comparison, figures tabulated by William Nordhaus (2005) suggest that the greatest regional differentiation for George Bush in 2004 was sixteen percentage points, based on the difference between Democratic support in the Southern and non-Southern states.

The works of Richard Wilson (2000) and Richard Simeon and David Elkins (1974) suggest that these differences in Canada may be due to deep variations in regional political cultures. Wilson, for example, develops the Hartzian notion of English and French "fragments" as founding cultures into an extended series of diverse cultural developments that is coterminous with different provincial boundaries (Hartz 1964). Since different regions of the country were settled by different cultures, which continue to develop in particular directions at different rates, this reality has varying political implications. Likewise, Simeon and Elkins (1974) supply evidence of regional variations in efficacy, trust, and involvement, which provide further reasons to expect differences in political behaviour.

When we systematically examine voting differentials over time, we find that different regions of the country do indeed support different political parties at varying rates and that, similar to the religious-secular divide, regional effects tend to be a relatively powerful motivating force. For example, support for the Liberals is typically above the country average in Atlantic Canada (greater than +8.0 points; Table 7.1). On the other hand, the worst region for the Liberals in Canada in terms of vote share has been the Prairies, where they average 13.5 points below their countrywide level of voter support. It is interesting to note, however, that not all regional effects have been consistent over time. As Richard Johnston details in his chapter in this volume, it was not until the first victory by Brian Mulroney in 1984 that the decline of the Liberals in Quebec became marked, and the pattern of Liberal over-performance in Ontario became more prominent. Ontario is an important battleground for determining the identity of the governing party in Canada, and vote differentials in that province indicate that the Liberals were more successful in attracting voter support in Ontario during the Jean Chrétien years than in earlier years. This fact was probably also partly facilitated by the divisions in Conservative ranks that existed during this time.

The Conservatives, on the other hand, have consistently performed best in the Prairies, particularly if one moves beyond the basic evidence presented in Table 7.2 and aggregates the Progressive Conservatives with the Reform and Canadian Alliance parties that formed during the Chrétien period. Conversely, Quebec almost consistently has been the Conservatives' worst region (−10.6 points; Table 7.2). In fact, if one excludes the exceptional 1988 election, the Conservative differential in Quebec drops even further (to −13 points). Turning to the NDP, the key evidence suggests that this party typically receives above-average support in British Columbia (+11.3 points; Table 7.3) and below-average support in Quebec (−7.5 points).

What is evident from all of these findings is that the average magnitude of regional effects is far larger than class effects. It is important to caution, however, that in certain instances the data presented in Tables 7.1, 7.2, and 7.3 may not be entirely representative. For example, the summary statistics presented in these tables group the Atlantic provinces together because the sample sizes for each individual province within this region on a year-to-year basis are relatively small.[4] Yet, there are clearly differences among the Atlantic provinces and, indeed, within them (for example, the Avalon peninsula versus the Newfoundland outports and Acadia versus the St. John Valley in New Brunswick). Likewise, the Prairie provinces are aggregated, while it is quite evident that there are sustaining differences between political cultures in Alberta, Saskatchewan, and Manitoba. Also, Edmonton is different from Calgary, Vancouver Island is distinctive from the BC interior, and both Quebec and Ontario can be meaningfully divided into at least five sub-regions apiece.

There is hardly a province in Canada where clear internal sub-regional patterns are present, and it is not surprising that more detailed analysis on regional voting in Canada has begun to emerge. For example, Ailsa Henderson (2004) improves upon Simeon and Elkins's (1974) study of provincial political cultures by redefining a region in a way that transcends provincial boundaries. She argues that parts of Atlantic Canada (not all) and parts of Ontario can be grouped together into the same "region" because the Loyalists who migrated to these areas developed a similar political culture. Other more recent approaches to the study of regional voting are equally provocative. Fred Cutler (2002), for example, draws links between voter behaviour and economic conditions within regions with similar levels of economic activity. Likewise, there is also increasing interest in the urban-rural and urban-suburban cleavage, although we do not yet have uniform cross-time measures of urbanization in the CES (Cutler and Jenkins 2000; Thomas 2001; Walks 2005, 2006, 2007).

Gender

As the figures provided in the concluding chapter of this volume show, gender has not until recently received as much research attention among Canadian academics. Theories addressing this matter are based upon differing values and issue priorities, which, in turn, can result in distinct political behaviours (Inglehart and Norris 2003). For instance, one recent study shows that women are more concerned with social issues, while men have greater economic concerns and higher faith in market-oriented solutions to contemporary problems (Gidengil et al. 2005). But do differences such as these translate into variations in men and women's voting behaviour? And, if so, how do gender effects compare to class effects?

The cross-time evidence from the CES suggests that women are more supportive of the Liberal party than average Canadians (+2.0 points; Table 7.1). Moreover, since 1988, women have tended to provide above-average support to the NDP (+1.3 points; Table 7.3). The basis of this transition can be traced to the 24-25 October debates in the 1988 federal election campaign. The average level of support for the NDP in the ten days before the debates was 22 percent among women and 26 percent among men. In the ten days that followed these debates, these results shifted, and the average degree of support was 29 percent among women and 22 percent among men. The Liberal party's strategy to focus the election on the Canada-US Free Trade Agreement was the headline issue during the televised event, and the extent to which free trade would undermine some of Canada's cherished social programs became an important point of discussion. Given the NDP's credibility over the social welfare agenda, it should come as no surprise that they benefited considerably from this strategy, particularly among women who valued such concerns. Ultimately, the NDP captured forty-three seats during this election.

As for the Conservative party, the cross-time data suggest that it benefits from greater support among men. However, similar to the results reported earlier, these vote differentials are not very large (+1.5 points; Table 7.2). In fact, the greatest male-female vote differentials registered among Conservatives have been for the now defunct Reform and Canadian Alliance parties.

From 1993 to 2000, males were generally 3.0 points more likely to support the Reform and Canadian Alliance parties than average Canadians.[5] At around the same time, the above-average pattern of male support for the Progressive Conservative party was disrupted briefly when its base of supporters fractured between 1988 and 2004. However, by 2006, the predominance of male support for the Conservatives becomes apparent once again (see Table 7.2).

Furthermore, although not shown in this chapter, it is interesting to note that women in more traditional family roles (as homemakers, married, and with children) were more likely to vote for the Conservative party than for the Liberal party, whereas single women in the paid workforce and in less traditional family situations account for the more general offsetting pattern of Liberal support. These findings are generalizable as research in other countries shows a similar pattern. Unemployed married women are typically more conservative than women who are employed, especially those who are also unmarried (Iversen and Rosenbluth 2006; see also Connelly 2000). On the whole, the evidence presented here suggests that the average magnitude of gender effects has been slightly greater for the Liberals than for the Conservatives and the NDP, but these effects are not systematically more powerful than the effects of class.

Age

As suggested by Gidengil in the preceding chapter, age has been a factor more noted than discussed in analyses of Canadian electoral behaviour. It typically appears as a control in multivariate models of voter choice, but rarely does it draw much mention. The main exception, as Pammett argues in his chapter in this volume, is that age recently has been identified as a very important determinant of voter turnout (see also Blais et al. 2004). However, as a measure of electoral choice, the findings are not always consistent with the widespread perception that voters tend to become more conservative as they age. For example, in the United States, data show that Americans over the age of sixty-five are somewhat more disposed to support the Democrats, perhaps out of concern for social security and Medicare programs.[6] Moreover, at the younger end, the results are mixed. New voters are frequently more supportive of the Democrats, but exceptions to this pattern emerged during the Ronald Reagan era (Abramson, Aldrich, and Rohde 1986). This lack of consistent voting behaviour among American youth and also the general propensity for younger voters to support newer parties are seen as a possible reflection of their inexperience. That is, they lack long-term memories and do not necessarily associate a political party in its present form with what positions and directions it took in the past.

. In Canada, the results are not all that different. A systematic assessment of the cross-time evidence from the CES suggests an overall tendency of the over-sixty group to be more supportive of the Liberals than the general population, sometimes by amounts of five points or more, particularly in the years from 1984 onward (see Table 7.1). However, the Conservatives benefited from older voters (according to Table 7.2) prior to 1984 and after 2000. At the other end of the continuum, the NDP (+2.7 points; Table 7.3) and, in recent years, the Bloc Québécois (+3.3 points since 1993) regularly performed better among younger voters than with the general population. And other evidence suggests that this pattern applied to the Green party in 2006 (Brown 2009).

What these findings seem to suggest, therefore, is that smaller (and newer) parties in Canada tend to find greater acceptance among the young, due perhaps to their varying levels of partisan development (Butler and Stokes 1974). It should be noted, however, that this finding is not stable across different elections and that the Reform and Canadian Alliance parties consistently underperformed among the eighteen-to-thirty-four group. Relatively speaking, the average size of these age-based voting differentials is modest, and they are more comparable to those for class and gender than they are to those for religion or region.

Conclusion

In the earliest years of the CES and even before, social class received a disproportionate focus in scholarly attempts to understand the Canadian electoral process and voting behaviour. Then, the evidence began to suggest that class was not very relevant. An objective calibration of social class in terms of education and income levels shows systematically weak and inconsistent effects on party support over time. In relative terms, however, the data examined in this chapter suggest that the potential influence of these variables on vote is comparable to that of gender and age, although much less powerful than the effects had by the religious-secular and regional divides. Based on this evidence, it would seem inconsistent to suggest that more work with socio-demographic variables such as age and gender is required, but, then, to ignore class because of its perceived irrelevance. There are many prospective lines of class analysis that have yet to be explored, and there may still be much more that we stand to learn. In the future, it may be wise to pay more careful attention to context and class networks, as the discussion in the preceding chapter suggests that both may be important considerations.

Another point to take away from this analysis for future consideration is that the manner in which a variable is defined and categorized can determine just how much impact it seems to have on the voting process. Some determinants, gender being the most obvious, stand on their own. However, other variables such as subjective class, objective class, region and religion might attribute some of their current relevance to the way they have been categorized. For instance, region has long been classified by the criteria used in this chapter, but one should be open to the possibility that some other criteria might fine tune and enhance its potency in accounting for Canadian voting. Similarly, the Catholic-Protestant distinction, which has long been a subject of scholarly discussion but one that is under-theorized, might also be a "classificational" artifact. Protestants have been grouped together out of convenience because there are so many denominations that have relatively small memberships. This categorization of convenience may camouflage denominational distinctions that warrant attention. Also, the analysis reported in this chapter suggests that other religious and secular groups may be worthy of further analysis.

NOTES

1 The 1974 and 1979 CES included a subjective measure of class: "which of the following five social classes would you say you were in: upper class, upper-middle class, middle class, working class, or lower class?" This item was not repeated in the 1980 election survey but was included in 1984. And subsequent election studies have omitted this item.

2 We start with the 1974 study because previous waves of the CES did not operationalize education and income in a standardized manner.

3 Differentials are a simple and easily interpretable tool. However, differentials may not always be representative because sample sizes for certain subgroups may not be sufficient. This is a limitation of this type of analysis that needs to be kept in mind.

4 See the Introduction of this volume for a more detailed breakdown.

5 Separate tables showing the vote differentials for the Reform, Canadian Alliance, and Bloc Québécois parties can be obtained upon request from the authors.

6 Any connection between age and voting among Americans may also reflect a cohort effect.

REFERENCES

Abramson, Paul R., John H. Aldrich, and David W. Rohde. 1986. *Change and Continuity in the 1984 Elections*. Washington, DC: CQ Press.

Alford, Robert R. 1963. *Party and Society: The Anglo-American Democracies.* Chicago: Rand McNally.

Archer, Keith. 1985. "The Failure of the New Democratic Party: Unions, Unionists, and Politics in Canada." *Canadian Journal of Political Science* 18: 353-66.

Blais, André, Elisabeth Gidengil, Neil Nevitte, and Richard Nadeau. 2004. "Where Does Turnout Decline Come From?" *European Journal of Political Research* 43: 221-36.

Butler, David, and Donald E. Stokes. 1974. *Political Change in Britain.* London: Macmillan.

Connelly, Marjorie. 2000. "Who Voted: A Portrait of American Politics." *New York Times* 12 November 2000, WK4.

Cutler, Fred. 2002. "Local Economies, Local Policy Impacts and Federal Electoral Behaviour in Canada." *Canadian Journal of Political Science* 35: 347-82.

Cutler, Fred, and Richard W. Jenkins. 2000. "Where One Lives and What One Thinks: Implications of Rural-Urban Opinion Cleavages for Canadian Federalism." Paper presented to the Transformation of Canadian Political Culture and the State of the Federation Conference, Institute of Intergovernmental Affairs, Queen's University, Kingston, 13-14 October 2000.

Gidengil, Elisabeth. 2002. "The Class Voting Conundrum." In Douglas Baer, ed., *Political Sociology: Canadian Perspectives*, 274-87. Don Mills, ON: Oxford University Press.

Gidengil, Elisabeth, André Blais, Joanna Everitt, Patrick Fournier, and Neil Nevitte. 2006. "Back to the Future? Making Sense of the 2004 Canadian Election outside of Quebec." *Canadian Journal of Political Science* 39: 1-25.

Gidengil, Elisabeth, Matthew Hannigar, André Blais, and Neil Nevitte. 2005. "Explaining the Gender Gap in Support for the New Right." *Comparative Political Studies* 38: 1171-95.

Hartz, Louis. 1964. *The Founding of New Societies.* New York: Harcourt, Brace and World.

Henderson, Ailsa. 2004. "Regional Political Cultures in Canada." *Canadian Journal of Political Science* 37: 595-615.

Hunter, Alfred A. 1982. "On Class, Status, and Voting in Canada." *Canadian Journal of Sociology* 7: 19-39.

Inglehart, Ronald, and Pippa Norris. 2003. *Rising Tide: Gender Equality and Cultural Change around the World.* New York: Cambridge University Press.

Iversen, Torben, and Frances Rosenbluth. 2006. "The Political Economy of Gender: Explaining Cross-National Variation in the Gender Division of Labor and the Gender Voting Gap." *American Journal of Political Science* 50: 1-19.

Lambert, Ronald D., and Alfred A. Hunter. 1979. "Social Stratification, Voting Behaviour, and the Images of Canadian Federal Political Parties." *Canadian Review of Sociology and Anthropology* 16: 287-304.

Lenski, Gerhard, and Jean Lenski. 1978. *Human Societies: An Introduction to Macrosociology.* New York: McGraw-Hill Ryerson.

Macpherson, C.B. 1953. *Democracy in Alberta: Social Credit and the Party System.* Toronto: University of Toronto Press.

Nordhaus, William. 2005. "The Profile of an Election, 2004: Outcomes and Fundamentals." *Economist's Voice* 2(3), Berkeley Electronic Press, http://www.bepress.com/ev/vol2/iss2/art3.

Ogmundson, Rick. 1975. "Party Class Images and the Class Vote in Canada." *American Sociological Review* 40: 506-12.

Simeon, Richard, and David J. Elkins. 1974. "Regional Political Cultures in Canada." *Canadian Journal of Political Science* 7: 397-437.

Thomas, Timothy L. 2001. "An Emerging Party Cleavage: Metropolis vs. The Rest." In Hugh G. Thorburn and Alan Whitehorn, eds., *Party Politics in Canada*, 8th edition, 431-42. Toronto: Prentice Hall.

Walks, Alan R. 2005. "The City-Suburban Cleavage in Canadian Federal Politics." *Canadian Journal of Political Science* 38: 383-413.

–. 2006. "The Causes of City-Suburban Political Polarization? A Canadian Case Study." *Annals of the Association of American Geographers* 96: 390-414.

–. 2007. "The Boundaries of Suburban Discontent? Urban Definitions and Neighbourhood Political Effects." *Canadian Geographer* 51: 160-85.

Wilson, John. 1968. "Politics and Social Class in Canada: The Case of Waterloo South." *Canadian Journal of Political Science* 1: 288-309.

–. 1974. "The Canadian Political Cultures: Towards a Redefinition of the Nature of the Canadian Political System." *Canadian Journal of Political Science* 7: 438-83.

Wilson, Richard W. 2000. "The Many Voices of Political Culture: Assessing Different Approaches." *World Politics* 52: 246-73.

8

Quebec versus the Rest of Canada, 1965-2006

RICHARD NADEAU AND ÉRIC BÉLANGER

The Canadian Election Studies (CES) are more than just a vast inquiry into voting behaviour. They are also a critical data source for studying the evolution of various divides within Canada, as described in the preceding two chapters. One of the most important of these has been the cleavage between Quebec and the rest of Canada (ROC). In this chapter, we organize the political dynamics of over four decades into three periods, each representing different phases in the evolution of the Quebec/ROC divide. For each phase, we draw on various CES-related studies and publications, focusing mainly on research describing the similarities and differences in peoples' outlooks and the determinants of electoral behaviour. Our goal is to answer the following four questions: What have the CES taught us about the nature and evolution of the Quebec/ROC cleavage? Has the gap between these two communities widened or has it decreased with time? What have we learned about voting behaviour in these two regions? And what can we suggest about the future of this divide?

1965-80: A Quebec More Conservative and More Liberal, a Canada Less Conservative and Less Liberal

The major works based on the CES from 1965 to 1980 led to two noteworthy paradoxes (van Loon 1970; Schwartz 1974; Simeon and Elkins 1974; Sniderman, Forbes, and Melzer 1974; Meisel 1975; Curtis and Lambert

1976; Clarke et al. 1979, 1984). The first is that support for the Liberal party was higher in Quebec than in the other Canadian provinces, even though Quebec was more conservative than the ROC (Meisel 1975). Second, Quebecers, to whom the question of identity is central, expressed less favourable feelings toward their own province than other Canadians did toward their respective provinces (Clarke et al. 1979).

A More Conservative Quebec

The most complete study on the thinking of Quebecers and other Canadians during this period was led by John Meisel (1975). This study was based on the 1965 and 1968 federal elections, and it developed a fascinating portrait of Quebec and Canada during the late 1960s. Several outlooks were explored, including the importance of religion, moral liberalism, authoritarianism, tolerance, centralism (the respective importance given to federal and provincial governments), interest in international issues, and feelings toward, and cynicism about, politics as measured by respondents' attitudes about the 1968 election.[1]

Quebec during the 1960s stands out from the ROC in terms of its religious sentiments (measured by religious practice, the homogeneity of social contacts, and expenses devoted to religious organizations) as well as its moral outlooks (measured by opinions expressed toward divorce, homosexuality, and the death penalty). For example, more than half of Quebecers (56 percent) were located on the highest category of Meisel's religiosity scale compared to only 22 percent of respondents from the ROC. Forty-one percent of Quebecers fell into the lowest category of Meisel's moral liberalism scale, whereas only 28 percent of those outside of Quebec matched that same mindset. Relative to the ROC, Quebec voters at the time had less of an interest in international issues (only 37 percent of Quebecers expressed an interest for international affairs as compared to 63 percent in the ROC) and a much more pronounced sense of cynicism toward politics (see Meisel 1975).

Quebecers' support for tough measures to maintain law and order (as indicated by support for sanctions against people breaking a law for religious reasons and for police action during illegal strikes), however, was less pronounced than it was for other Canadians (only 28 percent of Quebecers were highly supportive of these measures as compared to 47 percent in the ROC). Also, support for sovereignty was marginal in Quebec at that time (9 percent), and the autonomist sentiment (measured by the level of government

perceived to be handling the most important problem affecting the respondent personally and by the importance attached to various corresponding
federal and provincial offices) was only slightly more pronounced than in
the ROC (39 percent of respondents in the ROC expressed a high level of
support for the centralization of powers versus 32 percent in Quebec).

Other studies conducted at the time match and nuance these character-
izations. For example, Richard van Loon (1970) concludes from the 1965
election study that francophones give a little more importance to their provincial government, which may explain their weaker levels of participation
and interest during federal elections. He associates such differences, in part,
with the weaknesses of the education system in Quebec. Richard Simeon
and David Elkins (1974), in their study of provincial political cultures, also
found that francophones in Quebec were characterized by weaker levels of
political interest and efficacy, a much more pronounced sense of cynicism,
but a stronger attachment to their provincial government. They argued that
these differences were partly attributable to a socio-economic deficit (in
terms of education and income) that existed in Quebec at that time. And
James Curtis and Ronald Lambert (1976) noted that a weaker political participation rate and lower levels of interest in public affairs was particularly
notable among Quebec women, and that this behaviour may be linked to the
late granting of voting rights to this group.

The work of Harold Clarke and his collaborators (1979) rounds out this
initial comparison by reaffirming and fleshing out some of what has already
been suggested. As noted earlier by Thomas Scotto and his colleagues in
their chapter in this volume, the 1974 election study sought to gauge the
relative importance given to federal and provincial governments and included direct measures of Quebecers' and Canadians' feelings toward their
province and Canada. The empirical evidence presented by these authors
also suggests that the autonomist sentiment (having a more favourable dis-
position toward the provincial as opposed to the federal government) was
only slightly more pronounced in Quebec than in the other provinces.
Clarke and his colleagues indicated at the time that this was one of the most
revealing results reported in their book: francophone Quebecers were as
positive about Canada as they were about their province (rating 72 in both
cases on a thermometer scale ranging from 0 to 100, where 100 indicates
very positive). Even more surprising was their finding suggesting that
francophone Quebecers were actually less positive about their province
than other Canadians were about their respective provinces (rating 81 on
average on the same thermometer scale).

Thanks to the CES, the overall picture that can be drawn from this comparison of Quebecers and the ROC from 1965 to 1980 is both enlightening and astonishing.[2] As a society, Quebec appears more religious, more conservative, and less interested in international issues and politics more generally than the ROC. It is also a society where cynicism toward politics is greater (Meisel 1975), and the autonomist sentiment is tempered (at least until the 1970s).

The Dominance of the Liberal Party

Another major finding that stems from this initial period points to the dominance of the Liberal Party of Canada and its leader in Quebec. Part of this conclusion is grounded in electoral outcomes, and part of it is rooted in the measurement of identification with the federal parties. Major studies of this period, namely those conducted by Meisel (1975), Clarke and his collaborators (1979, 1984), as well as the work of Paul Sniderman, H.D. Forbes, and Ian Melzer (1974), all underline that the Liberal party's partisan pool in Quebec was stronger than that of its adversaries. Indeed, a substantial portion of Quebecers during this period identified themselves with the Liberal party, recognized themselves in its policies, and supported the party come election time. It is true that the partisan identification of Quebec voters was sometimes depicted as being weaker, less stable, and not as strongly linked to the vote than in the ROC, but the Liberal party still dominated Quebec during this time both in terms of voters and identifiers (the Liberals held nearly 83 percent of the seats in the province between 1965 and 1980).

Other notable determinants of voting patterns include language, place of birth, religion, and the rural/urban divide. Meisel showed that support for the Liberal party was not only high among non-francophone Quebecers and massive among immigrants but also strong among Quebec French speakers and French speakers in the ROC. In addition, religion seemed to play a more important role in influencing voting behaviour in the ROC than in Quebec, as there was a greater contrast between Catholics and Protestants in the ROC than in Quebec. And support for more conservative party formations, such as the Social Credit party in Quebec and the Progressive Conservative (PC) party elsewhere in Canada, was consistently reported to be stronger outside of large urban areas.

The vitality in Quebec of the Social Credit movement during the 1960s and part of the 1970s was a distinctive feature of Quebec politics. Between 1965 and 1979, the Social Credit party attracted the support of nearly 20 percent of Quebecers (with a peak of 24 percent in 1972) and was represented by a significant number of members of parliament (more than ten on average). The CES also helps to shed some light on the profile of the Social Credit voter in Quebec. The works of Mildred Schwartz (1974) and Meisel (1975), for example, have noted that support for the Right-leaning Social Credit party was strong among the less well-off strata of the population. This observation has led several researchers to conclude that the class vote was weaker in Quebec than in the ROC. Others have suggested that it was simply reversed – in the sense that in Quebec it was a Right-wing party that had the support of voters who were generally thought to be more inclined to turn to a Left-wing alternative (that is, blue collar workers, the less fortunate, and the less educated citizens). As Meisel (1975, 7) puts it, "in a sense, the class role performed by the NDP elsewhere in Canada is assumed in Quebec by the rallying of the Créditistes."

Still, the domination of the Liberal party in Quebec stood in contrast to the more volatile nature of its support in the ROC. Consequently, it is not surprising that researchers observed that the effects of short-term determinants of the vote were less important in Quebec than anywhere else in Canada during this period. For instance, Daniel Guérin and Richard Nadeau (1998, 559) concluded from their study of economic voting during the Pierre Trudeau years that the "fidelity of francophone Quebecers to the Liberal Party of Canada has inhibited the expression of an economic vote during this period and that this particular behaviour of Quebecers has led to a dilution of the economic vote in the whole of Canada." This assessment is similar to observations that emanate from later works that suggest that the impact of the national unity issue on the vote in Quebec is overpowering. As will be seen in the following discussion, the impact of both long-term social cleavages and short-term determinants on voting decisions in the later periods was partly muted in Quebec by the growing relevance of the nationalism debate and the push for sovereignty.

1984-92: The Brian Mulroney Years

At first blush, the Mulroney years seemed to suggest a rapprochement between Quebec and the ROC. Breaking away from their traditional fidelity toward the Liberal party, Quebecers joined with other Canadians to elect two majority PC governments in 1984 and 1988. Quebecers and Canadians again voted in the same direction in 1992, this time to reject the Charlottetown Accord. Yet, this apparent convergence was mostly on the surface. Quebec's support for the PC party during the 1980s was in large part attributable to a rejection of the Liberal party's constitutional positions. The

Charlottetown Accord was rejected by both regions for opposing reasons: Quebecers estimated the deal to be insufficient and other Canadians believed the offer to be too generous for Quebec.

Perhaps best described as a transitional period, the Mulroney years marked the end of a "Solid Quebec" on the federal scene.[3] During this time, Quebec ceased to constitute an essential component of the Liberal party's electoral coalition. More precisely, francophone Quebecers put an end to their massive support of that party and distinguished themselves from two other clienteles that remained faithful to the Liberals, namely non-francophone Quebecers and francophones outside Quebec. A new generation of voters had started to transform the political scene. Quebec was becoming less conservative, and the sovereignty issue was beginning to impose itself as a major determinant of vote choice.

A More Affirmed Nationalism

As was the case during the mid-1960s to the early 1980s, studies based on the CES highlight various interesting differences between citizens in Quebec and the ROC during the mid-1980s. For example, francophones were more prone than anglophones to attach some significance to the notion of social class, and the former were less inclined to believe in their chances of promotion through social mobility. Paradoxically, however, such perceptions were still not readily applied to the political scene, as attested to by an inferior understanding of the concepts of Left and Right and by the fact that the class vote was not highly relevant in Quebec (Lambert et al. 1986, 1987). Another difference has to do with political engagement. Lambert and his colleagues concluded that Quebecers continued to be less interested in politics when compared to other Canadians (Lambert et al. 1988). In addition, Quebecers still expressed a softer opinion on crime. Forty-one percent agreed with the statement that "capital punishment is never justified." In the ROC, only 30 percent felt the same way. Quebecers were also more supportive than others in the ROC of the idea that "government should do more for ethnic minorities" (44 percent in Quebec versus 28 percent in the ROC).

Perhaps the most notable differences between Quebecers and other Canadians during the mid-1980s were over-competing visions of nationalism, or what Sylvia Bashevkin (1990) refers to as the pan-Canadian and Quebecois nationalisms. Pan-Canadianists sought to protect the sovereignty of Canada in the face of the United States by maintaining a strong federal presence in the country's politics and by controlling foreign investments. Quebecois nationalism, on the other hand, was less driven by the fear of

Americanization than by a will to see the Quebec government enjoy wider political autonomy.

During this period, two events that occurred almost simultaneously – the Meech Lake Accord and the Free Trade Agreement with the United States – exacerbated tensions between Quebecers and the ROC on these two competing visions of nationalism. Clarke and his collaborators (1991) and Richard Johnston and his team (1992) showed that Quebecers were more favourable to the Free Trade Agreement, more favourably disposed toward the United States, and less preoccupied with the political and economic consequences of such a treaty than those in the ROC. Moreover, the failure of the Meech Lake Accord was interpreted by many Quebecers as a refusal by other Canadians to fully and formally recognize their specific national identity. As a consequence, Quebecers' autonomist sentiment, which was shown in earlier studies to be barely higher in Quebec than in the other provinces, was expressed with much more intensity by the end of the 1980s (Clarke and Kornberg 1993). The population's overall feelings toward the Quebec and Canadian communities had also changed. By the time of the Charlottetown Accord Referendum, the gap in francophone Quebecers' evaluations of Quebec and Canada reached unprecedented levels.

It is important to note, however, that not all of the evidence reported during this time points exactly in the same direction. In certain respects, the data suggest that Quebec and the ROC grew more alike. For example, differences in religiosity and moral conservatism, which were significant at the time of the election of Pierre Trudeau, had essentially disappeared. The percentage of people attending church (on a monthly basis) was slightly lower in Quebec (44 percent) than in the ROC (49 percent), and the proportion of respondents agreeing that "religion is an important part of my life" was the same (70 percent) in both regions. Furthermore, opinions about abortion in Quebec and the ROC were now virtually undistinguishable, with 49 percent of Quebecers expressing the view that abortion is a personal choice (41 percent answered that it should be available if needed and 10 percent felt that it should never be permitted) as compared to 47 percent in the ROC (the percentages favouring conditional access and unconditional opposition were again almost identical to those in Quebec, at 41 percent and 12 percent, respectively). In addition, nearly half of Quebecers (46 percent) expressed the opinion that everyone would be better off if more women pursued careers of their own instead of staying at home (26 percent said the

opposite). This tilt toward feminist orientations appeared slightly less pronounced in the ROC (the percentages for the "career" and "home" options
outside Quebec were 38 percent and 26 percent, respectively).[4] Finally, attitudes in Quebec and the ROC toward the respective role of the state and
the private sector displayed hardly any difference. Around one in three (32
percent in Quebec versus 36 percent in the ROC) believed that everyone
profits when businesses are allowed to make as much money as they can,
and almost half (49 percent in Quebec versus 48 percent in the ROC)
thought that governmental regulation of business is necessary.

Same Vote, Different Motivations
With growing tensions over differing nationalistic tendencies, why would
Quebecers and those in the ROC exhibit similar voting patterns from the
mid-1980s to the early 1990s? As mentioned earlier, both groups of voters
supported the PCs in 1984 and 1988 and rejected the Charlottetown Accord
in 1992. As discussed further by Richard Johnston in the next chapter of this
volume, a detailed analysis of these two groups' political behaviour shows
that the motivations behind these choices were actually very different. The
first difference relates to weaker partisan ties found in Quebec as compared
to the ROC. Examining the evolution of party attachments between 1965
and 1991, Clarke and Allan Kornberg (1993) observed a sharp decline in
party identification in both Quebec and the ROC, but they have also noted
that the proportion of non-partisans was higher in Quebec than in the ROC
(43 percent and 24 percent, respectively; for a similar conclusion based on
different indicators, see Johnston et al. 1992). These authors deduced that
this settling of party identification was mainly due to the decline of the
Liberal party in Quebec – a decline not entirely compensated at the time by
the emergence of the PC party.

   In addition, constitutional preoccupations had much more influence on
Quebecers than other Canadians during the period from 1984 to 1992.
Looking at election studies conducted from 1974 to 1993, Clarke and his
colleagues (1991, 1996) noted that Quebecers have often opted for the party
that seemed the most capable of dealing with constitutional issues. The
Liberal party was perceived as such during the 1970s, followed by the PC
party during the 1980s, and by the Bloc Québécois since the 1993 election.

   Johnston et al's (1992, 1996) analysis of the 1988 election and the
Charlottetown Accord Referendum led to similar conclusions. Analyzing
the determinants of party identification at the time of the 1988 election,

these authors showed that the factors structuring party attachments were different in Quebec than in the ROC. Three dimensions were relevant in the ROC, namely a commercial dimension (dispositions toward the Free Trade Agreement and the strengthening of ties with the United States), a national dimension (measured by attitudes toward the role that the French should play in Canada, the Official Languages Act, and immigration), and a class dimension (attitudes toward unions, the privatization of Air Canada, and the funding of daycare centres).[5] The first, and sharpest, difference in Quebec was the absence of a class dimension (Johnston et al. 1992, 102). Partisan preferences in Quebec were basically structured around two, rather than three, dimensions. The first dimension is the commercial policy one and it was largely determined by the same factors as in the ROC. However, the second dimension, relating to nationalism, showed substantive differences in Quebec. It excluded attitudes toward official languages and immigration and included orientations toward Quebec sovereignty.

The analysis of the determinants of the 1992 referendum further highlights the effect of the Quebec sovereignty issue (Johnston et al. 1996). The Quebec electorate at the time was essentially split into three groups: the non-francophones (massively favourable to the YES side), the sovereignist francophones (largely favourable to the NO side), and the non-sovereignist francophones (divided between the two options). In this instance, feelings toward Quebec also weighed heavily on voters in the ROC, and disagreement over the Charlottetown Accord's two central clauses appears to have been decisive. "The problem," argue Johnston and his colleagues (1996, 276), "may have been the compounding of objectionable Quebec-related features, especially piling the 25 percent guarantee on top of the distinct society clause."

In some respects, it appeared as though the very calculus of voting in Quebec and the ROC was now different. The vote in Quebec was related more to group rationality than in the ROC. Quebecers were more likely to vote as one block so as to maximize their electoral weight (this argument has been proposed to explain the 1988 election outcome). In this way, the national unity/Quebec sovereignty issue seemed to detract from the influence of other determinants on the vote choice of Quebecers. This same type of interpretation is also evident in subsequent analyses. For example, Lynda Erickson and Brenda O'Neill (2002) claim that the emergence of a modern gender gap (a positive bias among women toward Left-leaning parties) in the ROC at the beginning of the 1990s did not occur in Quebec due to the polarization of opinions around the national question.[6] In addition, the works of Guérin and Nadeau (1998), Jean-François Godbout and Éric

Bélanger (2002), and Fred Cutler (2002), lead to similar assessments. Economic voting may have been absent, or weaker, in Quebec compared to the ROC because of the importance of the constitutional issue.

1993-2006: The Great 1993 Divide

The 1993 federal election profoundly transformed the party system in Canada. The system known as "two-party-plus" ceded its place, if only for a limited time, to an environment where five parties began to compete. Differences between francophone Quebecers, non-francophone Quebecers, and francophones outside Quebec were reaffirmed. However, the divergence of electoral choices in Quebec and in the ROC was now more striking. Canadians were about to elect four successive Liberal governments, while francophone Quebecers set their hearts on the Bloc Québécois.

The distinction between Quebecers and other Canadians is reflected in the investigations of CES data conducted over this period. Although it was common during the Trudeau and Mulroney years to analyze the voting behaviour of the Canadian population as a whole, or to consider Quebec as a region among others, this practice is now the exception. Most analyses today on Canadian voting behaviour rest on the premise that Quebec and the ROC form different political markets, which need to be analyzed separately (for example, Blais et al. 1995; Gidengil et al. 1999, 2006).

An Image Taking Shape

The rise of anti-party sentiments and political distrust in Western Canada at the start of the 1990s partly explains the breakthrough of the Reform party in 1993 (Bélanger 2004a; Bélanger and Nadeau 2005). Works based on the 1997 election not only confirm this trend but also show that in Quebec there was a mobilization effect created by the emergence of the Bloc Québécois (Gidengil et al. 2001, 2002). The evidence indicates that in the 2000 election, Quebecers continued to display less interest in federal politics than other Canadians (Gidengil et al. 2004). Our own analysis of the 2006 election study confirms and nuances this picture. Quebec voters still appear to be slightly less informed and less interested in federal politics than voters in the ROC, but their opinions toward parties, politicians, and the capacity of the political system to respond to the needs of citizens are now more in line with those in the ROC.

André Blais and his colleagues (2002a; Nevitte et al. 2000) provide a more contemporary comparison of Quebec and the ROC, looking at several dimensions that tap people's outlooks toward moral conservatism, feminism, law and order, state interventionism, the importance of religion, racial minorities, and Quebec sovereignty, and they suggest that with the exception of the latter there are no strong differences on such matters between Quebecers and other Canadians. Some qualifications to this statement are necessary, however. An analysis of the 2000 election study shows that, compared to other Canadians, Quebec citizens are less conservative, more favourable to feminism, more open to racial minorities, more detached from religion, more favourable to a "soft" approach on crime, and, perhaps surprisingly, less favourable to state intervention in general and better disposed toward private sector involvement in the health care domain (Blais et al. 2002a).

Results from our own analysis of the 2004 and 2006 CES, using a slightly different categorization of orientations, are largely similar.[7] Quebecers' moral and religious conservatism appears less pronounced than that of other Canadians, in that Quebecers are more favourable to abortion (73 percent compared to 55 percent in the ROC) and same-sex marriage (64 percent compared to 53 percent in the ROC), and nearly two out of three say that they give less importance to religion in their life (64 percent). Just like they have in the past, Quebecers continue to be more opposed to capital punishment (55 percent compared to 46 percent in the ROC) and to the use of repressive measures on young offenders (44 percent compared to 53 percent in the ROC). Quebecers are also more favourable to limiting the use of firearms to just policemen and the military (69 percent compared to 54 percent in the ROC) and more opposed to the elimination of the gun registry (51 percent compared to 32 percent in the ROC).

Other results confirm that a larger proportion of Quebecers than other Canadians say they wish to do more for racial minorities (61 percent compared to 47 percent in the ROC). Also, analyses of responses to questions tapping the respective roles that governments and private businesses should have in society are a bit more ambiguous but still consistent with the findings from 2000 (see Blais et al. 2002a). And beyond these distinctions, there are few differences between Quebecers and other Canadians in their perceptions of unions and businesses as well as on the issue of taking personal responsibility, particularly when it comes to one's own economic problems. However, Quebecers do appear to be more inclined than people in the ROC to entrust the private sector with the entire responsibility of creating jobs (45 percent compared to 32 percent in the ROC), which is again a surprising finding, particularly in a province where it has traditionally been argued that the preferred model of economic development is one where the state should play a significant role.

Views toward Canada's foreign policy have been much less explored in the past, but two questions from more recent CES point to significant differences between Quebec and the ROC on this subject. The first deals with military spending. Quebecers are much less likely than other Canadians to wish for more defence spending (19 percent compared to 51 percent in the ROC), a result that suggests that Canadians outside Quebec may hold very different visions of Canada's role on the international scene. A second difference deals with feelings toward the United States. Ever since the involvement of the United States in Iraq in 2003, Quebecers appear less favourable toward their southern neighbours than other Canadians (average scores of 51 for Quebec and 61 for the ROC on a feeling-thermometer scale ranging from 0 to 100, where 100 means being favourable).

Recall that levels of attachment toward Quebec and Canada among francophone Quebecers were similar in 1974 (scores of 72 on two thermometer scales ranging from 0 to 100). A little less than twenty years later, in the aftermath of the Meech Lake Accord debacle and at the time of the debate on the Charlottetown Accord, an important gap appeared between their levels of attachment to Quebec (increasing to 79) and to Canada (falling to 61). A mere fifteen years later, things changed again. This time, attachment to Quebec remained at the same level (at 79), but appreciation of Canada is clearly on the rise (now at 74). This evolution suggests that the massive victories of the Bloc Québécois in the 1993 and 2004 federal elections may best be explained by a generally negative feeling toward the Canadian political community following the failure of the Meech Lake Accord in the first case and by frustration toward the Liberal Party of Canada (but not Canada itself) following the sponsorship scandal in the second case.[8] These findings notwithstanding, data from the CES do indicate that Quebecers continue to attach more importance to their provincial government than other Canadians do. They are more prone to believe that the provincial government is the most important political entity in their life (66 percent compared to 52 percent in the ROC), and they are clearly more inclined to prefer a strong provincial government to a strong federal one (the proportions are, respectively, 73 percent and 19 percent in Quebec, against 42 percent and 45 percent in the ROC).

Different Political Markets, Different Behaviours
Investigations of the CES during the 1993 to 2006 period show a number of significant differences in voting motivations in Quebec and the ROC. The first relates to socio-demographics. Age and language prove to be the most

salient social divisions in Quebec, but cleavages related to religion, region, birth place (born in Canada or outside), gender, place of residence (rural or urban), and social class all exert a significant influence in the ROC (see Nevitte et al. 2000; O'Neill 2001; Erickson and O'Neill 2002; Blais et al. 2002a; Brym et al. 2004).

A second difference deals with party images, feelings of attachment toward them, and the effect of party identification on vote choice. Outside of Quebec, the image of federal parties seems better defined, partisan attachments appear deeper, and the impact of party identification on voting more pronounced (see Nadeau et al. 2001; Blais et al. 2002a). A third difference lies in the relative impact of various local factors (candidates or regional economic conditions) and other short-term factors (the evolution of the economic situation, for example), both of which seem more important in the ROC than in Quebec (see Cutler 2002; Godbout and Bélanger 2002; Blais et al. 2002b, 2003).

A fourth difference, which actually helps explain the first three, is the weight that the sovereignty issue has in structuring partisan and electoral choices in Quebec. Many studies demonstrate that this issue both fosters electoral cleavages (age and language are the main socio-economic determinants of support for sovereignty) and weakens the effects of other short-term determinants (such as the economic situation) and of long-term forces (such as party identification or ideological orientation) (see Nevitte et al. 2000; Blais et al. 2002a). For example, Bélanger (2004b) shows that during the 1993 election anti-party sentiments helped to explain the Reform party's success in the West, whereas sovereignty support was the main determinant of the Bloc Québécois's upsurge. Scotto, Laura Stephenson, and Kornberg (2004) conclude that the most important political issues in Quebec and the ROC in the 1997 election were sovereignty in the former and social issues in the latter. Blais and his colleagues (2002a) offer a similar account in the context of the 2000 election by showing that ideological positionings on moral conservatism and state intervention have exerted much less influence in Quebec than in the ROC.

Conclusion: 2006 and Beyond
Our assessment of over four decades of research on the Quebec/ROC cleavage, based on the CES, points to four main conclusions. The first is that the differences in outlooks between these two communities continue to exist today but that they are not the same differences that used to exist in the past.

For instance, the Quebec that voted for Pierre Trudeau and Réal Caouette in 1968 was different from the ROC because of its socio-economic lag, its religious past, and its traditional association with the party of the French Canadians, namely the Liberal Party of Canada. The Quebec which casts more than 45 percent of its votes in favour of the Bloc Québécois (on average between 1993 and 2006), sets itself apart from the ROC with its slightly more progressive outlooks, its developing appreciation for the private sector, and its project of making Quebec an independent state.

The second conclusion has to do with the resilience of the sovereignty issue. Under various circumstances, this factor has proven to be an important determinant of voting behaviour in Quebec. During the Mulroney and Bloc Québécois years, in particular, there were several distinctive determinants of vote choice, such as socio-economic cleavages, party identification, values, and issues. However, the sovereignty issue, due to ongoing debates about the renewal of federalism and Quebec nationalism, continued to occupy centre stage.

The third conclusion, which is perhaps a bit overshadowed by the framing of the present chapter around the notion of differences, is that over time Quebec and the ROC have also grown closer on several points. For example, both societies over the last decades have undergone similar shifts toward secularism, moral liberalism, and more openness toward feminism and minorities. In fact, most of the remaining differences between Quebec and Canada (apart from the sovereignty issue) are now more a matter of degree.

The fourth and final conclusion deals with the significance of the 2006, 2008, and 2011 election outcomes for the future of Quebec-ROC relations. The constant decline of the Bloc Québécois, the collapse of the Liberal vote, and the breakthroughs of Stephen Harper's Conservative party and, especially, Jack Layton's NDP during these elections perhaps foreshadow a new electoral period in Quebec. After having supported the Liberal party for several years, Quebecers turned to the PC party over the course of a transition period that lasted for two elections (1984 and 1988). It may be possible that they are about to do the same with the Bloc Québécois, after nearly two decades of domination by this party. If this is the case, we may be about to witness an important fragmentation of the vote in Quebec and a relative decline of sovereignty as a factor structuring electoral choices in this province. As they did in the past, future CES will undoubtedly be able to help us shed important light on these ongoing developments.

NOTES

1 With hindsight, it is possible today to express some reservations regarding John Meisel's (1975) opinion categories (for instance, the decision to distinguish authoritarianism from law and order) as well as his choice of indicators to measure certain dimensions of political behaviour (such as the joint use of attitudes toward the death penalty in both his moral liberalism and authoritarianism scales). One also notices the absence of other dimensions, such as the support and opposition for state intervention or *laissez-faire* economic policies. Still, the value of Meisel's study for understanding the differences between Quebec and the rest of Canada (ROC) during the Pierre Trudeau era remains truly exceptional.

2 It was common during this time to analyze the behaviour of all francophone Canadians – Quebecers and those outside Quebec – together because of their common support for the Liberal party. It was also common to invoke the socioeconomic deficit of Quebecers to explain their lower level of interest in politics. The fact that these types of analyses are absent from the study of contemporary voting behaviour is also an indication of the extent to which the Quebec/ROC cleavage has evolved.

3 The label "Solid Quebec," which is sometimes used by Canadian political scientists, took its origins in the expression "Solid South," which was used in the United States to refer to the massive dominance of the Democratic party in the American South from the post–Civil War period through the mid-1960s (see Bakvis and Macpherson (1995) for a discussion of this parallel).

4 Interestingly, significant proportions of respondents in both regions were also uncertain about this question.

5 *Official Languages Act*, RSC 1985, c 31 (4th Supp).

6 See the two preceding chapters in this volume for more details on the gender gap.

7 All results in this section, with three exceptions, come from the 2006 election study. Findings relating to young offenders, racial minorities, and the relative importance of the federal and provincial governments are based on the 2004 election study.

8 The "sponsorship scandal" refers to allegations of government misconduct on a program put into place after the 1995 Quebec Referendum, aimed at promoting the visibility of Canada and of the federal government in Quebec. The Gomery Commission, appointed to investigate these allegations, eventually documented cases of fraud involving publicity agencies and members of the Liberal Party of Canada.

REFERENCES

Bakvis, Herman, and Laura G. Macpherson. 1995. "Quebec Block Voting and the Canadian Electoral System." *Canadian Journal of Political Science* 28: 659-92.

Bashevkin, Sylvia. 1990. "Solitudes in Collision? Pan-Canadian and Quebec Nationalist Attitudes in the Late 1970s." *Comparative Political Studies* 23: 3-24.

Bélanger, Éric. 2004a. "Antipartyism and Third-Party Vote Choice: A Comparison of Canada, Britain, and Australia." *Comparative Political Studies* 37: 1054-78.

–. 2004b. "The Rise of Third Parties in the 1993 Canadian Federal Election: Pinard Revisited." *Canadian Journal of Political Science* 37: 581-94.

Bélanger, Éric, and Richard Nadeau. 2005. "Political Trust and the Vote in Multiparty Elections: The Canadian Case." *European Journal of Political Research* 44: 121-46.

Blais, André, Elisabeth Gidengil, Agnieszka Dobrzynska, Richard Nadeau, and Neil Nevitte. 2003. "Does the Local Candidate Matter?" *Canadian Journal of Political Science* 36: 657-64.

Blais, André, Elisabeth Gidengil, Richard Nadeau, and Neil Nevitte. 2002a. *Anatomy of a Liberal Victory. Making Sense of the Vote in the 2000 Canadian Election.* Peterborough, ON: Broadview Press.

Blais, André, Richard Nadeau, Elisabeth Gidengil, and Neil Nevitte. 2002b. "The Impact of Issues and the Economy in the 1997 Canadian Federal Election." *Canadian Journal of Political Science* 35: 409-21.

Blais, André, Neil Nevitte, Elisabeth Gidengil, Henry Brady, and Richard Johnston. 1995. "L'élection de 1993: le comportement électoral des Québécois." *Revue québécoise de science politique* 27: 15-50.

Brym, Robert J., John W.P. Veugelers, Jonah Butovsky, and John Simpson. 2004. "Postmaterialism in Unresponsive Political Systems: The Canadian Case." *Canadian Review of Sociology and Anthropology* 41: 291-317.

Clarke, Harold D., Jane Jenson, Lawrence LeDuc, and Jon H. Pammett. 1979. *Political Choice in Canada.* Toronto: McGraw-Hill Ryerson.

–. 1984. *Absent Mandate: The Politics of Discontent in Canada.* Toronto: Gage.

–. 1991. *Absent Mandate: Interpreting Change in Canadian Elections.* Toronto: Gage.

–. 1996. *Absent Mandate: Canadian Electoral Politics in an Era of Restructuring.* Toronto: Gage.

Clarke, Harold D., and Allan Kornberg. 1993. "Evaluations and Evolution: Public Attitudes toward Canada's Federal Political Parties, 1965-1991." *Canadian Journal of Political Science* 26: 287-311.

Curtis, James E., and Ronald D. Lambert. 1976. "Voting, Election Interest, and Age: National Findings for English and French Canadians." *Canadian Journal of Political Science* 9: 293-307.

Cutler, Fred. 2002. "Local Economies, Local Policy Impacts and Federal Electoral Behaviour in Canada." *Canadian Journal of Political Science* 35: 347-82.

Erickson, Lynda, and Brenda O'Neill. 2002. "The Gender Gap and the Changing Women Voter in Canada." *International Political Science Review* 23: 373-92.

Gidengil, Elisabeth, André Blais, Joanna Everitt, Patrick Fournier, and Neil Nevitte. 2006. "Back to the Future? Making Sense of the 2004 Canadian Election outside of Quebec." *Canadian Journal of Political Science* 39: 1-25.

Gidengil, Elisabeth, André Blais, Richard Nadeau, and Neil Nevitte. 1999. "Making Sense of Regional Voting in the 1997 Canadian Federal Election: Liberal and Reform Support outside Quebec." *Canadian Journal of Political Science* 32: 247-72.

–. 2002. "Change in the Party System and Anti-Party Sentiment." In William Cross, ed., *Political Parties, Representation, and Electoral Democracy in Canada*, 68-86. Don Mills, ON: Oxford University Press.

Gidengil, Elisabeth, André Blais, Neil Nevitte, and Richard Nadeau. 2001. "The Correlates and Consequences of Anti-Partyism in the 1997 Canadian Election." *Party Politics* 7: 491-513.

–. 2004. *Citizens.* Vancouver: UBC Press.

Godbout, Jean-François, and Éric Bélanger. 2002. "La dimension régionale du vote économique canadien aux élections fédérales de 1988 à 2000." *Canadian Journal of Political Science* 35: 567-88.

Guérin, Daniel, and Richard Nadeau. 1998. "Clivage linguistique et vote économique au Canada." *Canadian Journal of Political Science* 31: 557-72.

Johnston, Richard, André Blais, Elisabeth Gidengil, and Neil Nevitte. 1996. *The Challenge of Direct Democracy: The 1992 Canadian Referendum.* Montreal: McGill-Queen's University Press.

Johnston, Richard, Henry E. Brady, André Blais, and Jean Crête. 1992. *Letting the People Decide: Dynamics of a Canadian Election.* Montreal: McGill-Queen's University Press.

Lambert, Ronald D., James E. Curtis, Steven D. Brown, and Barry J. Kay. 1986. "Canadians' Beliefs about Differences between Social Classes." *Canadian Journal of Sociology* 11: 379-99.

–. 1987. "Social Class, Left/Right Political Orientations, and Subjective Class Voting in Provincial and Federal Elections." *Canadian Review of Sociology and Anthropology* 24: 526-49.

Lambert, Ronald D., James E. Curtis, Barry J. Kay, and Steven D. Brown. 1988. "The Social Sources of Political Knowledge." *Canadian Journal of Political Science* 21: 359-74.

Meisel, John. 1975. *Working Papers on Canadian Politics.* Montreal: McGill-Queen's University Press.

Nadeau, Richard, André Blais, Elisabeth Gidengil, and Neil Nevitte. 2001. "Perceptions of Party Competence in the 1997 Election." In Hugh Thorburn and Alan Whitehorn, eds., *Party Politics in Canada,* 8th edition, 413-30. Toronto: Prentice Hall.

Nevitte, Neil, André Blais, Elisabeth Gidengil, and Richard Nadeau. 2000. *Unsteady State: The 1997 Canadian Federal Election.* Don Mills, ON: Oxford University Press.

O'Neill, Brenda. 2001. "A Simple Difference of Opinion? Religious Beliefs and Gender Gap in Public Opinion in Canada." *Canadian Journal of Political Science* 34: 275-98.

Schwartz, Mildred A. 1974. "Canadian Voting Behaviour." In Richard Rose, ed., *Comparative Electoral Behavior,* 543-617. New York: Free Press.

Scotto, Thomas J., Laura B. Stephenson, and Allan Kornberg. 2004. "From a Two-Party-Plus to a One-Party-Plus? Ideology, Vote Choice, and Prospects for a Competitive Party System in Canada." *Electoral Studies* 23: 463-83.

Simeon, Richard, and David J. Elkins. 1974. "Regional Political Cultures in Canada." *Canadian Journal of Political Science* 7: 397-437.

Sniderman, Paul M., H.D. Forbes, and Ian Melzer. 1974. "Party Loyalty and Electoral
Volatility: A Study of the Canadian Party System." *Canadian Journal of Political
Science* 2: 268-88.
van Loon, Richard. 1970. "Political Participation in Canada: The 1965 Election."
Canadian Journal of Political Science 3: 376-99.

The Structural Bases of Canadian Party Preference
Evolution and Cross-National Comparison

RICHARD JOHNSTON

The Canadian party system is peculiar, and its peculiarity is subject to debate. A widely circulated image is of a system in "stable dealignment" (LeDuc 1984). As discussed and emphasized further by Harold Clarke and Allan Kornberg in the next chapter in this volume, the roots of the system are commonly thought to be shallow,[1] and so are many Canadians' ties to parties (see also Clarke et al. 1996). The weak social base reflects, in turn, the policy similarity of the major parties, a claim supported at least during earlier years by Ian Budge and his colleagues (2001). The system, therefore, is prone to shocking electoral swings. These stylized facts were characterized years ago as the "textbook theory" (Sniderman, Forbes, and Melzer 1974). But the stylization sits uneasily with other, apparently contradictory facts. The system has been routinely dominated by one party, the Liberals, and this fact would seem to suggest deep roots (Blais 2005). Data from party conventions and candidate surveys indicate sharp policy differences (Cross and Young 2002). Voters are similarly able to detect that the policy stakes in Canadian elections are high (Bélanger 2003), and claims about weak ties between individuals and parties may rest on a measurement artifact (Johnston 1992).

This chapter argues that these seemingly contradictory claims can be reconciled. Doing so requires that we respond to Mildred Schwartz's plea for a return to political sociology (outlined in her chapter in this volume).

When the data from the Canadian Election Studies (CES) are properly arranged, they show that the width of cleavages in Canadian party preference is typical for the consolidated party systems of Anglo-American democracies. However, it also reveals what is truly untypical: the domination of Canada's cleavage structure by cultural forces.[2] Equally critical is the fact that the direction of the key cultural gaps reverses at the boundary between Quebec and the rest of Canada (ROC).[3] This division produces, or accommodates, the greatest peculiarity of all – the domination of the Canadian system by a party of the centre. From this domination flow the historically weak policy differences between the major parties and the alternation between long-lived Liberal governments, on the one hand, and violent electoral swings, on the other.

The Canadian System in Comparative Context

The obvious comparators to the Canadian polity are the consolidated systems produced by single-member plurality or majority institutions. Table 9.1 compares Canada with the United States, Great Britain, and Australia, for which roughly comparable survey data span at least four decades. Each country appears twice, with data from an early study (typically from the 1970s) and from a post-2000 one. The comparison captures four elements in the underlying structural basis of each system: the width of the largest economic cleavage; the width of the largest cultural cleavage; the width of the largest geographic contrast; and an indicator of the overall power of social structure in accounting for party preference. For each contrast, the table gives the "shift," which is the difference in the likelihood of supporting a party made by an individual's membership in a social category, as opposed to non-membership. Also indicated is the category in question and the party most affected by it. For example, for Canada in 1974, the widest economic difference reflected union membership – a union member was 0.102 (or 10.2 percentage points) more likely than a non-union person to support the New Democratic party (NDP). In the same year, a Roman Catholic was 0.184 (18.4 percentage points) less likely than a non-Catholic to support the Progressive Conservative (PC) party. All of these values derive from a multivariate probit estimation and indicate the difference made for a survey respondent who is otherwise typical of the survey sample as a whole. The overall predictive power of the social structure is given by $\hat{R}^2$, the "pseudo R^2" for the underlying probit regression.[4] Most estimations feature a standard suite of indicators for "industrial revolution" cleavages: farm status;

union membership; manual employment; and income. Some "national revolution" contrasts are also common to most countries: Catholic/non-Catholic and no religion/any religion contrasts.[5] For Canada, language – "official" and "other" – is also a factor, and, in the United States, race and (in 2004) Hispanic ethnicity are factors.[6] Geography is represented by dummy variables for large historically distinct regions: Atlantic Canada, Quebec, and the West; the US South; Scotland, Wales, and Northern England; and Victoria and Western Australia. All of these factors are relatively fixed in themselves and, for extended periods, in their effects. Each refers to a group or place that parties and candidates can target and thus can be a potential building block for electoral coalitions.[7]

In country after country, the most consequential non-geographic cleavage typically represents a conditional difference of fifteen to twenty percentage points in the likelihood of some party's support. This observation is as true of the class-polarized British and Australian systems as it is of the supposedly brokerage-dominated US and Canadian ones.[8] It is true that the Canadian system is less structured by economic factors than the others, since, for the other countries, the dominant factor is usually either manual employment, union membership, or income. It is not true, however, that the Canadian system is peculiarly based on geography. Geography plays a bigger role in Canada than in Australia or the United States, to be sure, but not a bigger role than in Great Britain. Note too that the power of social structure to predict variance in outcomes varies remarkably little from country to country. On average, about 10 percent of the variance is explained. Canada exhibits the weakest explanatory power in 1974, but only by a small margin. In 2004, the Canadian system seems more impressively structured, particularly in comparison to Great Britain and Australia.[9]

Continuity, Change, and Geographic Contingency
The true Canadian peculiarity is threefold: (1) the system is dominated by cultural factors; (2) the key cultural factors interact with residence in or out of Quebec; and (3) this combination yields a system uniquely dominated by a party of the centre. This section explains the first and second elements in detail. The third element will animate the concluding discussion. The first estimation strategy involves pairwise comparison between parties, effected by multinomial probit. Paired comparison allows the system's multi-dimensionality to emerge. Some of this characteristic can appear simply through a rich set of independent variables, but the pairwise strategy

TABLE 9.1

The Canadian system in comparative context

Country/Year	Class			Culture[b]			Geography			R^2
	Shift	Factor	Party	Shift	Factor	Party	Shift	Factor	Party	
Canada										
1974	0.102	Union	NDP	−0.184	Catholic	Conservative	−0.173	West	Liberal	0.093
2004	0.119	Union	NDP	−0.153	No religion	Conservative	−0.191	West	Liberal	0.118
Great Britain										
1974	0.312	Manual	Labour	0.192	No religion	Labour	−0.256	Wales	Conservative	0.134
2005	0.109	Manual	Labour	−0.083	No religion	Conservative	−0.190	Scotland	Conservative	0.053
United States[a]										
1972	−0.151	Income	Republican	−0.086	Catholic	Republican	0.135	US South	Republican	0.108
2004	−0.242	Income	Republican	0.222	Evangelical Protestant	Republican	0.047	US South	Republican	0.129
Australia										
1967	0.228	Union	Labor	0.136	Catholic	ALP	0.082	Western Australia	Liberal	0.126
2004	0.205	Union	Labor	0.033	Catholic	ALP	0.032	Western Australia	Liberal	0.039

Notes: Estimation by probit regression; cell entries are absolute values of the largest marginal effect in the indicated category. All data are drawn from the election studies for each indicated country during specific years. Exceptions are for the United States in 1972 and Great Britain in 1974, where the data are drawn from *Political Action*, eight-country study, http://dx.doi.org/10.3886/ICPSR07777.v1.

a Presidential elections.

b Categoric group must represent at least 15 percent of the sample.

shows how different dimensions govern the contrasts between different party pairs (Whitten and Palmer 1996).[10]

Given the claim of geographic contingency, discussed in the preceding chapter by Richard Nadeau and Éric Bélanger, analyses are performed separately for Quebec and the ROC. Within each place, analyses are initially divided by period according to the menu of the parties. Outside Quebec, this division dictates three periods: 1965 to 1988, when the menu featured the Liberals, the PCs, and the NDP; 1993 to 2000, the years of deconsolidation when the Reform and Canadian Alliance parties were added to the mix; and 2004 to 2006, the reconsolidated system with the Canadian Alliance and PCs now united as the Conservative party. In Quebec, the number of periods is effectively two: 1965 to 1988, when the three national parties shared the field with Social Credit; and 1993 to 2006, years of three-party competition, as Social Credit officially disappeared, the NDP effectively did so as well, and the Bloc Québécois entered the arena. Although the Conservatives changed their official organization between 2000 and 2004, there is little evidence that this changed the party's actual or potential appeal in Quebec. The critical fact about Quebec seems to be the continuity of the Bloc Québécois for all the years since 1993.[11]

Canada outside Quebec

In the 1965-88 period, the following were the basic polarities (as shown in Table 9.2).

- The dominant forces were cultural and mostly pitted the Liberals against the Progressive Conservatives (PCs). The Catholic/non-Catholic contrast was the most consequential, both in that it yielded a big marginal effect and in that Catholics are a big minority. Even with religion controlled, ethno-linguistic contrasts were also sharp and all tended in the same direction – French Canadians, Eastern Europeans, southern Europeans, and non-Europeans were significantly more likely than northern Europeans and the British/Canadian-only/don't know reference category to be Liberals as opposed to PCs.
- The NDP was always the middle party, usually closer to the Liberals. The one cultural axis on which the NDP controlled a pole was religiosity. These findings lend further support to those presented by Barry Kay and Andrea Perrella in this volume. Respondents of no religion were more likely than all others to support the NDP and less likely than all others to support the PCs. In this case, the Liberals were very close to the PCs.

TABLE 9.2

Structural foundations outside Quebec, 1965-88

	Conservative vs Liberal		NDP vs Liberal		NDP vs Conservative	
Union	−0.001	(0.047)	0.521	(0.052)	0.510	(0.051)
Farm	0.295	(0.075)	0.009	(0.091)	−0.285	(0.087)
French	−0.283	(0.084)	−0.090	(0.096)	0.193	(0.099)
Northern European	−0.035	(0.060)	0.025	(0.068)	0.060	(0.066)
Eastern European	−0.313	(0.071)	−0.125	(0.078)	0.187	(0.078)
Southern European	−0.796	(0.141)	−0.386	(0.145)	0.410	(0.160)
Non-European	−0.573	(0.126)	−0.225	(0.137)	0.348	(0.142)
Catholic	−0.623	(0.052)	−0.299	(0.060)	0.324	(0.061)
No religion	0.026	(0.086)	0.612	(0.089)	0.585	(0.083)
West	0.427	(0.048)	0.515	(0.054)	0.088	(0.052)
Atlantic	0.056	(0.057)	−0.490	(0.074)	−0.546	(0.074)
Intercept	0.208	(0.040)	−0.752	(0.047)	−0.960	(0.046)
χ^2	849.052					
N	8,241					

Source: 1965-88 Canadian Election Studies.
Notes: Estimation by multinomial probit. Entries in parentheses are asymptotic standard errors.

- In the economic domain, the PC party has traditionally anchored a pole. The identity of the other polar party has not been consistent, however. Union families were much more likely than others to support the NDP and much less likely than others to support the PCs. But the Liberals exerted no more attraction for union families (*qua* union families) than the PCs did. The PCs were the party of farm families. Although the farm/non-farm difference was not as great as the union/non-union divide, the PC party was alone at the pro-farm pole. During these years, the Liberals and the NDP were essentially indistinguishable on the farm/non-farm axis.
- The NDP was distinctively a party of the West and not a party of Atlantic Canada. The PCs were relatively strong in both regions. The Liberals were weak in the West, matched the PCs in Atlantic Canada, and, by implication, were (even then) the party of Ontario.

TABLE 9.3
Structural foundations outside Quebec, 1993-2000

	Conservative vs Liberal	NDP vs Liberal	NDP vs Conservative	Reform vs Liberal	Reform vs Conservative	Reform vs NDP
Union	-0.184 (0.085)	0.404 (0.088)	0.587 (0.098)	-0.201 (0.078)	-0.017 (0.090)	-0.605 (0.092)
Farm	0.151 (0.201)	-0.121 (0.243)	-0.272 (0.255)	0.396 (0.175)	0.245 (0.194)	0.517 (0.237)
French	-0.249 (0.160)	0.068 (0.162)	0.317 (0.187)	-0.297 (0.155)	-0.048 (0.182)	-0.365 (0.182)
Northern European	0.109 (0.123)	-0.049 (0.138)	-0.157 (0.149)	0.475 (0.105)	0.367 (0.120)	0.524 (0.135)
Eastern European	-0.044 (0.144)	0.243 (0.145)	0.287 (0.164)	0.205 (0.122)	0.249 (0.145)	-0.038 (0.146)
Southern European	-0.118 (0.241)	-0.092 (0.270)	0.026 (0.305)	-0.074 (0.218)	0.044 (0.262)	0.018 (0.287)
Non-European	-0.341 (0.157)	-0.406 (0.172)	-0.065 (0.193)	-0.824 (0.156)	-0.482 (0.180)	-0.417 (0.192)
Catholic	-0.468 (0.101)	-0.424 (0.111)	0.045 (0.123)	-0.508 (0.094)	-0.040 (0.110)	-0.084 (0.118)
No religion	-0.148 (0.114)	0.135 (0.116)	0.283 (0.130)	-0.079 (0.101)	0.069 (0.116)	-0.214 (0.118)
West	0.259 (0.091)	0.718 (0.101)	0.459 (0.112)	0.816 (0.082)	0.558 (0.095)	0.098 (0.105)
Atlantic	0.444 (0.120)	0.598 (0.135)	0.154 (0.145)	-0.494 (0.140)	-0.939 (0.149)	-1.093 (0.161)
Intercept	-0.659 (0.087)	-1.451 (0.103)	-0.792 (0.112)	-0.487 (0.081)	0.172 (0.093)	0.964 (0.108)
χ^2	461.667					
N	2,868					

Source: 1993-2000 Canadian Election Studies.
Notes: Estimation by multinomial probit. Entries in parentheses are asymptotic standard errors.

- A final point worth noting about Table 9.2 relates to the intercepts – the value on the PC versus Liberal contrast is positive, a reminder that outside Quebec the PC party was consistently stronger in this period than the Liberal party. This finding reinforces the discussion presented in the preceding chapter.

The deconsolidation of 1993 changed few of the underlying structural features of the old system, and such changes as occurred foreshadowed the system put in place in 2004. Table 9.3 shows that the most interesting elements refer to the new Reform party (which later became the Canadian Alliance):

- On the Catholic/non-Catholic axis, Reform/Canadian Alliance was the most polarized against the Liberals, more so than against the PC remnant.
- The Reform/Canadian Alliance party was most favoured by the oldest "immigrant" group, northern Europeans. This is the only time this group emerges as distinct, and Reform seemed to peel northern Europeans away from every other party. Reform was least favoured by the newest "immigrant" group, non-Europeans. The Reform/Liberal gap for this group was almost 1.5 times as wide as the PC/Liberal gap was in the earlier period.
- Reform was distinctively a party of farm families, however much their numbers had dwindled. The Reform/NDP gap was almost twice as great as the PC/NDP gap had been. The distance from Reform/Canadian Alliance to the Liberals was one-third greater than the old one from the PCs to the Liberals.
- Reform was, of course, distinctively a party of the West.

As shown in Table 9.4, the following are the structural changes that accompanied the resurrection of the united Conservative alternative in 2004:

- Although the Catholic/non-Catholic contrast persists, it is not as powerful as it once was. Its effect appears to have been cut roughly in half. The same is also true of an ethnic distinction that strongly overlaps the religious one – southern Europeans remain disproportionately Liberal but only about half as distinctive as before. Eastern Europeans, formerly aligned with the Liberals, are no longer a politically distinct group. French Canadians and non-Europeans outside of Quebec, in contrast,

TABLE 9.4

Structural foundations outside Quebec, 2004-06

	Conservative vs Liberal		NDP vs Liberal		NDP vs Conservative	
Union	−0.185	(0.083)	0.403	(0.088)	0.588	(0.086)
French	−0.396	(0.151)	−0.282	(0.164)	0.113	(0.167)
Northern European	−0.154	(0.125)	−0.083	(0.138)	0.071	(0.130)
Eastern European	−0.018	(0.158)	−0.100	(0.177)	−0.082	(0.166)
Southern European	−0.487	(0.194)	−0.290	(0.211)	0.197	(0.215)
Non-European	−0.926	(0.137)	−0.341	(0.140)	0.585	(0.147)
Catholic	−0.302	(0.099)	−0.128	(0.110)	0.174	(0.108)
No religion	−0.434	(0.103)	0.436	(0.106)	0.870	(0.104)
West	0.738	(0.086)	0.604	(0.094)	−0.134	(0.091)
Atlantic	−0.371	(0.124)	−0.059	(0.134)	0.312	(0.139)
Intercept	0.333	(0.079)	−0.685	(0.090)	−1.019	(0.088)
χ^2	310.671					
N	2,459					

Source: 2004-06 Canadian Election Studies.
Notes: Estimation by multinomial probit. Entries in parentheses are asymptotic standard errors.

are more distinctly tied to the Liberals than before. Non-Europeans, of course, are much more numerous than in the earlier period. For the most part, then, the Liberals assemble much the same coalition as before, but the ethnic components of this coalition have gained prominence relative to the central religious one.

- Religiosity, as such, has also gained prominence, and the NDP/Conservative contrast is bigger than ever. However, the Liberals have moved – where before they were indistinguishable from the Conservatives, now the party has moved almost exactly half the distance toward the NDP.
- In the economic domain, the NDP remains as polarized against the Conservatives as before, although not as much as they were against the Reform and Canadian Alliance parties. The Liberals appear to have moved away from the Conservatives, in the sense that union families are now significantly more likely than non-union ones to choose the Liberals over the Conservatives, but the Liberal/NDP gap is still twice as great as

the Liberal/Conservative one. Farmers have disappeared from view. They do not appear in Table 9.4 and are no longer routinely identifiable in the CES. The next section shows that they have also ceased to be politically distinct.

- The geographic deck has been shuffled dramatically. The West is more distinct than before in relation to all of the parties. The Liberals are even more shut out than in the earlier period. The new Conservatives, reflecting the Reform/Canadian Alliance transition, are both more distinctly Western themselves and more Western than the NDP. The NDP, considerably rejuvenated in the West relative to the 1990s, is now also a party of Atlantic Canada.

To sum up, although the 1993-2000 deconsolidation disrupted some of the older system's features, the rebirth of a nationally competitive Conservative alternative resurrected most of them. Continuity is more impressive than discontinuity. The biggest qualitative change was in geography. Otherwise, changes to the old structure were at the margin, as certain features gained strength and others lost it.

The very richness of the pairwise display in Tables 9.2 to 9.4 carries a price in complexity. At the same time, pooling of elections into two or three periods masks possible shifts within periods. The discussion thus elided much temporal detail, so Figures 9.1 to 9.4 bring that detail back. As the figures pull large amounts of information together, they require preliminary explication. To allow for fine-grained temporal analysis, estimation shifts back to the binomial form rather than the form that is used in the model of Tables 9.2-9.4. As already mentioned, this approach averages the effects for a given party across all of the alternative parties. Values in the figures depict marginal effects, defined as for Table 9.1, for all of the key structural elements and for all of the relevant parties. Underlying estimations are multivariate and specific to each year. For the figures, effect coefficients are grouped by variable and arrayed across consecutive years, so that the election-by-election evolution of a cleavage can be presented for the entire period. The lines link estimated values for a given party, and all parties appear on the same graph.

Figure 9.1 presents the system's religious dimensions. The "Catholic" panel confirms the diminished power of the cleavage for the Liberals and suggests that the critical year was 1974.[12] After 1974, the cleavage stabilized. Indeed, it widened in the 1990s, with the emergence of the Reform and the Canadian Alliance parties. In 2004, the cleavage shrank again and was

FIGURE 9.1

Religious cleavages outside Quebec (marginal effects estimated from year-by-year multivariate probit regression, binomial by party)

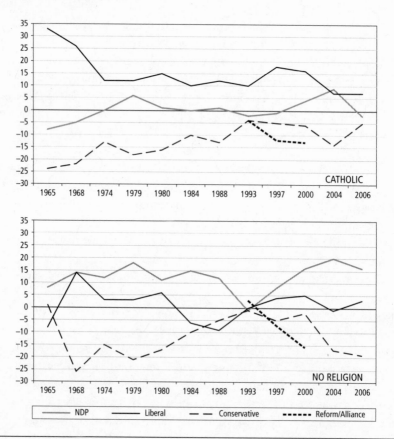

Source: 1965-2006 Canadian Election Studies.

unchanged in 2006.[13] It is tempting to infer that each shift reflects repositioning of the Liberals (and sometimes the Conservatives) on issues with moral content. The mid-1970s drop may reflect the Liberal party's role in the *Criminal Code* amendments on divorce and abortion. The 2004 Liberal shift follows debate on gay marriage, on which the Liberal party changed sides.[14]

The story for voters with no religion is one of short-term flux but long-term resilience. As is already clear, the poles are controlled by the NDP and the Conservatives. The small coefficient for the Liberal-Conservative pairing in Table 9.2 disguises the considerable movement by the Liberals and the small movement by the Conservatives. The Liberals move back and forth, making them sometimes indistinguishable from the NDP and sometimes indistinguishable from the Conservatives. All parties momentarily landed in the same place in 1993. Gaps re-emerged in 1997, with Reform occupying the place once held by the Conservatives. With the union of the Right, the new Conservative party assumed the Reform/Canadian Alliance position.

In the patterns for French Canadians outside Quebec and for post-war immigrant groups, according to Figure 9.2, the influence of Brian Mulroney looms large. Building on the efforts of Robert Stanfield and Joe Clark, Mulroney set out to make his party inclusive on the Liberal model. For French Canadians and southern Europeans, he largely succeeded, and he erased, or came close to erasing, long-standing differences. For non-Europeans, he at least made his party converge on the NDP. No good turn goes unpunished, however, and the gap – especially for non-Europeans – reappeared in the 1990s, with Reform usurping the old PC position. The new Conservatives have inherited the Reform/Canadian Alliance position, and the gap with the Liberals is wider than ever. It is wider partly because of the lack of clarity on the Liberal/NDP side in the early years, and there is reason to suspect that this is partly a sampling issue – in the early years, the number of non-European respondents was very small.[15] Now, the group is an important electoral building block, with the Liberal party being the main beneficiary.

The economic realm in Figure 9.3 is a combination of inanition and stability. Inanition describes the farm/non-farm axis. Parties have shifted ground, but, most importantly, farm families have essentially disappeared from the CES, reflecting the evaporation of the sector as a source of employment. Stability describes the union/non-union axis. Although the Liberal party moves back and forth, it was closer to the Conservative party most of the time and certainly was so in 2006. In the 1990s, the overall weakness of both the Conservatives and the NDP reduced the impact of union membership, although the Reform and Canadian Alliance parties picked up some of the slack. In the 2000s, everything old is new again, and the gaps are as great as ever.

The regional pattern, as we have already seen, shifted dramatically, and no party has been immune. Figure 9.4 organizes the regional data differently from the non-geographic axes in the earlier panels. Here, each panel refers

FIGURE 9.2

Ethno-linguistic cleavages outside Quebec (marginal effects estimated from year-by-year multivariate probit regression, binomial by party)

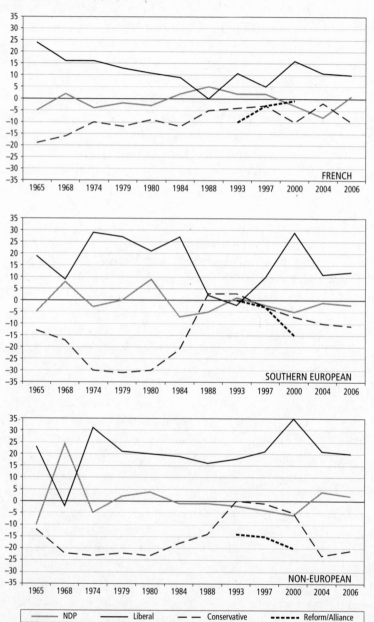

Source: 1965-2006 Canadian Election Studies.

FIGURE 9.3

Economic cleavages outside Quebec (marginal effects estimated from year-by-year multivariate probit regression, binomial by party)

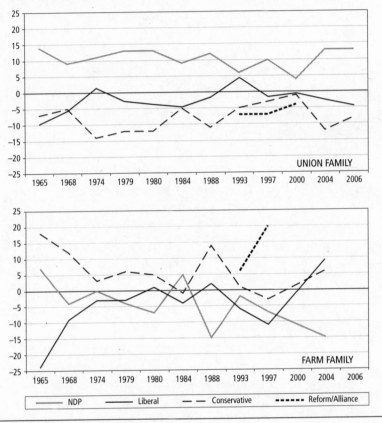

Source: 1965-2006 Canadian Election Studies.

to a single party and arrays marginal effects for both the West and the Atlantic provinces, with Ontario as the reference category. The NDP panel shows how the party moved east – it gathered up a reaction to the budgets of Paul Martin during the mid-1990s and so did particularly well in Atlantic Canada in 1997. In later years, its Atlantic share faded back toward the Ontario baseline. Liberal dynamics are partly complementary. The party dropped in Atlantic Canada as the others rose and then bounced back. This repeated an earlier episode, produced by Robert Stanfield's emergence as Tory leader. In the West, despite occasional plateaus and recoveries, the Liberal trajectory has been basically downward.[16]

FIGURE 9.4

Geographic cleavages outside Quebec (marginal effects estimated from year-by-year multivariate probit regression, binomial by party)

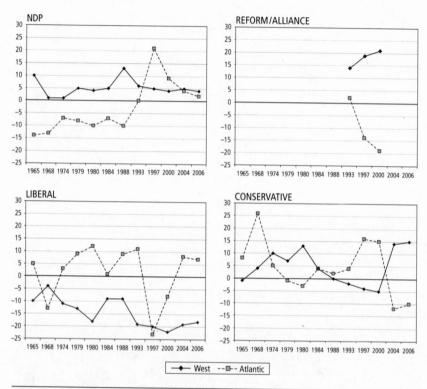

Source: 1965-2006 Canadian Election Studies.

In part, the Liberals' Western decline in the 1990s mirrors the rise of the Reform party. Reform emerged almost fully fledged as a Western vehicle in 1993, and it gained more ground in the region in 1997 and 2000. Strikingly, it became progressively more repellent to Atlantic Canada. This paved the way for the weakness of the new Conservative party in the same region. Although the party lost its advantage of having Stanfield as leader after his retirement, it was never distinctively unwelcome in Atlantic Canada before 2004. In 1997, it benefited from reaction to the Martin budgets, and the leadership transition from Jean Charest to Joe Clark did not hurt. Of course, the West had ceased to be distinctively hospitable, a shift that predated the 1990s, having begun under Brian Mulroney. But the new

Conservatives inherited a large portion of the Westernism *pur et dur* of the Reform and Canadian Alliance parties.[17]

Quebec

The story for Quebec is simpler but more dramatic. In the early period (1965-88), party competition was radically unbalanced (as was pointed out in the preceding chapter) but dimensionally complicated. In the later period, the province became competitive, and, as it did so, the choices simplified. Where Tables 9.5 and 9.6 force the boundary between systems to lie between 1988 and 1993, Figure 9.5 shows that the shift began in the 1980s. The old system in Quebec featured four parties, but before 1984 only the Liberals had serious pretensions, which is demonstrated in Table 9.5. These four parties tapped four dimensions of choice. However, on none of these dimensions was the party ordering the same. The Liberal party and Social Credit party controlled poles on two of the four dimensions, but only on one dimension were they polarized against each other.

Significantly, the Liberal/Social Credit polarization was on the most critical dimension: language. Even in the old system, although the Liberal party was dependent on Quebec for its quasi-permanent lock on power, it was distinctively not the party of francophones within the province. All of the other parties were more French than the Liberals, and the most distinctively French party was Social Credit. The Conservatives were somewhat more distinctly French than the NDP. Of course, the Conservative party was much more consequential than the NDP in Quebec, even before 1984. What the multivariate estimation picks up is the conditional effect: relative to its generally weak base, the Quebec NDP was a quite distinctively French party. This point can be made more generally: given the weakness of the other parties in this era, the Liberal party was almost always the plurality or majority choice among Quebec francophones – those that voted at least. It simply enjoyed even bigger shares among non-francophones.

Religion produced a different ordering. Again, Social Credit anchored one end, as both the most distinctively Catholic voting party and the least irreligious. Next in line in this period was the Liberal party, both quite Catholic and hardly irreligious. The Conservatives, as in the rest of the country, anchored the non-Catholic end, while the NDP, as elsewhere, controlled the no-religion pole.

The union/non-union dimension polarized the NDP against the Liberals. Again, this is not to say that union members were mostly NDP supporters, just that they were distinct in the support that they gave. The distinctively

TABLE 9.5

Structural foundations in Quebec, 1965-88

	Conservative vs Liberal	NDP vs Liberal	Social Credit vs Liberal	NDP vs Conservative	Social Credit vs Conservative	Social Credit vs NDP
Union	0.419 (0.075)	0.592 (0.094)	0.216 (0.105)	-0.173 (0.098)	-0.203 (0.108)	-0.376 (0.122)
Farm	0.215 (0.149)	-0.660 (0.280)	0.245 (0.192)	-0.874 (0.284)	0.030 (0.199)	0.905 (0.307)
French	0.457 (0.143)	0.365 (0.181)	1.718 (0.441)	-0.092 (0.193)	1.260 (0.446)	1.352 (0.458)
Catholic	-0.338 (0.167)	-0.073 (0.220)	0.237 (0.408)	0.266 (0.232)	0.576 (0.412)	0.310 (0.434)
No religion	0.472 (0.295)	1.211 (0.335)	0.206 (0.672)	0.739 (0.336)	-0.266 (0.672)	-1.004 (0.688)
Intercept	-0.850 (0.118)	-1.868 (0.166)	-3.485 (0.482)	-1.017 (0.174)	-2.635 (0.484)	-1.617 (0.496)

X^2 118.581
N 2,803

Source: 1965-88 Canadian Election Studies.

Notes: Estimation by multinomial probit. Entries in parentheses are asymptotic standard errors.

TABLE 9.6

Structural foundations in Quebec, 1993-2006

	Conservative vs Liberal		Bloc Québécois vs Liberal		Bloc Québécois vs Conservative	
Union	0.097	(0.102)	0.458	(0.090)	0.360	(0.097)
French	0.906	(0.150)	2.551	(0.191)	1.645	(0.207)
Catholic	0.267	(0.195)	0.986	(0.246)	0.719	(0.264)
No religion	0.232	(0.256)	1.450	(0.286)	1.217	(0.310)
Intercept	−1.507	(0.169)	−3.099	(0.274)	−1.591	(0.287)
χ^2	280.080					
N	2,158					

Source: 1993-2006 Canadian Election Studies.
Notes: Estimation by multinomial probit. Entries in parentheses are asymptotic standard errors.

non-union shop was the Liberal party. In absolute numbers, the party of unionized Quebecers was the Conservatives. The rural cast of Social Credit is confirmed by the farm/non-farm dimension, although Conservative support was also quite rural. As in the ROC, the NDP was a distinctively urban-industrial party.

In the later period (1993-2006), as can be seen in Table 9.6, one of the four dimensions effectively disappears. This is the farm/non-farm contrast.[18] Two of the four pre-1993 players also disappear – the Social Credit party disappears entirely and the NDP disappears, effectively, from Quebec.[19] In place of both parties is the Bloc Québécois. And on the remaining axes of choice, the polarity is always the same – the Liberals anchor one pole and the Bloc Québécois, the opposite one. The Conservatives are always the middle party. This is true even in the oddly complicated domain of religion. The Conservatives are now more Catholic than the Liberals (in contrast to the earlier period) but less so, at least in terms of raw identification, than the Bloc Québécois. They are less irreligious than the Bloc Québécois, which comes as little surprise. However, they are also more irreligious than the Liberals, which is surprising.[20] On the union/non-union dimension, the Conservatives and Liberals are indistinguishable and the Bloc Québécois seems to have benefited from this support.

Figure 9.5 shows that the old system in Quebec was cracking in the 1980s. The figure is simpler than its ROC counterparts. As a result of collinearity

FIGURE 9.5

Linguistic and economic cleavages in Quebec (entries are percentage-point differences between groups by year)

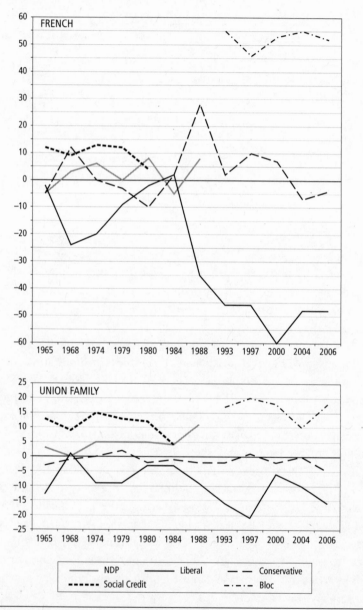

Source: 1965-2006 Canadian Election Studies.

and small numbers, year-specific estimations often collapsed. For example, in some years, not one non-francophone respondent claims to have voted for Social Credit. This token of the language cleavage's very power causes the estimation to drop the critical respondents. The estimation that results is thus both misleading and statistically weak. In light of this result, the best way to proceed is to focus on the two most critical axes, language and unionization, and present simple between-group differences.

The most dramatic shift is on the language axis. The 1968 election did foreshadow what was to come – a dramatic widening of the language gap, reflecting, presumably, Pierre Trudeau's sharpening of a rights-based conception of a language policy pitted against the Conservatives' dramatic but temporary commitment to a "two nations" conception of Canada. Aside from 1968, differences before 1988 were never massive, partly because the alternatives to the Liberal party were so weak. As Social Credit evaporated, the Liberals increased their relative drawing power among francophones. However, in 1988, the language cleavage blew wide open. In that year, the gap for the Liberals was nearly as great as it became – and stayed – after 1993. For the next several elections, the Conservatives were disproportionately French. In 1988, this majority added up to a large absolute share. In 1993 and after, with the advent of the Bloc Québécois, the Conservatives' distinctively French character did not help much. With the Bloc Québécois now firmly anchoring the nationalist pole – and bringing large numbers of hitherto inert sovereignists into the federal electorate (Johnston 2005) – the linguistic gap in the province became massive. The Conservatives reverted to the middle ground. The further reconfiguration of the party in 2003 pushed the party back in an anglophone direction, at least for the time being.

In the world of unionization, Quebec continues to be a distinct society. The Liberal party still anchors the non-union pole, in contrast to the situation elsewhere. The Bloc Québécois has gathered up all of the pieces that formerly engaged in feeble competition for the other pole and made itself the party of the province's union movement. Indeed the union/non-union gap in Quebec – idiosyncratically framed as it is – is wider than in the ROC.

Discussion

Notwithstanding changes in party nomenclature, the polarities of Canadian elections endure. The polarities are not trivial, neither in the width of the gaps or in the substantive stakes. Change in the system's social base tracks changes in economy and society. One example of economic change is the weakened position of farmers. In 1965, farm families still constituted a significant fraction of the electorate. By 2000, their numbers were tiny. Social evolution is indicated by the increased power of ethnicity relative to religion. Even in 1965, the Catholic/non-Catholic contrast had a whiff of staleness. The subsequent weakening of a cleavage with little resonance in policy differences among the parties makes perfect sense. For all that, the changes preserved much of the logic of earlier decades. Cultural factors still have primacy and order the parties roughly as before. Regional differences have sharpened, but earlier patterns are still evident.

The social bases of the system are quite complex, in that different dimensions of the social structure order the parties differently. Multiplicity in the underlying dimensionality of a party system is not unusual, but what *is* unusual is the fractionalization of the Canadian system, relative to its Anglo-American comparators. This observation, in turn, makes possible the variety in the parties' dimensional orderings. The reason for this fractionalization must be sought elsewhere than in this chapter. However, one implication of the fractionalization – and, I suspect, one cause of it – is the peculiar strength of the Liberal party. And this is the Canadian system's other major peculiarity – its historic domination by a party of the centre. It is always tempting to attribute the party's dominance to its very centrism. In most countries, however, parties of the centre are electorally weak (Macdonald, Listhaug, and Rabinowitz 1991).[21] In André Blais's (2005) catalogue of the four most successful political parties in the world, two are clearly on the right and one is clearly on the left. The Liberals are the sole party of the centre. The fact that they are indeed of the centre is confirmed by the tracking in the study by Ian Budge and his colleagues (2001, Figure 1.5). Before the 1970s, both the Liberals and the PCs look centrist. After the 1970s, the PCs pull to the right, but the Liberals stay in the middle, sometimes leaning right, sometimes the other way. Canadian voters also see the system this way. When asked to place themselves on a Left-Right scale and then to place the parties on the same scale, the mean imputation for the Liberals is almost identical to respondents' mean self-location.[22]

How is this possible? I submit that the answer lies in this chapter's ensemble of estimations and images on the core "national" questions. The Liberal party is *not* centrist – or is not responded to as if it were – on the ethno-religious components of the cleavage structure. However, its relative positioning on these components is the opposite inside and outside Quebec. Outside Quebec, it is still the party of Catholics and French Canadians, joined by the ethnic or religious minorities that pose, or have posed, "deep diversity" challenges. This mix is complicated, but an underlying logic of accommodativeness is detectable (see Abu-Laban and Nieguth (2000) for a start on working out this logic).[23] In Quebec, the Liberal party is more than ever the party of non-francophones. In this province, the party now also anchors the right side of the economic spectrum, even as it is the most secular in its support base. To put matters crudely, outside Quebec, the Liberals are the party of accommodating Quebec. Inside Quebec, they are the party of accommodating Canada. Taking the country as a whole, this position is defensible and, indeed, coherent, and it is the centrist position on the national question – again taking the country as a whole. This helps explain why the Liberal party is peculiarly credible on the question (Bélanger 2003). It is striking, though, that Eric Bélanger's finding is arguably about the management of the issue. Often managing the issue requires not talking about it, at least not out of doors, which is another commonly observed feature of Canadian politics. However, the Liberal party might not have survived to be credible in this way were the electorate not segmented between Quebec and the ROC.

Coherent and defensible though this position is for the Liberal party, it leaves its chief rivals caught on the horns of a dilemma. On the national question, the NDP and the Conservatives can trump the Liberals only by playing the ends against the middle. The NDP did this before the Bloc Québécois marginalized that party in Quebec. The NDP's modest base in that province was essentially sovereignist, certainly opposed to the party's generally centralist posture outside Quebec.[24] Perhaps fortunately for the NDP, the party was essentially faking it – a feint in Quebec to enhance its credibility elsewhere. In government, the Conservatives actually had to live with the consequences of the ends-against-the-middle strategy, and the major consequence was the party's collapse in 1993. However, this boom-and-bust cycle is a longer-standing pattern, even if the 1993 manifestation was especially dramatic. The Liberal command of the centre has forced the Conservatives to alternate between "me-tooism," which implicitly concedes Liberal ownership of the issue, and the internally centrifugal strategy that can deliver power but only as a poisoned chalice.

NOTES

This chapter uses data from every one of the Canadian Election Studies (CES) since 1965 and so is indebted to all the principal and co-investigators as well as to the studies' various sources of financial support, most notably the Canada Council and the Social Sciences and Humanities Research Council (SSHRC) of Canada. Research for this chapter was supported by the SSHRC, the Provost and Dean of Arts at the University of British Columbia, and the School of Arts and Sciences and the Annenberg Public Policy Center at the University of Pennsylvania. As usual, Amanda Bittner saved my bacon more than once. Comments from Brenda O'Neill were especially helpful. All of the foregoing institutions and persons are exempt from responsibility for errors of analysis or interpretation in this chapter.

1 See also Elisabeth Gidengil's chapter in this volume.

2 Cultural forces are commonly important where votes are counted by a proportional representation formula, but, as the next section shows, they are not typically dominant in single-member plurality systems (Caramani 2004).

3 See the preceding chapter for more details on the relevance of this regional divide.

4 Estimation is by "dprobit" in Stata. For each system, the determination is made from a set of binomial estimations, party by party. The effect is for an indicated party relative to all others in the system taken together. This determination glosses over the fact that the relative power of factors shifts when parties are considered pairwise, a matter considered in detail later in this chapter. The setups also assume that the effect of no factor is conditional on any other factor, which is unlikely to be true in general and, as the rest of this chapter emphasizes, is certainly not true for Canada. I decided, however, to keep matters reasonably simple for the cross-national comparisons. Even in this simple form, the estimations deploy seven to ten free parameters, depending on the country and the decade. A detailed account of the estimations is available from the author on request.

5 The "national" versus "industrial" revolution nomenclature originates with Lipset and Rokkan (1967).

6 Although the "largest" contrast is usually just the biggest marginal effect, I imposed a further constraint that the smaller side to the contrast must comprise at least 15 percent of the electorate. Intuitively, a small group that is very distinct is not necessarily more consequential than a group that is somewhat less distinct but much larger.

7 In some respects, this chapter parallels the chapter by Barry Kay and Andrea Perrella in this volume. Our chapters differ somewhat in demographic focus, however. Kay and Perrella consider age and gender factors, whereas this chapter does not. Age, regrettably, is not fixed, a fact driven home by the girths and hairlines of the older contributors to the CES forum. Gender exhibits short-term instability in its effects through the years of the CES (Gidengil 2007). It is also useful to contrast this chapter's strategy with the chapter by Harold Clarke and Allan Kornberg. Their objective is to pin down as many individual voters as possible. This goal leads them to a more eclectic mix of social structural factors and to move much closer on the causal chain to the vote. So where they are concerned to account for *voters*, this chapter is concerned with the party *system*, hence its more austere setup.

8 If anything, the comparison understates the polarization of the US system as the massive black/white contrast is removed from the table by the 15 percent threshold (see note 6 in this chapter).

9   Strikingly, all of the systems exhibit seemingly small $\hat{R}^2$ values. In part, this observation reflects the lowball values derived by the McFadden's calculation used in Stata. The real issue, however, is that the four systems in question are relatively consolidated. This ensures that the variances to be "explained" are large by world standards. This is an artifact of how variances of proportions are calculated: var $(p) = p\,(1\text{-}p)$. The variance increases as $p \to 0.50$, and parties in consolidated systems are much more likely to do this than are parties in fractionalized systems. This fact is worth pondering, as it casts an eerie shadow upon three decades of claims about the weak basis of the Canadian system. One piece of commonly cited evidence is Canada's low standing in the variance-explained columns of Table 1 in Richard Rose's study (1974). A classic instance of such a citation is made by Lawrence LeDuc (1984, 407). Never mentioned, as far as I can tell, is this awkward fact – on Rose's table Canada outranks its Anglo-American comparators.

10 For a sensitive discussion of this logic also applied to the Canadian case, see Gidengil et al. (2005). The estimation in this study follows Alvarez and Nagler (1998), who point out that the multinomial logistic strategy advocated by Guy Whitten and Harvey Palmer is equivalent to a sandwich of pairwise binomial logistic regressions. As such, it imposes an independence-of-irrelevant-alternatives assumption on the calculation that is unrealistic given the very interaction between party pairings and underlying dimensionality. Multinomial probit imposes no such restriction. All this said, using probit rather than logit makes little difference to the relative magnitudes of coefficients, certainly not enough to disturb this chapter's conclusions. Probit is computationally much more demanding than logit, requiring as it does numerical integration of bivariate normal distributions.

11 As discussed in the chapter by Thomas Scotto, Mebs Kanji, and Antoine Bilodeau in this volume, it is important to bear in mind that there are methodological differences among the CES and thus among the periods. This too may have some effect on any cross-time analysis.

12 For all we know, 1972 might be the critical year. The absence of an official 1972 election study means that this chapter cannot draw a definitive conclusion.

13 This is consistent with the report by Elisabeth Gidengil et al. (2006).

14 The fact that the Roman Catholic Church of John Paul II and Benedict XVI has increased its own emphasis on moral issues may also be relevant.

15 This could also reflect the geographic clustering of early samples. See the chapter by Scotto, Kanji, and Bilodeau in this volume for more details.

16 The party is able to extract seats from the urban West but mainly because of the fragmentation of the rest of the vote.

17 Although not all of it. The mere fact of reconstitution with power as its object deprived the new Conservative party of some of its Western edge, creating room for the New Democratic party (NDP). In Figure 9.4, compare the 2000 endpoint of the Reform/Canadian Alliance series with the 2004 and 2006 values for the Conservatives.

18 It disappears from the CES, at least. Whether or not the power of the Union des Producteurs Agricoles has also waned is an interesting question.

19 The NDP's 2007 by-election victory in Outremont may signal a rebirth. The one earlier NDP by-election victory in Quebec by Phil Edmonston did not prove to be a harbinger, however.
20 See the preceding chapter for a description of some shifts in outlooks that may be linked to these findings.
21 Their electoral weakness may still leave them critical to government formation. In relatively fractionalized party systems based on proportional representation, governments almost always cover the median, and this implies that a party or parties of the centre are included in the ruling coalition (Powell 2000). What is unusual is a party of the centre that can govern by itself.
22 Based on analyses by the author with data from the 2004 CES.
23 It is difficult to see a sharp reflection of this in public opinion data, especially for Catholics, as André Blais (2005) reminds us. So far, we have done well at saying what the Catholic cleavage is not: not just ethnicity in disguise (Irvine 1974); not just a residue of socialization pressures in the family of origin (Johnston 1985); not a strong issue complex (Blais 2005); and not just a response to religious bias in candidate selection (ibid.).
24 See, for instance, the analysis of the 1988-93 vote flows in Johnston (2005, Table 3), which indicates that "virtually the entire 1988 Quebec NDP vote switched to the Bloc" (ibid., 47).

REFERENCES

Abu-Laban, Yasmeen, and Tim Nieguth. 2000. "Reconsidering the Constitution, Minorities and Politics in Canada." *Canadian Journal of Political Science* 33: 465-97.

Alvarez, R. Michael, and Jonathan Nagler. 1998. "When Politics and Models Collide: Estimating Models of Multiparty Elections." *American Journal of Political Science* 42: 55-96.

Bélanger, Éric. 2003. "Issue Ownership by Canadian Political Parties 1953-2001." *Canadian Journal of Political Science* 36: 539-58.

Blais, André. 2005. "Accounting for the Electoral Success of the Liberal Party in Canada." *Canadian Journal of Political Science* 38: 821-40.

Budge, Ian, Hans-Dieter Klingemann, Andrea Volkens, Judith Bara, and Eric Tanenbaum. 2001. *Mapping Policy Preferences: Estimates for Parties, Electors, and Governments, 1945-1998.* Oxford: Oxford University Press.

Caramani, Daniele. 2004. *The Nationalization of Politics: The Formation of National Electorates and Party Systems in Western Europe.* Cambridge, UK: Cambridge University Press.

Clarke, Harold D., Jane Jenson, Lawrence LeDuc, and Jon H. Pammett. 1996. *Absent Mandate: Canadian Electoral Politics in an Era of Restructuring,* 3rd edition. Toronto: Gage.

Cross, William, and Lisa Young. 2002. "Policy Attitudes of Party Members in Canada: Evidence of Ideological Politics." *Canadian Journal of Political Science* 35: 859-80.

Gidengil, Elisabeth. 2007. "Beyond the Gender Gap." *Canadian Journal of Political Science* 40: 815-31.

Gidengil, Elisabeth, André Blais, Joanna Everitt, Patrick Fournier, and Neil Nevitte. 2006. "Back to the Future? Making Sense of the 2004 Election outside Quebec." *Canadian Journal of Political Science* 39: 1-25.

Irvine, William P. 1974. "Explaining the Religious Basis of the Canadian Partisan Identity: Success on the Third Try." *Canadian Journal of Political Science* 7: 560-63.

Johnston, Richard. 1985. "The Reproduction of the Religious Cleavage in Canadian Elections." *Canadian Journal of Political Science* 18: 99-113.

–. 1992. "Party Identification Measures in the Anglo-American Democracies: A National Survey Experiment." *American Journal of Political Science* 36: 542-59.

–. 2005. "Canadian Elections at the Millennium." In Paul Howe, Richard Johnston, and André Blais, eds., *Strengthening Canadian Democracy*, 19-61. Montreal: Institute for Research on Public Policy.

LeDuc, Lawrence. 1984. "Canada: The Politics of Stable Dealignment." In Russell J. Dalton, Scott C. Flanagan, and Paul Allen Beck, eds., *Electoral Change in Advanced Industrial Democracies: Realignment or Dealignment?* 402-24. Princeton, NJ: Princeton University Press.

Lipset, Seymour Martin, and Stein Rokkan. 1967. "Cleavage Structures, Party Systems, and Voter Alignment: Cross-National Perspectives." In Seymour Martin Lipset and Stein Rokkan, eds., *Party Systems and Voter Alignments*, 1-64. New York: Free Press.

Macdonald, Stuart Elaine, Ola Listhaug, and George Rabinowitz. 1991. "Issues and Party Support in Multiparty Systems." *American Political Science Review* 85: 1107-31.

Powell, G. Bingham, Jr. 2000. *Elections as Instruments of Democracy: Majoritarian and Proportional Visions*. New Haven, CT: Yale University Press.

Rose, Richard, ed. 1974. *Electoral Behavior: A Comparative Handbook*. New York: Free Press.

Sniderman, Paul M., H.D. Forbes, and Ian Melzer. 1974. "Party Loyalty and Electoral Volatility: A Study of the Canadian Party System." *Canadian Journal of Political Science* 7: 268-88.

Whitten, Guy D., and Harvey D. Palmer. 1996. "Heightening Comparativists' Concern for Model Choice: Voting Behavior in Great Britain and the Netherlands." *American Journal of Political Science* 40: 231-60.

10 The Valence Politics Model of Electoral Choice

HAROLD D. CLARKE AND ALLAN KORNBERG

Scores of articles, books, and conference papers have been written about the factors that drive voting behaviour in Canada's federal and provincial elections (see the appendix in this volume for some examples). Although differing considerably in specifics, many of these contributions have been rooted in three types of models. As mentioned in previous chapters, the theoretical perspectives guiding the specification of these models come from sociology and social psychology as well as "soft" rational choice theories informed by contemporary political psychology. The latter endow voters with agency but do not require them to adhere to the strict canons of instrumental rationality posited in neo-classical microeconomic theories. In this chapter, we pay particular attention to the development of a variant of the soft rational choice approach known as the valence politics model. We use data from recent surveys of the Canadian electorate to evaluate challenges to the valence politics model, and we conclude with a summary of the key points from our analysis.

Absent Mandates and Valence Politics Models

Scholars of political parties have long argued that in Canada the Liberals and Conservatives are brokerage organizations, whose long-running dominance is due largely to their ability to exploit the country's deep-seated ethno-linguistic and regional cleavages for political advantage (for example,

Engelmann and Schwartz 1967; Schwartz 1974; Meisel 1975). They do this by brokering policy deals among national and sub-national (political and socio-economic) elites, with the two "heavyweight" provinces, Ontario and Quebec, dominating the process to their advantage at the expense of the Atlantic provinces and the West as well as working-class people in all parts of the country.

Not surprisingly, variants of this argument have been ideologically charged. Marxists and other left-of-centre scholars have lamented the practice of brokerage politics, claiming that it obfuscates the fundamental class cleavage in Canadian society (for example, Brodie and Jenson 1988). These critics charge that, rather than being occasions for genuine policy debate, election campaigns generate political rhetoric that confuses voters about their genuine interests. Masters of the brokerage game, the major parties successfully thwart progressive politics, thereby perpetuating a "vertical mosaic" of wealth, status, and power (Porter 1965).

Harold Clarke and his colleagues (1996) contended that – its non-trivial normative aspects aside – the brokerage politics model can be developed into a powerful positive theory of electoral choice. The data that Clarke and his colleagues gathered through the 1974, 1979, and 1980 Canadian Election Studies (CES) provided three empirical building blocks for the argument. First, the evidence indicated that many Canadians had flexible partisan attachments.[1] Individual-level partisan change was ongoing rather than the product of unusual periods of party-system realignment. Moreover, party identifications changed in response to the same kinds of short-term leader and issue forces that affected the vote itself (Stewart and Clarke 1998).[2]

Second, when given an opportunity to designate important election issues, voters repeatedly emphasized what Donald Stokes (1963, 1992) termed valence issues. Unlike position issues, such as women's reproductive rights, same-sex marriage, taxation-social spending trade-offs, or more general Left-Right ideological positions – all of which have "pro-con" qualities and are the cornerstones of Downsian spatial models of party competition (Downs 1957), valence issues are one-sided, meaning that there is effectively only one ideal point. Nearly everybody has the same preference. For example, when it comes to the economy, virtually everyone favours low levels of inflation and unemployment and a wealthy, rather than a poor, society. Similarly, in Canada and most other mature democracies, an abundant supply of publicly funded health care, affordable access to educational opportunities, and a diverse range of other public services are in strong demand. Terrorism, crime, and corruption are also good examples, with overwhelming majorities viewing these activities as unmitigated "bads" that governments of all ideological stripes must strive to eliminate.

According to Stokes, valence issues typically have high salience in elections, and claims by rival parties and their leaders that they can "deliver the goods" dominate campaign discourse. In their empirical analyses of the Canadian context, Clarke and his colleagues (1996) found that valence issues were always very much on voters' minds, and judgments about which party was best able to handle the problems associated with salient valence issues had powerful effects on voting. Conversely, however, the electoral politics of valence issues often failed to provide winning parties with mandates to pursue coherent and innovative policy agendas (hence the title of Clarke et al's volume, *Absent Mandate*).

Third, data from the 1970s and 1980 also showed party leader images to be very important determinants of voting behaviour. In fact, Clarke and his colleagues' (1979, 1996) multivariate analyses revealed that leader images were among the strongest predictors of the vote. However, since their analyses were based on data that were gathered during the 1970s and early 1980s, one might be tempted to attribute this finding to the presence of one unusually salient politician – Pierre Trudeau – who was initially widely popular and subsequently became a highly polarizing figure. But, this inference would be incorrect. The effects of leader images on electoral choice were very general, with figures as different as Ed Broadbent, Kim Campbell, Joe Clark, Brian Mulroney, and John Turner all exerting very significant effects on party choice. This result is consistent with work in political psychology by Paul Sniderman, Richard Brody, and Philip Tetlock (1991; see also Lupia and McCubbins 1998). Using leader images as cues for making decisions in a context where reliable information about important topics is in short supply, Canadian voters react by seeking a "safe pair of hands" to guide the ship of the state.

In the 1980s and 1990s, Clarke and his colleagues tested their brokerage politics–inspired model of electoral choice and these three building blocks in a series of investigations conducted as part of the Political Support in Canada (PSC) project (for example, Kornberg and Clarke 1992; Clarke, Kornberg, and Wearing 2000). Unlike the CES, the PSC study was designed to investigate sources of support for Canada's political regime and community as well as federal and provincial political parties and leaders. The key feature of the PSC study was an ongoing series of countrywide cross-sectional and panel surveys. These surveys began in 1983, and the most recent one was conducted at the time of the 2011 federal election.

Recent Challenges

Although both the CES and the PSC offer strong support for the valence politics model, interesting challenges have been articulated in recent years. Two such challenges concern the measurement and dynamics of partisanship. Recall from Thomas Scotto, Mebs Kanji, and Antoine Bilodeau's chapter in this volume that Richard Johnston and his colleagues (1992) have argued that a change in question wording (changing the end of the basic party identification question from "or what" to "none of these") reduces the number of partisans while enhancing the measured stability of partisanship.[3] While this question-wording conjecture is plausible, survey experiments that we have conducted suggest that the reduction in partisans is generally quite modest (see Table 10.1). In these experiments, one random half of a countrywide survey was asked the traditional party identification question, and a second random half was asked the revised question crafted by Johnston and his colleagues. Moreover, panel data, including data from four waves of the 2004 and 2006 CES, which use the revised question wording, show substantial cross-time instability in party identification. A majority of panelists report either changing the direction of their party identification (20 percent) or moving between identification and non-identification (35 percent) over a brief span of time. Another 33 percent are directionally stable identifiers, and 12 percent are stable non-identifiers.

Furthermore, a direct comparison of rates of instability using the question-wording experiment conducted in the 2000 and 2002 PSC panel surveys shows virtually no difference between the traditional and revised questions. As Figure 10.1 indicates, 59.6 percent of the 2000-02 panelists who were asked the traditional party identification question reported stable identifications. Among panelists who were asked the revised party identification question, the percentage who were stable was virtually identical – 59.4 percent. In addition, if panelists who said they were not identifiers in response to the first question in the party identification battery but then indicated that they felt closer to a party (in question 2) are counted as identifiers, the percentages of stable identifiers as measured by the traditional and revised questions were 60.2 and 58.6, respectively.

A second, related challenge concerns the possibility that the observed incidence of partisan change in time t to time t + i turnover tables is largely

TABLE 10.1

Responses to the party identification question (traditional and revised versions)

	2000 (pre)		2000 (post)		2002	
Party identification	Traditional	Revised	Traditional	Revised	Traditional	Revised
Liberal	33.6	29.2	35.7	29.9	40.2	31.8
Progressive Conservative	10.5	7.9	7.9	7.2	10.2	10.5
NDP	7.1	5.1	6.2	7.6	9.0	6.6
Canadian Alliance	10.8	9.6	16.5	14.6	11.5	15.5
Bloc Québécois	8.4	6.4	6.0	8.3	8.6	9.1
Reform	3.6	0.1	4.5	0.0	0.0	0.0
Other	0.0	0.7	0.0	1.8	0.8	0.0
Total identifiers	74.0	59.0	76.8	69.4	79.5	73.5
Independent	1.8	1.1	0.2	0.7	1.4	1.2
None	14.5	31.9	16.7	25.8	13.9	21.5
Do not know	9.6	8.1	6.4	4.3	4.3	3.8
N	1,808	1,766	468	446	487	
Chi-Square	219.76		45.93		21.90	
P	.00		.00		.01	
v	.25		.22		.14	

Source: 2000 and 2002 Political Support in Canada surveys.

an artifact of random measurement error (for example, Green, Palmquist, and Schickler 2002). Again, analyses of the data beg to differ.[4] Even after controlling for random measurement error, there are very sizeable groups of partisan movers (ranging in size from 41 percent to 45 percent) to be found in both the CES and the PSC studies (see Figure 10.2). To sum up then, neither a revised question wording or a control for random measurement error turns Canadians into Michigan-style party identifiers – that is, persons with stable partisan attachments.

A third challenge concerns the issues and choice sets that parties offer the voters. After the demise of the venerable "two-party-plus" system, which featured the long-lived Liberal-Progressive Conservative (PC) duopoly (Epstein 1964), some observers have argued that position issues became more important than in the past (for example, Blais et al. 2002; Scotto,

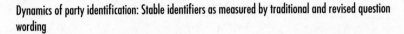

FIGURE 10.1

Dynamics of party identification: Stable identifiers as measured by traditional and revised question wording

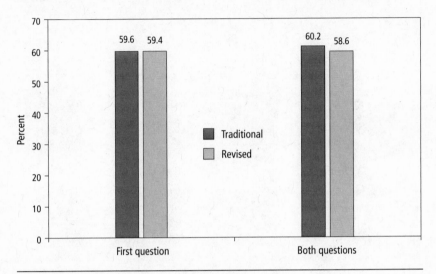

Source: 2000-02 Political Support in Canada surveys.

Stephenson, and Kornberg 2004). Certainly, the Reform party, the Canadian Alliance, and the newly minted Conservative party have been branded by their opponents and media commentators as being more right-of-centre than the PCs, and, by espousing sovereignty, the Bloc Québécois offers Quebecers a quintessential, and highly consequential, position issue (see Richard Nadeau and Éric Bélanger's chapter in this volume). Moreover, several position issues, including abortion, gun control, immigration, same-sex marriage, and Canada-US relations have achieved very substantial media coverage during recent federal elections.

These considerations notwithstanding, evidence from recent surveys indicates that voters' issue agendas remain heavily oriented toward classic valence issues such as health care and the economy, and that these issues were supplemented in 2004 and 2006 by the sponsorship scandal, which is also a valence issue (virtually everyone views corruption as a bad thing)! The point is illustrated in Figure 10.3, which summarizes answers to open-ended questions asking respondents to designate what they considered to be the most important issue in the 2006 federal election. Moreover, despite the increased clarity of choices on position issues offered by the new party

FIGURE 10.2

Mover and stayer chains in four-wave, mixed Markov latent class analyses

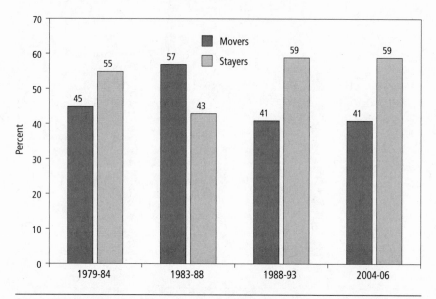

Source: 1979-2006 Canadian Election Studies and Political Support in Canada surveys.

system, analyses indicate that the same trio of partisanship, valence issues, and leader images dominates multivariate models of party choice in Canada (Clarke et al. 2005, 2006; Clarke, Kornberg, and Scotto 2009).

To be sure, there are statistically significant effects associated with positional issues (such as those mentioned earlier), but these effects do not negate the impact of the valence variables. In this regard, Figure 10.4 documents the ability of various predictors to affect the probability of voting Conservative in 2006.[5] With all other predictor variables held at their means (continuous variables) or at zero (party identification, party closest on most important issue, and regional dummy variables), as feelings about Stephen Harper vary from their lowest to their highest values, the probability of voting for the Conservative party increases by fully seventy-nine points. Selecting the Conservative party as closest on the most important (typically valence) issue enhances the probability of voting for the Conservatives by a lesser, but still very substantial, forty-one points. The effects of position issues such as the desirability of closer/looser ties with the United States, the desirability of same-sex marriage, and the taxation/public services

TABLE 10.2

Rival models of electoral choice: Analyses of voting in the 2006 Canadian federal election

	McFadden R^2	McKelvey R^2	Percentage correctly classified	AIC[a]
Liberal models				
Socio-demographics	.05	.10	72.5	3,731.38
Position issues	.02	.04	72.5	3,819.64
Valence politics	.53	.71	89.3	1,871.13
Composite model	.57	.75	89.5	1,757.64
Conservative models				
Socio-demographics	.03	.05	66.5	4,118.36
Position issues	.22	.36	74.9	3,321.18
Valence politics	.59	.73	90.0	1,774.83
Composite model	.62	.77	89.6	1,665.05
NDP models				
Socio-demographics	.06	.12	78.8	3,265.57
Position issues	.06	.12	78.7	3,221.46
Valence politics	.45	.59	89.1	1,925.04
Composite model	.48	.64	90.1	1,842.29
Bloc Québécois models				
Socio-demographics	.04	.07	57.9	2,247.82
Position issues[b]	.34	.45	80.1	1,536.15
Valence politics	.55	.71	87.2	1,063.92
Composite model	.58	.74	87.8	524.46

Source: 2006 Political Support in Canada survey.
a   Smaller values indicate better model performance.
b   Includes Quebec sovereignty.

trade-off are not trivial, but they are considerably smaller – twenty-two, twelve, and twenty-three points, respectively.

The explanatory power of the valence politics variables (party identification, party closest on most important issue, party leader effect) is also demonstrated in Table 10.2. These data show that the valence model easily bests positional rivals. Regardless of whether one is trying to explain Liberal, Conservative, NDP, or Bloc Québécois voting, the valence politics model always prevails. For example, for Conservative voting, the McFadden R^2 for the valence politics model is .59. The comparable statistics for the positional issue and socio-demographic variables models are .22 and .03, respectively.

FIGURE 10.3

Most important issues: 2006 Canadian Election Studies and Political Support in Canada studies

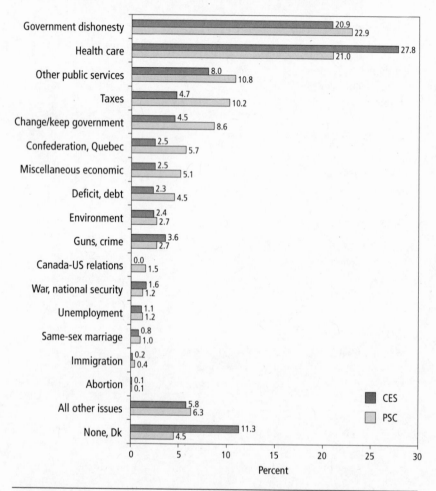

Source: 2006 Canadian Election Studies and Political Support in Canada surveys.

Similarly, the percentages of respondents whose voting is correctly pre-dicted are 90.0 percent for the valence politics model, as compared to 74.9 percent for the position issue model and 66.5 percent for the socio-demographic model. This is not to say that the valence politics model has the playing field all to itself. Rather, as Table 10.2 indicates, a composite model that includes significant predictors for all of the rival models has

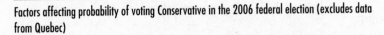

FIGURE 10.4

Factors affecting probability of voting Conservative in the 2006 federal election (excludes data from Quebec)

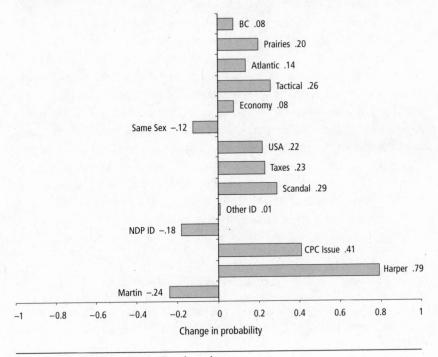

Source: 2006 Political Support in Canada study.

slightly higher R^2s and better (that is, smaller) model selection (AIC) values (see Burnham and Anderson 2002).

Conclusion: Studying Electoral Choice in Canada in the Twenty-First Century

Since their inception, the CES and PSC projects have exhibited a strong interest in the dynamics of political choice. Data gathered by these projects have enabled analysts to depict medium- and short-term movements in party support and to test competing claims about why voters do what they do. We argue that overall the results of these investigations provide strong support for what has become known as the valence politics model. The model has two key scientific virtues: it is conceptually parsimonious, and it provides a statistically powerful explanation for voting in particular elections and the dynamics of party support over time (Zellner, Keuszenkamp, and McAleer 2001; Achen 2003). In comparative statistical analyses, the valence politics model easily bests its rivals. Positional issue and socio-demographic models are not irrelevant to electoral choice, but their effects are clearly weaker than those associated with the valence politics model.

It bears emphasis that the story told by the valence politics model is not one where voters are unthinking objects of ponderous social forces. Rather, voters are endowed with agency, without being subject to unattainable Laplacean computational requirements. Being smart enough to know that they are not smart enough, voters rely on heuristic devices, including partisanship and leader images to make choices in a political world where stakes are high and uncertainty abounds. Our comparative research indicates that Canadians are not unique – valence voting and valence politics also dominate in Britain, the United States, and elsewhere (see Clarke, Kornberg, and Scotto 2009; Clarke et al. 2004, 2009). The theories and methods developed for studying Canadian voting and elections travel well.

NOTES

1 For more details on flexible partisanship, see the chapters provided by Lawrence LeDuc and Thomas Scotto, Mebs Kanji, and Antoince Bilodeau in this volume.
2 Similar findings have been documented in the United States and Britain (see, for example, Achen (2002); Clarke et al. (2004); Fiorina (1981); Franklin and Jackson (1983)).
3 See also the preceding chapter.
4 Data from four waves of countrywide panel surveys are analyzed using mixed Markov, latent, class-generalized "mover-stayer" models (see Hagenaars and McCutcheon (2002) for a discussion of this technique). For a detailed application, see Harold Clarke et al. (2004, chapter 6).
5 Changes in probabilities are calculated by varying a predictor variable across its range while holding other predictors at their means (in the case of continuous variables) or at zero (for dummy variables). Probabilities are computed using the CLARIFY program (Tomz, Wittenberg, and King 1999).

REFERENCES

Achen, Christopher. 2002. "Parental Socialization and Rational Party Identification." *Political Behaviour* 24: 151-70.
–. 2003. "Toward a New Political Methodology: Microfoundations and ART." *Annual Review of Political Science* 5: 423-50.
Blais, André, Elisabeth Gidengil, Richard Nadeau, and Neil Nevitte. 2002. *Anatomy of a Liberal Victory: Making Sense of the Vote in the 2000 Canadian Election.* Toronto: Broadview Press.

Brodie, Janine, and Jane Jenson. 1988. *Crisis, Challenge and Change: Party and Class in Canada Revisited*. Ottawa: Carleton University Press.

Burnham, Kenneth P., and David R. Anderson. 2002. *Model Selection and Inference: A Practical Information-Theoretic Approach*. New York: Springer.

Clarke, Harold D., Jane Jenson, Lawrence LeDuc, and Jon H. Pammett. 1979. *Political Choice in Canada*. Toronto: McGraw-Hill Ryerson.

–. 1996. *Absent Mandate: Canadian Electoral Politics in an Era of Restructuring*, 3rd edition. Toronto: Gage.

Clarke, Harold D., Allan Kornberg, John MacLeod, and Thomas Scotto. 2005. "Too Close to Call: The 2004 Canadian Federal Election." *PS: Political Science and Politics* 38: 247-53.

Clarke, Harold D., Allan Kornberg, and Thomas J. Scotto. 2009. *Making Political Choices: Canada and the United States*. Toronto: University of Toronto Press.

Clarke, Harold D., Allan Kornberg, Thomas Scotto, and Joe Twyman. 2006. "Flawless Campaign, Fragile Victory: Voting in Canada's 2006 Federal Election." *PS: Political Science and Politics* 40: 815-19.

Clarke, Harold D., Allan Kornberg, and Peter Wearing. 2000. *A Polity on the Edge: Canada and the Politics of Fragmentation*. Toronto: Broadview Press.

Clarke, Harold D., David Sanders, Marianne C. Stewart, and Paul Whiteley. 2004. *Political Choice in Britain*. Oxford: Oxford University Press.

–. 2009. *Performance Politics: Electoral Choice in Contemporary Britain*. Cambridge: Cambridge University Press.

Downs, Anthony. 1957. *An Economic Theory of Democracy*. New York: Harper and Row.

Engelmann, Frederick C., and Mildred A. Schwartz. 1967. *Canadian Political Parties: Origin, Character, Impact*. Scarborough, ON: Prentice-Hall.

Epstein, Leon D. 1964. "A Comparative Study of Canadian Parties." *American Political Science Review* 58: 46-60.

Fiorina, Morris. 1981. *Retrospective Voting in American National Elections*. New Haven, CT: Yale University Press.

Franklin, Charles H., and John E. Jackson. 1983. "The Dynamics of Party Identification." *American Political Science Review* 77: 957-73.

Green, Donald, Bradley Palmquist, and Eric Schickler. 2002. *Partisan Hearts and Minds: Political Parties and the Social Identities of Voters*. New Haven, CT: Yale University Press.

Hagenaars, Jacques, and Allan McCutcheon, eds. 2002. *Applied Latent Class Analysis*. Cambridge: Cambridge University Press.

Lupia, Arthur, and Matthew McCubbins. 1998. *The Democratic Dilemma: Can Citizens Learn What They Really Need to Know?* Cambridge: Cambridge University Press.

Johnston, Richard, André Blais, Henry E. Brady, and Jean Crête. 1992. *Letting the People Decide: Dynamics of a Canadian Election*. Stanford, CT: Stanford University Press.

Kornberg, Allan, and Harold D. Clarke. 1992. *Citizens and Community: Political Support in a Representative Democracy*. New York: Cambridge University Press.

Meisel, John. 1975. *Working Papers on Canadian Politics*, 2nd edition. Montreal: McGill-Queen's University Press.

Porter, John. 1965. *The Vertical Mosaic: An Analysis of Social Class and Power in Canada*. Toronto: University of Toronto Press.

Schwartz, Mildred A. 1974. *Politics and Territory: The Sociology of Regional Persistence in Canada*. Montreal: McGill-Queen's University Press.

Scotto, Thomas J., Laura B. Stephenson, and Allan Kornberg. 2004. "From a Two-Party-Plus to a One-Party-Plus? Ideology, Vote Choice, and Prospects for a Competitive Party System in Canada." *Electoral Studies* 23: 463-83.

Sniderman, Paul M., Richard A. Brody, and Philip E. Tetlock, eds. 1991. *Reasoning and Choice: Explorations in Political Psychology*. Cambridge: Cambridge University Press.

Stewart, Marianne C., and Harold D. Clarke. 1998. "Partisan Inconsistency and the Dynamics of Party Support in Federal Systems: The Canadian Case." *American Journal of Political Science* 41: 97-116.

Stokes, Donald E. 1963. "Spatial Models of Party Competition." *American Political Science Review* 57: 368-77.

Tomz, Michael, Jason Wittenberg, and Gary King. 1999. *CLARIFY: Software for Interpreting and Presenting Statistical Results*. Cambridge, MA: Department of Government, Harvard University.

Zellner, Arnold, Hugao A. Keuszenkamp, and Michael McAleer, eds. 2001. *Simplicity, Inference and Modelling*. Cambridge: Cambridge University Press.

11

Voting Turnout in a System of Multi-Level Governance

JON H. PAMMETT

Evidence of a decline in voting turnout in Canada first appeared in the early 1990s. From an average of 75 percent following the Second World War, turnout fell to 70 percent in 1993, 67 percent in 1997, 61 percent in 2000, and just over 60 percent in 2004, before rebounding modestly to 64.5 percent in 2006.[1] The prolonged nature of this decline has resulted in an increase in public and media attention. Political scientists have been frequently consulted for their explanations of this phenomenon and encouraged to speculate on its seriousness. This chapter explores a few of the ways in which this subject can be investigated using data from the Canadian Election Studies (CES) and presents some supporting evidence. It then briefly outlines the relevance of this evidence and presents some suggestions for future research.

Researching the Turnout Decline

Despite the centrality of the basic decision to vote or not to vote in elections, investigation of who votes and who does not has not often engaged the interest of the teams who have thus far designed the CES. In part, this could be because the surveys themselves do not pick up a full complement of non-voters, necessitating extensive weighting if the correct proportions of voters and non-voters are to be simulated in a representative investigation of the active and inactive electorate. Although a certain amount of analysis can be done by simply correlating the report of vote or no vote given by the respondent with their characteristics or attitudes, the reasons for abstention have much less analytic depth.

Not all of the CES ask non-voting respondents about why they did not cast a ballot. Moreover, in 2004 and 2006, the question was open-ended, but the answers were placed in a previously established set of codes that were collapsed from the full set of responses given in 2000. Although this coding strategy may have been more efficient, it could also have masked nuances and distorted trends that developed from one campaign to the next. Consider, for instance, the responses compiled in Table 11.1.[2] Note the erratic results. In 1997, fewer non-voters appear as disinterested in politics than were coded as such in the elections before or after it. Disinterest also appears to precipitously decline as a reason for not voting in 2004 and 2006, but there is a corresponding rise in those individuals saying that they are too busy, which to some degree is a rationalization of disinterest. In addition, there appears to be an increase in the proportion of non-voters who see the exercise of voting as being meaningless. However, since the electoral competition between the parties was arguably greater in 2004 and 2006 than in 2000, it is difficult to interpret why people might feel their vote did not count in the latter cases. Findings such as these make it difficult to put a great deal of faith in an interpretation of these "trends."

Likewise, when considering the role of negativity toward politics in non-voting, we can see that only with the 1997 election do significant numbers of people begin to be coded as not voting because they felt there were no appealing candidates, parties, leaders, or issues. But did feelings of negativity toward politics only emerge in 1997? And why did they dip in 2000 but rise again in 2004? It may be that differential coding decisions for similar responses produced this patchwork of results over time. Having said that, the open-ended answers listed under the "personal/administrative" heading that is given for not voting may be more reliable as these are relatively clear-cut reasons related to people's personal health or location, but even here we see what may be random fluctuations in the results. Although the general trend in both instances would seem to suggest a downward trajectory, the real extent to which sickness or absence are still the centrally important factors they were in the period prior to 1991 is not clear.

Voting at the Federal and Provincial Levels in Canada

As it stands, the CES might not be the most ideal or precise data source for studying in detail the attitudinal reasons behind voting turnout or abstention, which is to some degree understandable given that the primary focus

TABLE 11.1

Reasons for not voting (percentage)

		1968	1974	1980	1984	1997	2000	2004	2006
Lack of interest	Not interested	13.5	16.7	25.0	25.2	9.8	17.0	4.3	3.1
	Meaningless	–	6.9	4.8	–	–	4.4	17.2	19.4
	Forgot	0.5	1.6	1.1	1.8	2.3	1.7	–	–
	Too complicated	6.4	–	–	–	–	–	–	–
Negativity	No appealing candidates/parties	–	–	2.7	–	21.4	8.0	24.4	18.1
	Lack of confidence	–	–	–	–	–	5.4	–	–
	Lack of information	–	5.3	5.9	5.3	10.3	5.9	–	–
	Regional discontent	–	3.5	–	–	–	–	–	–
Personal/	Too busy	15.6	9.8	2.1	12.3	25.9	15.9	23.7	28.9
Administrative	Away	23.2	37.2	37.2	21.3	10.5	17.1	11.5	13.6
	Registration problems	2.3	2.0	8.5	10.4	–	8.8	1.9	2.1
	Illness	20.7	12.2	12.8	8.8	4.4	6.9	4.3	4.8
	Polling station problems	–	–	–	–	–	5.1	–	–
	Moving problems	–	–	–	–	–	1.9	–	–
Other	Religion	–	0.4	0.5	2.2	1.2	0.8	–	–
	Unclassified	17.8	6.0	–	5.5	14.2	1.0	12.7	10.1
N		392	450	188	511	571	478	418	199

Source: 1968-2006 Canadian Election Studies.

of the CES has been to examine the reasons for vote choice. However, because the CES are countrywide studies with large samples, they provide us
with opportunities to explore voting and non-voting habits in other respects. For instance, because Canadian scholars rarely have access to provincial election studies, and the CES ask a few questions about provincial
voting and non-voting, this data source may be helpful for examining voting
habits at different levels of the federal system.

Federal and provincial parties may benefit from the popularity, or suffer
from the unpopularity, of their counterparts at the other level in the Canadian federal system. However, studies of differential abstention are rarely
attempted, perhaps because differential partisan abstention does not seem
substantial enough, or long-standing enough, to amount to anything significant. Studies of local and national election turnout as well as abstention
in unitary states find little direct linkage between such behaviour at the two
levels (Abrial, Cautres, and Mandran 2003; Rallings and Thrasher 2003).
However, what does the evidence from the CES suggest?

The first point to note is that the aggregate turnout situation shows remarkably similar rates of voting at both the federal and provincial levels of
government, with a few exceptions that might be attributed to different political cultures, party systems, and the perceived competitiveness of particular electoral situations. In addition, there is an overall trend toward a decline
in voting rates at both levels. If we take as an initial hypothesis that there are
similar correlates of voting and non-voting at both levels within most provinces, we would not expect to find large numbers of people who are regular
voters at only one level of the federal system, despite the facts that opinions
differ as to which level of government is "most important" to citizens and
that voters may "feel closer" to one level as opposed to another. Feelings of
disassociation or negativity that inhibit voting may be generally applicable
to politics as practised at multiple levels of government. A multi-level governance situation provides several opportunities to practise, or abstain from
participating in, various political acts, and, as others have argued, once the
habits of voting or non-voting are established in young citizens entering the
eligible electorate they are likely to persist (Franklin 2004).

Figure 11.1 does not show a monotonic relationship, but this would be
expected given that the percentage of reported non-voters in any given survey is an under-reporting of the actual non-voting rate, often by a considerable margin. As documented in Thomas Scotto, Mebs Kanji, and Antoine
Bilodeau's chapter in this volume, there have been different methodologies
used in the CES over the years, which may make the long-term results less

FIGURE 11.1

Percentage of federal non-voters reporting non-voting in most recent provincial election

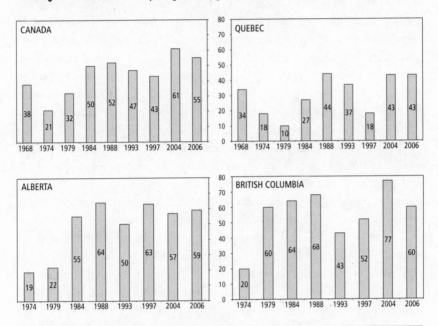

Note: In 1965, 1980, and 2000, some of these measures were unavailable.
Source: 1968-2006 Canadian Election Studies.

precise. Still, by simply observing those people who said they did not vote federally, we can see that the proportion who said they had not voted in the previous provincial election reaches 50 percent in the early 1980s. In the 2004 survey, the percentage was over 60 percent. What this evidence suggests is that people may be becoming more consistent in their non-voting behaviour at different levels of government.

The subsequent panels of Figure 11.1 compare non-voting behaviour between levels in certain provinces. Note that relative to the countrywide results, Quebec has a disproportionately low level of non-voting consistency. However, as outlined by Richard Nadeau and Éric Bélanger in this volume, given the polarized nature of politics in Quebec, it is not surprising that more people in this province who choose not to vote federally would still cast a vote in a provincial election. Some of the Quebec provincial elections in the 1970s and early 1980s were particularly momentous in this respect. Quebec respondents to the 1979 CES, for example, would have been looking back to the 1976 provincial election, which brought the independentist party of René Lévesque to power for the first time. Respondents to the 1984 survey would have referenced the provincial election of 1981, an election that sustained the Parti Québécois in power and one in which there was an 82 percent turnout. In 1988, respondents would have referenced the 1986 provincial election, where the provincial Liberal party regained power with a sweeping victory, and this outcome may be why the tendency to vote in this election was relatively lower. Notice, however, that after 2000 turnout patterns appear more stable, and the likelihood of voters abstaining in both federal and provincial elections is higher than it was in the past.

In Alberta, provincial turnout is consistently lower than at the federal level, a fact that is usually attributed to the non-competitive nature of the provincial party system in that province.[3] It is not surprising, therefore, that abstention tendencies in this province at both levels are more consistent than in Quebec. In British Columbia, despite the competitive nature of party politics at both levels of government, there is also a substantial degree of consistency in non-voting patterns, although the reported turnout at the provincial level is higher in some years than in others, especially during the early 1970s and 1990s. Still, in 2004, over three-quarters of federal non-voters also did not vote provincially. On the whole, therefore, much of this cross-time evidence, both countrywide and provincially, suggests that there may be an increased tendency toward withdrawing from electoral politics at both levels of the system.

Correlates of Federal and Provincial Voting

Another way of examining the consistency between voting and non-voting behaviour at the federal and provincial levels is to compare the determinants of voting at both levels. If we find similar relationships, we can have more confidence that we are dealing with non-voting as a more general phenomenon and not one that is engaged in for specific political reasons related to particular levels of government. As an illustration, let us look first at the relationship between voter turnout and age. Age is consistently shown to be the key variable in delineating electoral participation patterns, as large numbers of young people are found to have declined opportunities to vote in recent elections (Pammett and LeDuc 2003; Pammett and LeDuc 2004; LeDuc and Pammett 2006; see also Blais et al. 2002). Table 11.2 shows the reported voting rate of different age groups in the 2004 federal election and the preceding provincial election. This table, while it seriously over-represents the actual voting rate of all age groups, illustrates the same basic

TABLE 11.2

Voting/non-voting of age groups in 2004 federal election and preceding provincial election (percentage)

	Age						Cramer's
	18-25	26-35	36-45	46-55	56-64	65+	V
2004 federal election	68	79	85	89	94	95	.23*
Last provincial election	46	70	83	90	92	92	.35*

Source: 2004 Canadian Election Survey, N = 3109.

TABLE 11.3

Feelings of citizen duty and voting/non-voting in 2004 federal election and preceding provincial election (percentage)

Citizen's duty to vote	Voted both	Federal only	Provincial only	Neither
Strongly agree	85	67	64	35
Agree	13	24	26	35
Disagree	2	7	8	16
Strongly disagree	1	3	3	15

Source: 2004 Canadian Election Study – Question: "It is every citizen's duty to vote in federal elections," strongly agree to strongly disagree (N = 3074).
Note: Cramer's V = .23 – statistically significant at .01 level.

relationship between age and voting turnout at both the federal and provincial levels. Younger Canadians in both cases vote at lower rates than older ones. Moreover, this lower voting rate is not limited solely to the youngest cohort. Rather, the tendency to vote at lower levels extends itself to those in their thirties and even forties. Although these findings suggest a somewhat lower inclination to vote provincially than federally, the results overall mirror those from our earlier study of voting, which was based on the 2000 federal election (Pammett and LeDuc 2003).[4]

Table 11.3 expands this analysis by looking at feelings of "citizen duty" and different patterns of multi-level voting and non-voting. Citizen duty is the belief that voting is important for its own sake rather than an instrumental act to be engaged in for a specific purpose, such as to make a difference in the outcome. The question in this case asks respondents whether they agree or disagree that "it is every citizen's duty to vote in federal elections."

TABLE 11.4

Feelings of guilt and voting/non-voting in 2004 federal election and preceding provincial election (percentage)

Feel guilty?	Voted both	Federal only	Provincial only	Neither
Very	41	18	16	8
Somewhat	42	49	39	28
Not	17	33	45	65

Source: 2004 Canadian Election Study – Question: "If you didn't vote in a federal election would you personally feel guilty?" (N = 2,999).
Note: Cramer's V= .24 – statistically significant at .01 level.

Note that even though this question refers only to voting in federal elections, the assumption is that it also serves as an indication of voting more generally. The findings in this case indicate that of those who voted both federally and provincially, a full 85 percent strongly agreed with the statement. Voters who participated at only one level dropped to a two-thirds rate of strong agreement, though very few of these people actually disagreed with the statement. Conversely, of those who did not vote in either the federal or provincial election, over 30 percent reported disagreeing that citizens have a duty to vote in federal elections. This is further evidence to suggest participation in elections is probably interconnected and that a sense of duty to vote is likely a generalizable driving force.

Table 11.4 examines whether people would feel guilty if they did not vote in a federal election. Again, the assumption here is that feelings of guilt about not voting in a federal election are likely generalizable to the provincial level. The evidence in this case shows that most of those who voted both federally and provincially would have felt at least somewhat guilty had they not voted. However, those who did vote federally but had failed to exercise their franchise in the preceding provincial election were less sure that they would have felt guilty had they not cast a federal ballot in 2004. About half said they would have felt only "somewhat" guilty and a third said they would not have felt guilty. Those who had voted provincially but not federally were even less likely to feel guilty. In fact, almost half said they would not have felt even partially guilty. And, among those who did not vote on either occasion, 65 percent said they would not feel guilty. The interesting point here is not just that non-voters are less likely to admit they felt guilty but also that behaviour at different levels is linked to the same beliefs and that it is possible

TABLE 11.5

Perceived seriousness of youth non-voting, by voting/non-voting in 2004 federal election and preceding provincial election (percentage)

How serious?	Voted both	Federal only	Provincial only	Neither
Very	35	32	20	20
Quite	48	47	52	38
Not very	11	14	16	18
Not at all	6	8	11	24

Source: 2004 Canadian Election Study – Question: "About 25 percent of Canadians aged eighteen to twenty-four years old voted in the 2000 federal election. Is this a very serious ... problem?" (N = 3,012).
Note: Cramer's V = .12 – statistically significant at .01 level.

that such beliefs, in turn, may rationalize future non-voting, especially if multi-level governance systems provide added opportunities for behaviour to become ingrained and accepted.

A final table of this type (Table 11.5) reports the perceived seriousness with which people view the low voter turnout rate among young voters. In this case, the question primed respondents by pointing out that the 2000 voting rate among those who were less than twenty-five years old was about 25 percent, and it asked how serious this problem was. Predictably, more of those who had voted both federally and provincially thought the low voting rate among youth was a serious problem than those who had only availed themselves of one of the two voting opportunities. Non-voters in both elections were less sure that youth non-voting was a serious problem. It is interesting to note, however, that even among the latter group, more than a majority still thought that the problem was "quite serious." Although in both Tables 11.4 and 11.5 it appears that not voting federally is associated with more guilt and concern than not voting provincially. The wider evidence suggests that it is participation, or lack of it, that counts, not necessarily where the participation takes place.

To summarize, Table 11.6 presents the results of two regression analyses that predict turnout at each level. For the sake of brevity and illustration, the table uses ordinary least squares regression and an equal number of test variables for each election.[5] Although these are not theoretically specified models, there is currently no evidence to suggest that variables not present are particularly, or differentially, related to turnout decisions. The results in

TABLE 11.6

Regression analyses of selected predictors of federal and provincial voting/non-voting (beta coefficients only)

Predictors	Voted federally	Voted provincially
Age (+)	.14*	.20*
Education (+)	.08*	.04
Income (+)	.09*	.09*
Born in Canada	.03	.11*
Gender (F)	.01	.04
Citizen duty (+)	.28*	.26*
Non-voters no right to criticize (+)	.12*	.10*
Members of parliament lose touch (+)	.05	.03
Political efficacy	.02	.04
R^2	.159	.158
N	1,390	1,384

Source: 2004 Canadian Election Study.
* = statistically significant at .01 level.

this table indicate that with a few differences in degree, the same predictor variables explain similar amounts of variance in decisions to vote in the 2004 federal election and the preceding provincial election. For example, a sense of duty appears to be a relatively powerful motivating force in both cases, and another attitudinal statement – that non-voters have no right to criticize the government – is also statistically significant. The effects of various socio-demographic predictors are also broadly similar. Age and income are important at both levels, while education appears statistically significant only at the federal level. In addition, those not born in Canada are less likely to vote provincially but not federally, while a number of other potential predictors (gender, political efficacy, and a question related to trust) do not exert any significant predictive power at either level. Overall, this multivariate analysis provides additional reasons to believe that similar influences likely drive both voting and non-voting at different levels of government.

Other Types of Participation

Canadian surveys generally do not distinguish between levels of the political system when it comes to other types of political participation, such as

TABLE 11.7

Participatory actions of voters/non-voters in 2004 federal election and preceding provincial election (percentage)

Have done	Voted both	Federal only	Provincial only	Neither
Signed a petition	83	78	87	53
Joined in a boycott	31	29	32	13
Attended a lawful demonstration	24	22	21	5
Joined an illegal strike	6	4	10	2
Took part in an Iraq war demonstration	7	7	3	4
Expressed views	40	31	20	6
Joined a voluntary association	40	38	23	16

Source: 2004 Canadian Election Survey.

signing petitions, engaging in boycotts, or attending some kinds of demonstrations. We can, however, look briefly at the connections between patterns of federal and provincial voting and the propensity to engage in a variety of other participatory acts. In the past, Canadian studies have found that those who vote are more likely than those who do not vote to engage in all other kinds of participation, thus calling into question suggestions that a decline in voting may not be a withdrawal from public life as much as a shift in the arena of activity.[6] Similarly, Table 11.7, based once again on the 2004 Canadian election survey data, shows that in various instances those who voted in either the 2004 federal election or the preceding provincial election were more likely to participate in other ways than non-voters. This activity ranges from active membership in voluntary associations, to public expression of views on a variety of subjects, to attending lawful demonstrations. In other instances, however, the evidence suggests that even people who voted in just one election were as, if not more, inclined to sign a petition, join a boycott, join an illegal strike, or take part in a war demonstration. What is clear in all instances is that not voting in either election typically makes all other types of participation much less likely. Thus, even beyond the realm of voting, what this evidence suggests is that most types of participation seem to be positively related to each other, and this connection implies once again that they may stimulate each other. It seems that what others have suggested in the past may ring true – within a country, "participation is participation is participation" (Newton and Montero 2007, 222).

Conclusion

The burden of the evidence examined in this chapter points to participation, or lack of participation, in the Canadian federal system as being connected to more general socio-demographic and attitudinal trends, rather than being specific to any particular level of government. This may have implications for how we contend with the issue of declining voter turnout. The fact that declining voting turnout would seem to be associated at both levels of the federal system suggests that we would be well advised to look for causes and potential remedies with this in mind. It is debatable whether this makes the task of stabilizing voting rates and reversing the decline easier or more difficult. The multiple opportunities for voting presented by a federal system can just as easily ingrain habits of withdrawal and abstention as they can reinforce commitment to the act of voting. Nonetheless, a practical example of how we might implement this evidence is as follows. Campaigns of civic education designed to emphasize that abstention from participation leads to important decisions being made by those not held responsible by the citizenry at large should stress the relevance of all levels of government to daily life. Likewise, efforts to engage the public with opportunities for direct public participation in decision making must cut across the various levels of governance and should not be limited to, for example, local public meetings or provincial referendums.

Based on some of the results that we have derived from other dedicated surveys, it may help to make election campaigns at all levels more relevant to public concerns by drawing clearer relationships between issues discussed and the resulting policies adopted by governments. Furthermore, to reinforce the legitimacy of the process and reinstate the public's faith in institutions, evaluation and reform of legislatures and electoral systems should be debated on all levels. Through actions such as these, across all levels of government, the vicious cycles of participation decline might stand a better chance of being reversed. Also, once this change is initiated at one level, it is also more likely to spread to others.

To return to the CES, this experience of working on issues of voting turnout and participation occasions some suggestions for future studies. First, there should be more careful attention paid to the continuity of basic measures over time. One of the key arguments for carrying out studies at the time of each election is to provide cross-time indicators for examining trends that may rise or fall. Voting turnout is a prime example, and the basic indicators that measure why people vote or do not vote should be included in all studies. Furthermore, these measures should be phrased in the same manner and be coded in such a way that more, rather than less, information is available to the investigator. As the unsuccessful attempt in this chapter to put together a coherent account of the reasons for voting abstention over time illustrates, we can reconstruct the circumstances of important secular trends only if we are provided with the data in detail. Finally, consistent with the suggestion that Elisabeth Gidengil makes in her chapter in this volume, it would be desirable for political scientists studying elections using the CES to raise their sights somewhat higher than the particular factors that simply predict vote choice. Elections as institutions are falling in the public's estimation, not only in Canada but also in many other parts of the world. And this preliminary analysis suggests that falling voting rates may be but one symptom of a decline in political participation more generally. We should use our ingenuity to find innovative measures to shed light on the reasons for this decline and search out possible solutions to re-build Canadian democracy.

NOTES

1 Elections Canada has issued corrected estimates of turnout after taking into account various known anomalies with voting lists, such as duplicate names, deceased persons, and so on. In 2000, their corrected estimate of turnout was 64 percent, and in 2004 the corrected estimate was 61 percent. For purposes of comparability of figures over time, this chapter continues to use the original turnout rates. In addition, turnout statistics and figures used in this chapter represent percentages of registered voters rather than percentages of the eligible population.

2 The responses in Table 11.1 were divided into the same sixteen categories employed in a dedicated study conducted for Elections Canada in 2002 (Pammett and LeDuc 2003). This particular study identified three general reasons for why Canadians abstain from voting. First, substantial proportions of young non-voters identified a personal disinterest in politics as the main reason for abstention. Second, non-voting reflected negative opinions about political actors and political parties. Third, non-voting was related to the non-competitive nature of electoral contests.

3 From its beginnings as a province, Alberta has been considered to have a one-party dominant system. The classic work on this subject is by C.B. Macpherson (1962).

4 Although the distribution of these types of behaviour within the electorate is not very meaningful given the lack of accurate representation of voting in the sample, comparisons of the characteristics and attitudes of these different types of participants can still illuminate the factors that are associated with non-voting at the two levels of the Canadian federal system.

5 Ordinary least squares regression is used for the ease of interpretation. Logistic regression produces similar results.
6 Jon Pammett and Lawrence LeDuc (2003) report positive relationships between voting and other types of participation. Pippa Norris, in her book *Democratic Phoenix* (2002), asserts the thesis that participation patterns, particularly among youth, are shifting.

REFERENCES

Abrial, Stéphanie, Bruno Cautres, and Nadine Mandran. 2003. "France: Turnout and Abstention at Multi-Level Elections." *Democratic Participation and Political Communication in Systems of Multi-Level Governance*, Working Paper, Fifth Framework Research Programme, http://www.ucd.ie/dempart.

Blais, André, Elisabeth Gidengil, Richard Nadeau, and Neil Nevitte. 2002. *Anatomy of a Liberal Victory*. Peterborough, ON: Broadview.

Franklin, Mark N. 2004. *Voter Turnout and the Dynamics of Electoral Competition in Established Democracies since 1945*. Cambridge: Cambridge University Press.

LeDuc, Lawrence, and Jon H. Pammett. 2006. "Voter Turnout in 2006: More Than Just the Weather." In Jon H. Pammett and Christopher Dornan, eds., *The Canadian Federal Election of 2006*, 304-27. Toronto: Dundurn.

Macpherson, C.B., 1962. *Democracy in Alberta: Social Credit and the Party System*. Toronto: University of Toronto Press.

Newton, Kenneth, and Jose Ramon Montero. 2007. "Patterns of Political and Social Participation in Europe." In Roger Jowell et al., eds., *Measuring Attitudes Cross-Nationally: Lessons from the European Social Survey*, 205-38. London: Sage.

Norris, Pippa. 2002. *Democratic Phoenix: Reinventing Political Activism*. Cambridge: Cambridge University Press.

Pammett, Jon H., and Lawrence LeDuc. 2003. *Explaining the Turnout Decline in Canadian Federal Elections*. Ottawa: Elections Canada.

–. 2004. "Behind the Turnout Decline." In Jon H. Pammett and Christopher Dornan, eds., *The Canadian General Election of 2004*, 338-61. Toronto: Dundurn.

Rallings, Colin, and Michael Thrasher. 2003. "Turnout and Abstention at Multi-Level Elections in Great Britain." *Democratic Participation and Political Communication in Systems of Multi-Level Governance*, Working Paper, Fifth Framework Research Programme, http://www.ucd.ie/dempart.

PART 3

CONCLUSION

12

The Future of the Canadian Election Studies

ANTOINE BILODEAU, THOMAS J. SCOTTO, AND MEBS KANJI

The objectives of this volume were threefold. The first was to document the evolution of the Canadian Election Studies (CES) from 1965 to 2006. The narrative provided in Chapters 1 through 5 starts by describing how the CES began from the perspective of some of the main players who got the first studies off the ground. It also tracks the development of these surveys from a theoretical and methodological perspective, points out links to similar projects in other countries, describes the growing relevance of the CES both in Canada and abroad, and reveals some of the key challenges that lie ahead.

The second objective was to highlight some key findings, advances in thinking, and research opportunities that have emerged as a result of the CES. Chapters 6 through 11 take stock of over four decades of such insights. The CES have taught us a great deal about the long- and short-term determinants of electoral choice in Canada and about why voters vote the way they do. For example, Harold Clarke and Allan Kornberg's chapter in this volume shows how work that began in the 1970s and continues today has led us to the conclusion that short-term forces such as flexible partisanship, valence issue orientations and leader images are potent predictors of electoral choice.

At the same time, other chapters in this volume suggest that we should not yet shut the door on analyzing the long-term forces and other more deep-rooted sociological factors that influence political outlooks and preferences. First, as Richard Johnston as well as Richard Nadeau and Éric

Bélanger demonstrate, we can employ the CES to better understand the evolution of the cleavage between Quebec and the rest of Canada. For instance, some of the key findings in this area of inquiry indicate that there has been some cross-time convergence between these distinct communities on dimensions, such as religiosity and moral outlooks. Evidence also shows, however, that the two communities still continue to think differently in many respects and that they vote in inconsistent ways for different reasons than in the past. This information combined suggests that there may be further developments in this divide down the line and that research on regional differences is likely to continue to be relevant for some time to come.

Second, in their contribution to this volume, Barry Kay and Andrea Perrella suggest that when more data are available, we need to further unpack our current operationalization of key socio-demographic variables, such as region and religion, and re-examine the evidence in greater detail. Third, Elisabeth Gidengil's chapter suggests that we need to shift away from models that focus entirely on merely predicting the vote to those that seek to explain electoral choices by placing them in the context of their social networks. Designing election studies that take into consideration the fact that voters are social beings who interact with other social beings in multiple social contexts – as opposed to autonomous members of different socio-demographic groups – is a challenge, but it is one that would come with a high probability of bearing even more fruitful information than in the past.

Taking stock of four decades of CES-related research also clearly reveals some inadequacies of the CES. Some of these are the consequences of financial constraints. Others are the result of the ongoing tension between innovation and continuity, while others arise from changing priorities in research agendas. For instance, insufficient sample sizes frequently restrict deeper and more in-depth investigations, particularly of sub-regional and sub-provincial variations in political behaviour. Also, the exclusion or modification of questions over time often makes conducting longitudinal analyses complicated and sometimes impossible. And despite the central focus of the CES, these data are not always adequate for confidently accounting for all things relating to voting. More specifically, Jon Pammett's chapter shows that there are substantial limitations to employing CES data to study turnout, in part because the methodology of these studies is not designed to capture a representative sample of non-voters, and people are less than forthcoming when it comes to declaring themselves non-voters during an interview.

The third and final objective of this volume was to look toward the future after having taken a more reflective and systematic look at the past. The diverse contributions that constitute chapters in this volume, as well as the independent insights that we have gained from working with the CES and by editing this book, suggest that there is much that we still have to do. The introduction of this volume provides an inventory of the vast amount of data collected over a period of four decades. There are thousands of variables drawn from different time points, multiple topic areas, comparable cross-time data, long- and short-term panel data, and rolling cross-sectional data. Clearly, many possible perspectives remain through which these data can be investigated, and we must continue working to ensure that researchers in Canada and across the world keep probing the CES so that we can learn all that they are capable of teaching us.

In this regard, certain critical steps have already been put in place. The archiving of all data sets with full documentation in the Canadian Opinion Research Archive (CORA) at Queen's University is nearly complete, and the current CES investigators maintain an active and updated website with the latest study developments.[1] Also, the fact that CORA makes data readily available in STATA and SPSS formats and that the archive has made the data available via Nesstar – a web-based data analysis software – eases the effort of instructors who wish to bring the CES into the classroom. Continuing to ensure that these data receive maximum publicity and are easy to acquire and use should be key priorities well into the future.

In addition, another strategy might be to allow for greater input into the planning and design phase of these studies. The standard approach used by some teams in the past has been to invite members of the political science community to submit potential survey questions for consideration and to assemble teams of election study experts, again usually political scientists, from Canada and other places to provide suggestions and assess questionnaires before they go into the field. Such overtures, which can now be done virtually – as evidenced by the successful "online commons" process of vetting ideas for the US National Election Studies – will only serve to make the presence of the CES better known and attract a wider pool of researchers and insights.

Furthermore, in the future, a more aggressive strategy might be to find a way of more formally incorporating a broader array of disciplines into the planning mix, possibly by forming larger, more diverse research teams or advisory boards. As pointed out in more than one chapter in this volume, the composition of the CES teams has been largely dominated – with a few exceptions – by political scientists. Opening up to other disciplines might also increase the number of researchers interested in making sure that these data get utilized both more frequently and broadly. Of course, the details of such changes would have to be carefully worked out so that they do not divert the surveys away from their primary mission of helping us to better understand political behaviour in Canada but, rather, contribute to expanding and enriching productivity and the success of the CES project. Finally, and maybe most importantly, a more long-sighted approach for marketing this research tool more broadly would be to move toward making the CES a strategic resource, a strategy suggested by Richard Johnston and André Blais in their chapter. Not only would this development essentially secure a degree of funding for future studies, but it would go a considerable distance toward facilitating future research.

Analytically speaking, we also need to ask, "Where do we go from here?" To this point, short- and long-term forces that influence political attitudes and behaviours, particularly electoral choice, have been frequently studied alongside one another without enough attempts at integration. For four decades, we have asked repeatedly which of these two groups of factors are the most important in shaping Canadians' political behaviours. It may be time, however, to move beyond this dichotomy and to focus more on dynamics and heterogeneity. We need to look more at the "ties that bind" and link long- and short-term forces together. We have yet to discover how forces that are distant from the vote (for example, value systems, social networks, and religiosity) shape understanding in an individual's political world and manifest into attitudes and political behaviours. And it is possible that these processes might vary for different types of voters in Canadian society across different levels of government and points in time.

Studies of the differences in how men and women approach the political world represent a start in analyzing the behaviour of known subgroups in the Canadian electorate (Gidengil et al. 2003, 2005). Other scholars are contributing to this process by examining the differences and similarities in how old and young Canadians relate to political affairs (White 2010) and whether immigrants and Canadian-born citizens share similar views and understandings of politics and democracy (Bilodeau 2008; Bilodeau and Kanji 2010). But, there is still much more detailed analysis that has yet to be done. In addition, at this point we know precious little about how Canadians think about politics more generally and what motivates their thought processes during the "off season." What would therefore be ideal are more extensive multi-wave panel surveys, conducted both during electoral campaigns as well as when federal and provincial legislators are sitting in their respective legislatures rather than campaigning.

Deepening our investigation and widening our perspective to cover the "off season" between elections could most easily be achieved with a change in the data collection process and would likely involve a move away from costly interview modes such as face-to-face and telephone surveys. If Internet-hosted election studies prove acceptable and successful in Canada, they would almost certainly yield the larger sample sizes necessary to make meaningful inferences about subgroups, in varying contexts, across different levels of government. Also, because it is easier to retain respondents in Internet-based studies, it may be possible to construct lengthier panels that cover the times between election campaigns as well as the campaign themselves, and this possibility would facilitate a better understanding of the causes of change in political attitudes and behaviour over time.

Scholars are still carefully assessing the advantages and disadvantages of such a mode of interviewing and asking whether a delivery mode that is not yet available to all Canadians can cover the target population. But progress is being made in other nations, and we would be remiss to not at least consider the possibilities (compare Sanders et al. 2007). None of these proposed changes would discard earlier advances and breakthroughs. Nor would they represent a radical shift in trajectory. Quite the contrary, these suggestions might help to expand and further enrich what we have learned from the CES thus far.

Having looked back at the evolution of the overall CES project – how it began and how far it has come, the quantity and types of data that have been collected, the theoretical and methodological developments that have transpired, the challenges that lie ahead and the advances in technology that have come about, what we have learned, what we still do not understand and what we have yet to investigate, the advances in thinking, the continuous inspiration provided by new research curiosities – we would suggest that these surveys and data have played a significant role in building, shaping, and expanding the subfield of political behaviour in Canada, and, as a result, they have helped deepen the discipline of Canadian political science.

During the mid-1960s, only a handful of scholars in Canada were even interested in studying electoral choice and political behaviour more broadly (see Johnston and Blais in this volume). Now, it is common for most political science departments across the country to have at least one such specialist and to offer both undergraduate and graduate courses in these areas.

Some departments even offer more focused graduate training and degrees in the subfield of political behaviour. Such achievements would have likely been much slower to develop, perhaps even unattainable, without the distinctive analytic base provided by the CES (see Johnston and Blais in this volume) and the massive amount of literature that has been accumulated as a result (see the Appendix). From that perspective, the CES have already served as a strategic resource, and, therefore, it may well be time that we formally recognize it as such and take necessary measures to ensure the long-term survival and continued development of these studies.

NOTE

1 The websites are, respectively, http://www.queensu.ca/cora/ces.html and http://ces-eec.org/.

REFERENCES

Bilodeau, Antoine. 2008. "Immigrants' Voice through Protest Politics in Canada and Australia: Assessing the Impact of Pre-Migration Political Repression." *Journal of Ethnic and Migration Studies* 34(6): 975-1002.

Bilodeau, Antoine, and Mebs Kanji. 2010. "The New Immigrant Voter, 1965-2004: The Emergence of a New Liberal Partisan?" In Laura Stephenson and Cameron Anderson, eds., *Perspectives on the Canadian Voter: Puzzles of Influence and Choice*, 65-85. Vancouver: UBC Press.

Gidengil, Elisabeth, André Blais, Richard Nadeau, and Neil Nevitte. 2003. "Women to the Left? Gender Differences in Political Beliefs and Policy Preferences." In M. Tremblay and L. Trimble, eds., *Women and Electoral Politics in Canada*, 140-59. Oxford: Oxford University Press.

Gidengil, Elisabeth, Matthew Hennigar, André Blais, and Neil Nevitte. 2005. "Explaining the Gender Gap in Support for the New Right." *Comparative Political Studies* 38(10): 1171-95.

Sanders, David, Harold D. Clarke, Marianne C. Stewart, and Paul Whiteley. 2007. "Does Model Matter for Political Choice? Evidence from the 2005 British Election Study." *Political Analysis* 15(3): 257-85.

White, Stephen E. 2010. *Political Learning and the Pathways to Political Engagement: Experience Counts*. Ph.D. dissertation, Department of Political Science, University of Toronto.

Appendix
Four Decades of Publications Based on the Canadian Election Studies

ANTOINE BILODEAU, THOMAS J. SCOTTO,
AND MEBS KANJI

The reasons for this appendix are twofold. The first is to demonstrate the substantive contribution that the Canadian Election Studies (CES) have made in the past four decades to the study of political behaviour. The second is to provide a readily accessible reference tool for those who may wish to pursue a broader and more concrete understanding of the nature of the work that has been conducted using the CES. We realize that what we have presented in this volume is by no means the full extent of the research that has been conducted using these surveys. Therefore, we have listed in this appendix a more expansive range of works that have come out of the CES, classifying them according to twenty-one themes and ordering them by year of publication, to allow the reader to more efficiently navigate through this massive and impressive collection. The list, which begins on page 222, is an updated and amended version of a bibliography that was first compiled by Richard Johnston and Amanda Bittner in 2007. We would like to acknowledge Johnston and Bittner's efforts and clearly state that we remain solely responsible for the classification of the publications in the current appendix and for any errors or omissions.

Richard Johnston and André Blais's chapter in this volume makes the point that the number of CES-related publications has expanded dramatically over the years and this productivity has helped to establish a literature that was virtually non-existent in the past. What we would like to show in this appendix is that the substance of this contribution has shifted over time

FIGURE A.1

Relative weight of publications on short- and long-term influences on electoral choice

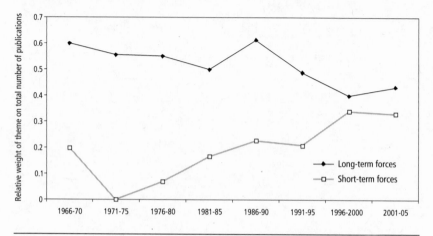

Note: These two categories are not exhaustive of all CES-related publications. See the reference list at the end of this Appendix for a more complete list of CES-related publications.
Sources: Publications (books, book chapters, and articles) using the Canadian Election Studies.

in demonstrable ways, and that the themes that were once at the centre of scholarly interest in the 1960s are no longer of primary concern.

Figure A.1 shows that since the early 1970s the relative weight of research publications on short-term forces went from being nearly absent to being the subject of about one-third of all CES-related publications. Conversely, the number of publications examining the effects of long-term forces on electoral choice has declined (from 60 percent of all CES-related publications when the CES began to just about 40 percent in the early twenty-first century). This is not to suggest that work on the long-term determinants of vote has become less relevant; it is just less prominent now that the subfield's overall content has expanded and diversified. Indeed, based on the discussion in the conclusion of this volume, it should be clear that interest in researching long-term forces is far from dead. Furthermore, it is important to remember that even though the relative number of articles on certain topics may have declined, their absolute number may have increased because of the sheer increase in number of publications utilizing these data over the forty-year period (again, see Richard Johnston and André Blais's chapter in this volume).

FIGURE A.2

Relative weight of publications on long-term influences on electoral choice (themes in decline)

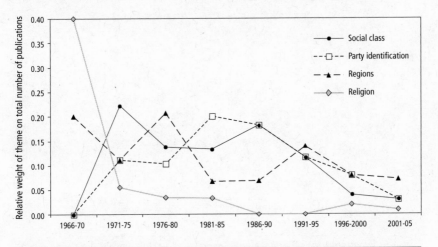

Note: Long-term influences on electoral choice also include the following themes that are not reported in this figure: political cultures and values. See the reference list at the end of this Appendix for a more complete list of publications on these specific themes.

Sources: Publications (books, book chapters, and articles) using the Canadian Election Studies.

Figure A.2 shows that among long-term forces there has been a declining emphasis on social class. During its peak in the early 1970s, work on social class made up almost 25 percent of the CES-based publications, whereas recently this type of research has almost disappeared. This finding is not surprising given that much of the analysis to date suggests that social class has only a modest influence on electoral choice (see the chapters by Elisabeth Gidengil, Barry Kay, and Andrea Perrella presented in this volume).

What may come as more of a surprise given all of the attention that has been allotted to this subject in other countries is the finding relating to the attention given to party identification. According to the data reported in Figure A.2, this line of research hit its peak in Canada during the 1980s, when analyses devoted to party identification made up about 20 percent of all CES-based publications. The relative weight of this research focus declined during the 1990s, and it fell below 5 percent in the early 2000s. While there is no clear explanation for this decline in interest, it may be that the work conducted by Harold Clarke and his colleagues, showing the flexibility of Canadian partisanship, has redirected scholars to focus their efforts

FIGURE A.3

Relative weight of publications on long-term influences on electoral choice (themes on the rise)

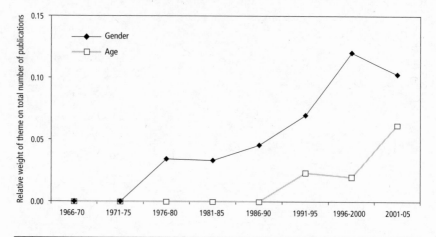

Note: See the reference list at the end of this Appendix for a more complete list of publications on these specific themes.
Sources: Publications (books, book chapters, and articles) using the Canadian Election Studies.

more squarely on examining the short-term influences on the vote. Likewise, the dealignment of the Canadian party system that occurred in the early 1990s may have been a contributing factor to the shift away from this research topic (see LeDuc's chapter in this volume).

The relative share of publications focusing on regions and regionalism also dipped over the years. CES-related work devoted to understanding regional dynamics went from constituting about 20 percent of all CES-related publications during the late 1960s and 1970s to less than 10 percent in the early 2000s. And studies relating to religion declined sharply from 40 percent of all work employing CES data between 1966 and 1970 to about 5 percent a decade later.

However, not all of the research that focuses on long-term forces is in relative decline. As indicated in Figure A.3, work relating to gender and its effects on electoral choice and political behaviour has become more prominent over the past two decades. This increased scholarly attention is likely connected to the emergence of feminist theories and their application to the study of politics (see Gidengil's chapter in this volume). This area of research went from being virtually non-existent in the 1960s, 1970s, and 1980s to constituting close to 10 percent of all CES-related publications

FIGURE A.4

Relative weight of publications on short-term influences on electoral choice

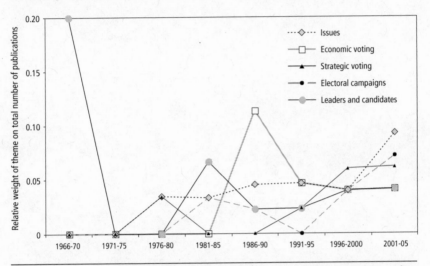

Note: Short-term influences on electoral choice also include work on the effects of the media,· which are not reported in this figure. See the reference list at the end of this Appendix for a more complete list of publications on these specific themes.

Sources: Publications (books, book chapters, and articles) using the Canadian Election Studies.

after 2000. In fact, the number of publications centring on gender between 2001 and 2005 (ten) was almost as great as the total number of works published on gender during the thirty-five-year period between 1965 and 2000 (thirteen). Moreover, among CES-related publications pertaining to the study of long-term forces, gender-based analyses currently sit at the top in terms of numerical output.

In a similar vein, the decline in voter turnout among the youth served as a catalyst for generating more CES-based work on younger generations (Howe 2003; O'Neill 2003; Blais, Gidengil, and Nevitte 2004; Rubenson et al. 2004). Since the mid-1980s, the proportion of CES-based publications on this subject rose to more than 5 percent overall. Furthermore, there are reasons to suppose that research on intergenerational differences, and their effects on electoral choice and political behaviour more broadly, is likely to continue to grow in the future (Kanji 2008).

Turning now to look more closely at a detailed breakdown of CES-based publications relating to short-term influences, Figure A.4 shows a cross-time increase in the proportion of publications relating to the influence of

FIGURE A.5

Relative weight of publications relating to participation, parties, political support, and referendums

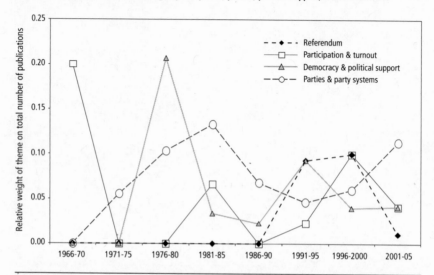

Note: See the list of references at the end of this Appendix for a more complete list of publications on these specific themes.

Sources: Publications (books, book chapters, and articles) using the Canadian Election Studies.

issues on electoral choice. Publications relating to strategic voting and electoral campaigns also grew markedly since the late 1980s and early 1990s. Currently, each of these three areas of research independently accounts for between 5 and 10 percent of all CES-related work. Taken together, they represent a major chunk of the current literature on electoral choice in Canada. By comparison, studies on economic voting, leaders, and candidates, which peaked at different points in time prior to the 1990s, currently each constitute about 5 percent of the current CES-based literature.

In addition to publications focusing on short- and long-term influences and electoral choice, there is a significant body of CES-related work that has developed on other topics such as political participation and voter turnout, parties and party systems, democracy and political support, and referendums. The evidence presented in Figure A.5, however, shows no clear and identifiable trends. Rather, work on these other subjects tends to peak and subside at various points in time. For instance, studies on democracy and political support and parties and party systems were most prevalent during the late 1970s. Over time, the relative proportion of studies published on democracy and political support changed from constituting 20 percent of output during the 1970s to less than 5 percent by the early 1980s. Work in this area picked up again slightly in the early 1990s but then declined shortly afterward. Similarly, studies on parties and party systems declined from a high of 12 percent during the early 1980s to below 5 percent by the late 1980s and early 1990s. In the mid-1990s, however, the proportion of publications on this subject increased once again and accounted for about 10 percent of the CES-based literature in the early 2000s.

Not surprisingly, work on the 1992 Charlottetown Referendum study reached a pinnacle in the mid- to late 1990s, after which interest in the scholarly analysis of these data subsided over time. Research on political participation and voter turnout also peaked during the late 1990s and was sustained into the 2000s, when it constituted about 5 percent of the literature derived from analyzing CES data.

Overall, we would synthesize the evolution of CES-based research output as follows: Over the course of the last four decades, the focus of CES-related research has shifted from being primarily concerned with the long-term determinants of Canadians' electoral choice to an expanding interest in the short-term dynamics of political change and political behaviour more generally.

REFERENCES

Blais, André, Elisabeth Gidengil, and Neil Nevitte. 2004. "Where Does Turnout Decline Come From?" *European Journal of Political Research* 43(2): 221-36.

Howe, Paul. 2003. "Where Have All the Voters Gone?" *Inroads Journal* 12: 74-83.

Kanji, Mebs. 2008. "The Generational Divide, Social Capital, and Political Support: Evidence from the World Values Surveys." *Journal of Comparative Policy Analysis: Research and Practice* 10(2): 47-74.

O'Neill, Brenda. 2003. "Examining Declining Electoral Turnout among Canada's Youth." *Electoral Insight* 5(2): 15-19.

Rubenson, Daniel, André Blais, Patrick Fournier, Elisabeth Gidengil, and Neil Nevitte. 2004. "Accounting for the Age Gap in Turnout." *Acta Politica* 39(4): 407-21.

CES-Based Publications

Articles, book chapters, and books only; each item is listed once only.

Election Post-Mortem

2005. Johnston, Richard. Canadian Elections at the Millennium. In *Strengthening Canadian Democracy*, ed. P. Howe, R. Johnston, and A. Blais, 19-61. Montréal: IRPP.

2004. Gidengil, Elisabeth, André Blais, Neil Nevitte, and Richard Nadeau. *Citizens*. Vancouver: UBC Press.

2002. Kanji, Mebs, and Keith Archer. The Theories of Voting and Their Applicability in Canada. In *Citizen Politics: Research and Theory in Canadian Political Behaviour*, ed. J. Everitt and B. O'Neill, 160-83. Don Mills, ON: Oxford University Press.

2002. Blais, André, Elisabeth Gidengil, Richard Nadeau, and Neil Nevitte. *Anatomy of a Liberal Victory: Making Sense of the Vote in the 2000 Canadian Election*. Peterborough, ON: Broadview.

2001. Pammett, Jon H., and Jill M. Vickers. The Canadian Election of 27 November 2000. *Australian Journal of Political Science* 36(2): 347-54.

2000. Nevitte, Neil, André Blais, Elisabeth Gidengil, and Richard Nadeau. *Unsteady State: The 1997 Canadian Federal Election*. Don Mills, ON: Oxford University Press.

1996. Swayze, Mikael Antony. Continuity and Change in the 1993 Canadian General Election. *Canadian Journal of Political Science* 29(3): 555-66.

1996. Clarke, H., Jane Jenson, Lawrence LeDuc, and Jon H. Pammett. *Absent Mandate: Canadian Electoral Politics in an Era of Restructuring*, 3rd edition. Agincourt, ON: Gage.

1995. Nevitte, Neil, Richard Johnston, André Blais, Henry E. Brady, and Elisabeth Gidengil. Electoral Discontinuity in Canada: The 1993 Federal Election. *International Social Science Journal* 47(4): 583-99.

1992. Johnston, Richard, André Blais, Henry E. Brady, and Jean Crête. *Letting the People Decide: Dynamics of a Canadian Election*. Stanford, CA: Stanford University Press.

1992. Gidengil, Elisabeth. Canada Votes: A Quarter Century of Canadian National Election Studies. *Canadian Journal of Political Science* 25(2): 219-48.

1991. Clarke, H., Jane Jenson, Lawrence LeDuc, and Jon H. Pammett. *Absent Mandate: Interpreting Change in Canadian Elections.* Agincourt, ON: Gage.

1987. Clarke, Harold, and M. Czudnowski, eds. *Political Elites in Anglo-American Democracies.* DeKalb: Northern Illinois University Press.

1984. Clarke, Harold, Jane Jenson, Lawrence LeDuc, and Jon H. Pammett. *Absent Mandate: The Politics of Discontent in Canada.* Agincourt, ON: Gage.

1979. Clarke, Harold, Jane Jenson, Lawrence LeDuc, and Jon H. Pammett. *Political Choice in Canada.* Toronto: McGraw-Hill Ryerson.

1975. Schwartz, Mildred A. Public Opinion and the Study of Canadian Society. In *Communications in Canadian Society,* 2nd edition, ed. Benjamin D. Singer. Toronto: Copp Clark.

1975. Meisel, John. *Working Papers in Canadian Politics,* 2nd edition. Montreal: McGill-Queen's University Press.

1973. Schwartz, Mildred A. Canadian Voting Behavior. In *Electoral Behavior: A Comparative Handbook,* ed. R. Rose, 543-617. New York: Free Press.

1972. Meisel, John. *Working Papers in Canadian Politics.* Montreal: McGill-Queen's University Press.

Methodological Issues

2005. Durand, Claire. Measuring Interviewer Performance in Telephone Surveys. *Quality and Quantity* 39(6): 763-78.

2002. Johnston, Richard, and Henry E. Brady. The Rolling Cross-Section Design. *Electoral Studies* 21(2): 283-95.

2001. Fournier, Patrick, André Blais, Richard Nadeau, Elisabeth Gidengil, and Neil Nevitte. Validation of Time of Voting Decision Recall. *Public Opinion Quarterly* 65(1): 95-107.

2001. Blasius, Jorg, and Victor Thiessen. The Use of Neutral Responses in Survey Questions: An Application of Multiple Correspondence Analysis. *Journal of Official Statistics* 17(3): 351-67.

2001. Blasius, Jorg, and Victor Thiessen. Methodological Artifacts in Measures of Political Efficacy and Trust: A Multiple Correspondence Analysis. *Political Analysis* 9(1): 1-20.

2000. Iyengar, Shanto, and Adam F. Simon. New Perspectives and Evidence on Political Communication and Campaign Effects. *Annual Review of Psychology* 51: 149-69.

2000. Brady, Henry E. Contributions of Survey Research to Political Science. *PS: Political Science and Politics* 33(1): 47-57.

2000. Bilodeau, Antoine. Which Party Will Win? Advantages and Weaknesses of a Numerical Question. *Bulletin de Méthodologie Sociologique* 67 (July): 5-24.

1993. Blais, André, and Elisabeth Gidengil. Things Are Not Always What They Seem: French-English Differences and the Problem of Measurement Equivalence. *Canadian Journal of Political Science* 26(3): 541-56.

1993. Bassili, John N. Response Latency versus Certainty as Indexes of the Strength of Voting Intentions in a CATI Survey. *Public Opinion Quarterly* 57: 54-61.

1989. Wiseman, Nelson. The National Election Studies Revisited. *Journal of Canadian Studies* 24(4): 141-47.

1989. Curtis, James E., Ronald D. Lambert, Steven D. Brown, and Barry J. Kay. On Lipset's Measurement of Voluntary Association Affiliation Differences between Canada and the United States. *Canadian Journal of Sociology* 14(3): 383-89.

1989. Archer, Keith. The Meaning and Demeaning of the National Election Studies. *Journal of Canadian Studies* 24(4): 122-40.

1987. Archer, Keith. A Simultaneous Equation Model of Canadian Voting Behaviour. *Canadian Journal of Political Science* 20(3): 553-72.

1986. Wiseman, Nelson. The Use, Misuse, and Abuse of the National Election Studies. *Journal of Canadian Studies* 21: 21-37.

1985. Goyder, John. Nonresponse on Surveys: A Canada-United States Comparison. *Canadian Journal of Sociology* 10(3): 231-51.

1983. Lambert, Ronald D. Question Design, Response Set, and the Measurement of Left/Right Thinking in Survey Research. *Canadian Journal of Political Science* 16(1): 135-44.

1978. Burke, Mike, Harold Clarke, and Lawrence LeDuc. Federal and Provincial Political Participation in Canada: Some Methodological and Substantive Considerations. *Canadian Review of Sociology and Anthropology* 15(1): 61-75.

1976. LeDuc, Lawrence. Measuring the Sense of Political Efficacy in Canada: Problems of Measurement Equivalence. *Comparative Political Studies* 8(4): 490-500.

1975. Elkins, David J., and Donald E. Blake. Voting Research in Canada: Problems and Prospects. *Canadian Journal of Political Science* 8(2): 313-25.

1974. LeDuc, Lawrence, Harold Clarke, Jane Jenson, and Jon Pammett. A National Sample Design. *Canadian Journal of Political Science* 7(4): 701-8.

1974. Elkins, David J. The Measurement of Party Competition. *American Political Science Review* 68(2): 682-700.

Participation, Parties, and Democracy

Referendums

2002. LeDuc, Lawrence. Opinion Change and Voting Behaviour in Referendums. *European Journal of Political Research* 41(6): 711-32.

2000. Mendelsohn, Matthew, and Fred Cutler. The Effect of Referendums on Democratic Citizens: Information, Politicization, Efficacy, and Tolerance. *British Journal of Political Science* 30(4): 685-98.

1997. Conley, Richard S. Sovereignty or the Status Quo? The 1995 Pre-Referendum Debate in Quebec. *The Journal of Commonwealth and Comparative Politics* 35(1): 67-92.

1996. Johnston, Richard, André Blais, Elisabeth Gidengil, and Neil Nevitte. *The Challenge of Direct Democracy.* Montreal: McGill-Queen's University Press.

1996. Clarke, Harold D., and Allan Kornberg. Choosing Canada? The 1995 Quebec Sovereignty Referendum. *PS: Political Science and Politics* 29(4): 676-82.

1996. Blais, André, Richard Johnston, Elisabeth Gidengil, and Neil Nevitte. La dynamique référendaire: Pourquoi les Canadiens ont-ils rejeté l'Accord de Charlottetown? *Revue Française de Science Politique* 46(5): 817-30.

1995. LeDuc, Lawrence, and Jon H. Pammett. Referendum Voting: Attitudes and Behaviour in the 1992 Constitutional Referendum. *Canadian Journal of Political Science* 28(1): 3-33.

1994. Clarke, Harold D., and Allan Kornberg. The Politics and Economics of Constitutional Choice: Voting in Canada's 1992 National Referendum. *The Journal of Politics* 56(4): 940-62.

1993. Johnston, Richard, André Blais, Elisabeth Gidengil, and Neil Nevitte. The People and the Charlottetown Accord. In *Canada: The State of the Federation, 1993,* ed. R.L. Watts and D.M. Brown, 19-43. Kingston, ON: Institute of Intergovernmental Relations.

1993. Johnston, Richard. An Inverted Logroll: The Charlottetown Accord and the Referendum. *PS: Political Science and Politics* 26(1): 43-48.

Political Participation and Voter Turnout

2005. Anderson, Cameron D., and Elizabeth Goodyear-Grant. Conceptions of Political Representation in Canada: An Explanation of Public Opinion. *Canadian Journal of Political Science* 38(4): 1029-58.

2004. Franklin, Mark N. *Voter Turnout and the Dynamics of Electoral Competition in Established Democracies Since 1945.* Cambridge: Cambridge University Press.

2003. Howe, Paul. Electoral Participation and the Knowledge Deficit. *Electoral Insight* 5(2): 20-25.

2002. Endersby, James W., Steven E. Galatas, and Chapman B. Rackaway. Closeness Counts in Canada: Voter Participation in the 1993 and 1997 Federal Elections. *Journal of Politics* 64(2): 610-31.

2000. Martinez, Michael D. Turning Out or Tuning Out? Electoral Participation in Canada and the United States. In *Canada and the United States: Differences That Count*, 2nd edition, ed. D. Thomas, 211-28. Peterborough, ON: Broadview.

1999. Matsusaka, John G., and Filip Palda. Voter Turnout: How Much Can We Explain? *Public Choice* 98(3-4): 431-46.

1999. Lapp, Miriam. Ethnic Group Leaders and the Mobilization of Voter Turnout: Evidence from Five Montreal Communities. *Canadian Ethnic Studies* 31(2): 17-42.

1997. Brians, Craig L. Residential Mobility, Voter Registration, and Electoral Participation in Canada. *Political Research Quarterly* 50(1): 215-27.

1996. Eagles, Munroe. The Franchise and Political Participation. In *Canadian Political Parties in Transition: Discourse, Organization, Representation*, 2nd edition, ed. B. Tanguay and A. Gagnon, 307-27. Scarborough, ON: Nelson Canada.

1993. Berch, Neil. Another Look at Closeness and Turnout: The Case of the 1979 and 1980 Canadian National Elections. *Political Research Quarterly* 46(2): 421-32.

1982. Zipp, John F., Richard Landerman, and Paul Leubke. Political Parties and Political Participation: A Reexamination of the Standard Socioeconomic Model. *Social Forces* 60(4): 1140-53.

1982. Uhlaner, Carole Jean. The Consistency of Individual Political Participation across Governmental Levels in Canada. *American Journal of Political Science* 26(2): 298-11.

1970. Van Loon, Richard. Political Participation in Canada: The 1965 Election. *Canadian Journal of Political Science* 3(3): 376-99.

Parties and Party Systems

2005. Dalton, Russell J., and Steven A. Weldon. Public Images of Political Parties: A Necessary Evil? *West European Politics* 28(5): 931-51.

2005. Clarkson, Stephen. *The Big Red Machine*. Vancouver: UBC Press.

2005. Bélanger, Eric, and Richard Nadeau. Political Trust and the Vote in Multiparty Elections. *European Journal of Political Research* 44(1): 121-46.

2004. Scotto, Thomas J., Laura B. Stephenson, and Allan Kornberg. From a Two-Party-Plus to a One-Party-Plus? Ideology, Vote Choice, and Prospects for a Competitive Party System in Canada. *Electoral Studies* 23(3): 463-83.

2004. Koop, Royce. Federal-Provincial Voting and Federal Integration in the Fourth Canadian Party System. *Federal Governance: A Graduate Journal of Theory and Politics* 4(1).

2004. Cross, William, and Lisa Young. The Contours of Political Party Membership in Canada. *Party Politics* 10(4): 427-44.

2004. Bélanger, Eric. The Rise of Third Parties in the 1993 Canadian Federal Election: Pinard Revisited. *Canadian Journal of Political Science* 37(3): 581-94.

2004. Bélanger, Eric. Antipartyism and Third-Party Vote Choice: A Comparison of Canada, Britain, and Australia. *Comparative Political Studies* 37(9): 1054-78.

2004. Alvarez, R. Michael, and Jonathan Nagler. Party System Compactness: Measurement and Consequences. *Political Analysis* 12(1): 46-62.

2001. Gidengil, Elisabeth, André Blais, Neil Nevitte, and Richard Nadeau. The Correlates and Consequences of Anti-Partyism in the 1997 Canadian Election. *Party Politics* 7(4): 491-513.

2001. Gidengil, Elisabeth, André Blais, Richard Nadeau, and Neil Nevitte. Changes in the Party System and Anti-Party Sentiment. In *Political Parties, Representation, and Electoral Democracy in Canada*, ed. W. Cross, 68-86. Toronto: Oxford University Press.

2000. Carty, R. Kenneth, William Cross, and Lisa Young. *Rebuilding Canadian Party Politics*. Vancouver: UBC Press.

1998. Nevitte, Neil, André Blais, Elisabeth Gidengil, Richard Johnston, and Henry E. Brady. The Populist Right in Canada: The Rise of the Reform Party of Canada. In *The New Politics of the Right: Neo-Populist Parties and Movements in Established Democracies*, ed. H-G. Betz and S. Immerfal, 173-202. New York: St. Martin's.

1997. Ellis, Faron, and Keith Archer. Reform at the Crossroads. In *The Canadian General Election of 1997*, ed. A. Frizzell and J. Pammett, 111-33. Toronto: Dundurn Press.

1993. Clarke, Harold D., and Allan Kornberg. Evaluations and Evolution: Public Attitudes toward Canada's Federal Political Parties, 1965-1991. *Canadian Journal of Political Science* 26(2): 287-311.

1992. Kornberg, Allan, and Harold D. Clarke. *Citizens and Community: Political Support in a Representative Democracy*. Cambridge: Cambridge University Press.

1988. Penniman, Howard Rae. *Canada at the Polls, 1984: A Study of the Federal General Elections*. Durham, NC: Duke University Press.

1988. Blake, Donald. Division and Cohesion: The Major Parties. In *Party Democracy in Canada: The Politics of National Party Conventions*, ed. G. Perlin, 32-53. Scarborough, ON: Prentice Hall.

1987. Clarke, Harold D., and Gary Zuk. The Politics of Party Popularity: Canada 1974-1979. *Comparative Politics* 19(3): 299-315.

1985. LeDuc, Lawrence. Partisan Change and Dealignment in Canada, Great Britain, and the United States. *Comparative Politics* 17(4): 379-98.

1985. Archer, Keith. The Failure of the New Democratic Party: Unions, Unionists, and Politics in Canada. *Canadian Journal of Political Science* 18(2): 353-66.

1984. LeDuc, Lawrence. Canada: The Politics of Stable Dealignment. In *Electoral Change in Advanced Industrial Democracies: Realignment or Dealignment?* ed. Russell J. Dalton, Paul Beck, and Scott Flanagan, 402-24. Princeton, NJ: Princeton University Press.

1983. Clarke, Harold. The Parti Québécois and Sources of Partisan Realignment in Contemporary Quebec. *Journal of Politics* 45(1): 64-85.

1980. Irvine, William P., and H. Gold. Do Frozen Cleavages Ever Go Stale? The Bases of the Canadian and Australian Party Systems. *British Journal of Political Science* 10(2): 187-218.

1980. Burke, Mike. Dimensions of Variation in Electoral Coalitions, 1965-1974. In *Small Worlds: Provinces and Parties in Canadian Political Life*, ed. David J. Elkins and Richard Simeon, 179-210. Toronto: Methuen.

1976. Jenson, Jane. Party Systems. In *The Provincial Political Systems: Comparative Essays*, ed. David J. Bellamy, Jon H. Pammett, and Donald C. Rowat, 118-31. Toronto: Methuen.

1974. Elkins, David J. The Perceived Structure of the Canadian Party Systems. *Canadian Journal of Political Science* 7(3): 502-24.

Democracy and Political Support

2005. Anderson, Christopher J., André Blais, Shaun Bowler, Todd Donovan, and Ola Listhaug. *Losers' Consent: Elections and Democratic Legitimacy.* Oxford: Oxford University Press.

2004. Hausegger, Lori, and Troy Riddell. The Changing Nature of Public Support for the Supreme Court of Canada. *Canadian Journal of Political Science* 37(1): 23-50.

2004. Docherty, David C., and Stephen White. Parliamentary Democracy in Canada. *Parliamentary Affairs* 57(3): 613-29.

2004. Archer, Keith. Redefining Electoral Democracy in Canada. *Election Law Journal* 3(3): 545-58.

2000. Howe, Paul, and David Northrup. Strengthening Canadian Democracy: The Views of Canadians. *Policy Matters* 1(5): 1-104.

1999. Bilodeau, Antoine. L'impact mécanique du vote alternatif au Canada: une simulation des élections de 1997. *Canadian Journal of Political Science* 32(4): 745-61.

1993. Nadeau, Richard, and André Blais. Accepting the Election Outcome: The Effect of Participation on Losers' Consent. *British Journal of Political Science* 23(4): 553-63.

1993. Brodie, Ian, and Neil Nevitte. Evaluating the Citizens' Constitution Theory. *Canadian Journal of Political Science.* 16(2): 235-59.

1992. Stewart, Marianne C., Allan Kornberg, Harold D. Clarke, and Alan Acock. Arenas and Attitudes: A Note on Political Efficacy in a Federal System. *The Journal of Politics* 54(1): 179-96.

1992. Clarke, Harold D., and Allan Kornberg. Do National Elections Affect Perceptions of MP Responsiveness? A Note on the Canadian Case. *Legislative Studies Quarterly* 17(2): 183-204.

1986. Monroe, Kristen, and Lynda Erickson. The Economy and Political Support: The Canadian Case. *The Journal of Politics* 48(3): 616-47.

1984. Clarke, Harold D., Allan Kornberg, and Marianne C. Stewart. Parliament and Political Support in Canada. *The American Political Science Review* 78(2): 452-69.

1980. Kornberg, Allan, Harold D. Clarke, and Lawrence Leduc. Regime Support in Canada: A Rejoinder. *British Journal of Political Science* 10(3): 410-16.

1980. Atkinson, Michael, William D. Coleman, and Thomas J. Lewis. Regime Support in Canada: A Comment. *British Journal of Political Science* 10(3): 402-10.

1979. Kornberg, Allan, Harold D. Clarke, and Marianne C. Stewart. Federalism and Fragmentation: Political Support in Canada. *The Journal of Politics* 41(3): 889-906.

1978. Madsen, Douglas. A Structural Approach to the Explanation of Political Efficacy Levels Under Democratic Regimes. *American Journal of Political Science* 22(4): 867-83.

1978. Kornberg, Allan, Harold D. Clarke, and Lawrence LeDuc. Some Correlates of Regime Support in Canada. *British Journal of Political Science* 8(2): 199-216.

1977. LeDuc, Lawrence. Political Behaviour and the Issue of Majority Government in Two Federal Elections. *Canadian Journal of Political Science* 10(2): 311-39.

Long-Term Factors

Political Culture, Values, and Ideology

2004. Brym, R.J., John Veuglers, Jonah Butovsky, and John Simpson. Postmaterialism in Unresponsive Political Systems: The Canadian Case. *Canadian Review of Sociology and Anthropology* 41(3): 291-317.

2002. Telford, Hamish, and H. Lazar, eds. *Canadian Political Culture(s) in Transition, Canada: The State of the Federation.* Montreal: McGill-Queen's University Press.

2002. Nevitte, Neil. *Value Change and Governance in Canada.* Toronto: University of Toronto Press.

2002. Erickson, Lynda, and David Laycock. Post-Materialism versus the Welfare State? Opinion among English Canadian Social Democrats. *Party Politics* 8(3): 301-25.

2002. Butovsky, Jonah. The Salience of Post-Materialism in Canadian Politics. *Canadian Review of Sociology and Anthropology* 39(4): 471-84.

2001. Turcotte, M. The Opposition of Rural and Urban a Thing of the Past? The Case of Moral Traditionalism. *Canadian Journal of Sociology – Cahiers Canadiens de Sociologie* 26(1): 1-29.

2000. Nevitte, Neil. Value Change and Reorientations in Citizen-State Relations. *Canadian Public Policy* 26 (Supplement: *The Trends Project*): S73-S94.

1996. Pelletier, R., and D. Guérin. Postmatérialisme et clivages partisans au Québec: Les partis sont-ils differents? *Canadian Journal of Political Science* 29(1): 71-109.

1990. Wohlfeld, Monika J., and Neil Nevitte. Postindustrial Value Change and Support for Native Issues. *Canadian Ethnic Studies* 22(3): 56-68.

1990. Baer, Douglas, Edward Grabb, and William Johnston. The Values of Canadians and Americans: A Rejoinder. *Social Forces* 69(1): 273-77.

1990. Baer, Doug, Edward Grabb, and William A. Johnston. The Values of Canadians and Americans: A Critical Analysis and Reassessment. *Social Forces* 68(3): 693-713.

1987. Bakvis, Herman, and Neil Nevitte. In Pursuit of Postbourgeois Man: Postmaterialism and Intergenerational Change in Canada. *Comparative Political Studies* 20(3): 357-89.

1986. Lambert, Ronald D., James E. Curtis, Steven D. Brown, and Barry J. Kay. In Search of Left/Right Beliefs in the Canadian Electorate. *Canadian Journal of Political Science* 19(3): 541-63.

1974. Wilson, John. The Canadian Political Cultures: Towards a Redefinition of the Nature of the Canadian Political System. *Canadian Journal of Political Science* 7(3): 438-83.

Party Identification

2004. Stephenson, Laura B., Thomas J. Scotto, and Allan Kornberg. Slip, Sliding Away or Le Plus Ça Change ... : Canadian and American Partisanship in Comparative Perspective. *The American Review of Canadian Studies* 34(2): 283-312.

2002. Blais, André, Elisabeth Gidengil, Richard Nadeau, and Neil Nevitte. Do Party Supporters Differ? In *Citizen Politics: Research and Theory in Canadian Political Behaviour*, ed. J. Everitt and B. O'Neill, 184-201. Don Mills, ON: Oxford University Press.

2001. Blais, André, Elisabeth Gidengil, Richard Nadeau, and Neil Nevitte. Measuring Party Identification: Britain, Canada, and the United States. *Political Behavior* 23(1): 5-22.

2000. Dalton, Russell J. The Decline of Party Identifications. In *Parties without Partisans: Political Change in Advanced Industrial Democracies,* ed. Russell J. Dalton and Martin P. Wattenberg, 19-36. New York: Oxford University Press.

1998. Stewart, Marianne C., and Harold D. Clarke. The Dynamics of Party Identification in Federal Systems: The Canadian Case. *American Journal of Political Science* 42(1): 97-116.

1998. Clarke, Harold D., and Marianne C. Stewart. The Decline of Parties in the Minds of Citizens. *Annual Review of Political Science* 1(1): 357-78.

1996. Bowler, Shaun, and David J. Lanoue. New Party Challenges and Partisan Change: The Effects of Party Competition on Party Loyalty. *Political Behavior* 18(4): 327-43.

1994. Bowler, Shaun, David J. Lanoue, and Paul Savoie. Electoral Systems, Party Competition, and Strength of Partisan Attachment: Evidence from Three Countries. *The Journal of Politics* 56(4): 991-1007.

1992. Johnston, Richard. Party Identification and Campaign Dynamics. *Political Behavior* 14(3): 311-31.

1992. Johnston, Richard. Party Identification Measures in the Anglo-American Democracies: A National Survey Experiment. *American Journal of Political Science* 36(2): 542-59.

1992. Clarke, Harold, and Allan Kornberg. Risky Business: Partisan Volatility and Electoral Choice in Canada, 1988. *Electoral Studies* 11(2): 138-56.

1991. Pammett, Jon. The Effects of Individual and Contextual Variables on Partisanship in Canada. *European Journal of Political Research* 19(4): 399-412.

1990. Uslaner, Eric M. Splitting Image: Partisan Affiliations in Canada's "Two Political Worlds." *American Journal of Political Science* 34(4): 961-81.

1990. Martinez, Michael D. Partisan Reinforcement in Context and Cognition: Canadian Federal Partisanships, 1974-79. *American Journal of Political Science* 34(3): 822-45.

1989. Uslaner, Eric M. Multiple Party Identifiers in Canada: Participation and Affect. *The Journal of Politics* 51(4): 993-1003.

1989. MacDermid, R.H. The Recall of Past Partisanship: Feeble Memories or Frail Concepts? *Canadian Journal of Political Science* 22(2): 363-75.

1988. Lambert, Ronald D., James E. Curtis, Steven D. Brown, and Barry J. Kay. The Left/Right Factor in Party Identification. *Canadian Journal of Sociology* 13(4): 385-406.

1987. Stevenson, H. Michael. Ideology and Unstable Party Identification in Canada: Limited Rationality in a Brokerage Party System. *Canadian Journal of Political Science* 20(4): 813-50.

1987. Clarke, Harold D., and Marianne C. Stewart. Partisan Inconsistency and Partisan Change in Federal States: The Case of Canada. *American Journal of Political Science* 31(2): 383-407.

1986. Lambert, Ronald D., James E. Curtis, Steven D. Brown, and Barry J. Kay. Effects of Identification with Governing Parties on Feelings of Political Efficacy and Trust. *Canadian Journal of Political Science* 19(4): 705-28.

1985. Clarke, Harold, and Marianne C. Stewart. Short-Term Forces and Partisan Change in Canada: 1974-80. *Electoral Studies* 43(1): 15-35.

1984. Martinez, Michael D. Intergenerational Transfer of Canadian Partisanships. *Canadian Journal of Political Science* 17(1): 133-43.

1984. LeDuc, Lawrence, Harold D. Clarke, Jane Jenson, and Jon H. Pammett. Partisan Instability in Canada: Evidence from a New Panel Study. *The American Political Science Review* 78(2): 470-84.

1982. Wattenberg, Martin P. Party Identification and Party Images: A Comparison of Britain, Canada, Australia, and the United States. *Comparative Politics* 15(1): 23-40.

1982. Blake, Donald E. The Consistency of Inconsistency: Party Identification in Federal and Provincial Politics. *Canadian Journal of Political Science* 15(4): 691-710.

1981. LeDuc, Lawrence. The Dynamic Properties of Party Identification: A Four-Nation Comparison. *European Journal of Political Research* 9(3): 257-68.

1980. LeDuc, Lawrence, Harold D. Clarke, Jane Jenson, and Jon H. Pammett. Partisanship, Voting Behavior, and Election Outcomes in Canada. *Comparative Politics* 12(4): 401-7.

1978. Elkins, David J. Party Identification: A Conceptual Analysis. *Canadian Journal of Political Science* 11(2): 419-35.

1976. Jenson, Jane. Party Strategy and Party Identification: Some Patterns of Partisan Allegiance. *Canadian Journal of Political Science* 9(1): 27-48.

1975. Jenson, Jane. Party Loyalty in Canada: The Question of Party Identification. *Canadian Journal of Political Science* 8(4): 543-53.

1974. Sniderman, Paul M., H.D. Forbes, and Ian Melzer. Party Loyalty and Electoral Volatility: A Study of the Canadian Party System. *Canadian Journal of Political Science* 7(2): 268-88.

Regions and Regionalism

2005. DeWiel, Boris. A Comparison of North-South and West-East Differences in Political Attitudes in Canada. *The Northern Review* 25-26 (Summer 2005): 71-81.

2004. Pickup, Mark, Anthony Sayers, Rainer Knopff, and Keith Archer. Social Capital and Civic Community in Alberta. *Canadian Journal of Political Science* 37(3): 617-45.

2004. Henderson, Ailsa. Regional Political Cultures in Canada. *Canadian Journal of Political Science* 37(3): 595-615.

2004. Gidengil, Elisabeth, André Blais, Richard Nadeau, and Neil Nevitte. Language and Cultural Insecurity. In *Quebec: State and Society,* 3rd edition, ed. Alain Gagnon, 345-67. Peterborough, ON: Broadview.

2003. O'Neill, Brenda, and Lynda Erickson. Evaluating Traditionalism in the Atlantic Provinces: Voting, Public Opinion and the Electoral Project. *Atlantis* 27(2): 113-22.

2002. Young, Lisa, and Keith Archer, eds. *Regionalism and Party Politics in Canada.* Toronto: Oxford University Press.

2001. Laycock, David. BC Voters and the Canadian Alliance in the 2000 Federal Election. *BC Studies* 129: 15-21.

2000. Dow, Jon K. A Comparative Spatial Analysis of Majoritarian and Proportional Elections. *Electoral Studies* 20(1): 109-25.

1999. Gidengil, Elisabeth, André Blais, Richard Nadeau, and Neil Nevitte. Making Sense of Regional Voting in the 1997 Canadian Federal Election: Liberal and Reform Support outside Quebec. *Canadian Journal of Political Science* 32(2): 247-72.

1998. Howe, Paul. Rationality and Sovereignty Support in Quebec. *Canadian Journal of Political Science* 31(1): 31-59.

1998. Hinich, Melvin J., Michael C. Munger, and Scott de Marchi. Ideology and the Construction of Nationality: The Canadian Elections of 1993. *Public Choice* 97(3): 401-28.

1995. Blais, André, Neil Nevitte, Elisabeth Gidengil, Henry E. Brady, and Richard Johnston. L'élection fédérale de 1993: Le comportement électoral des Québécois. *Revue québécoise de science politique* 27: 15-49.

1995. Bakvis, Herman, and Laura G. Macpherson. Quebec Block Voting and the Canadian Electoral System. *Canadian Journal of Political Science* 28(4): 659-92.

1994. Stewart, Ian. *Roasting Chestnuts: The Mythology of Maritime Political Culture.* Vancouver: UBC Press.

1994. Newman, Saul. Ethnoregional Parties: A Comparative Perspective. *Regional and Federal Studies* 4(2): 28-66.

1993. Curtis, James E., and Philip G. White. Proximity or Regional Cultures? A Re-Examination of Patterns of Francophone-Anglophone Liking of Each Other. *Canadian Journal of Sociology* 18(3): 303-11.

1991. Blais, André. Le clivage linguistique au Canada. *Recherches sociographiques* 32(1): 43-54.

1990. White, Philip G., and James E. Curtis. Language, Regions and Feelings toward Outgroups: Analyses for 1968 and 1984. *Canadian Journal of Sociology* 15(4): 441-62.

1990. Gidengil, Elisabeth. Centres and Peripheries: The Political Culture of Dependency. *Canadian Review of Sociology and Anthropology* 27: 23-48.

1989. Curtis, James E., Steven D. Brown, Ronald D. Lambert, and Barry J. Kay. Affiliating with Voluntary Associations: Canadian-American Comparisons. *The Canadian Journal of Sociology* 14(2): 143-61.

1982. Kornberg, Allan, and Keith Archer. A Note on Quebec Attitudes toward Constitutional Options. *Law and Contemporary Problems* 45(4): 71-85.

1981. Aunger, Edmund A. *In Search of Political Stability: A Comparative Study of New Brunswick and Northern Ireland.* Montreal: McGill-Queen's University Press.

1980. Ornstein, Michael D., H. Michael Stevenson, and A. Paul Williams. Region, Class and Political Culture in Canada. *Canadian Journal of Political Science* 13(2): 227-71.

1980. Johnston, Richard. Federal and Provincial Voting: Contemporary Patterns and Historical Evolution. In *Small Worlds: Provinces and Parties in Canadian Political Life,* ed. D. Elkins and R. Simeon, 31-78. Toronto: Methuen.

1980. Elkins, D.J., and R. Simeon. *Small Worlds: Provinces and Parties in Canadian Political Life.* Toronto: Methuen.

1977. LeDuc, Lawrence. Canadian Attitudes towards Quebec Independence. *Public Opinion Quarterly* 41(3): 347-55.

1977. Beck, Nathaniel, and John C. Pierce. Political Involvement and Party Allegiances in Canada and the United States. *International Journal of Comparative Sociology* 18: 23-43.

1976. Curtis, James E., and Ronald D. Lambert. Voting, Election Interest, and Age: National Findings for English and French Canadians. *Canadian Journal of Political Science* 9(2): 293-307.

1974. Simeon, Richard, and David J. Elkins. Regional Political Cultures in Canada. *Canadian Journal of Political Science* 7(3): 397-437.

1974. Schwartz, Mildred A. *Politics and Territory: The Sociology of Regional Persistence in Canada.* Montreal: McGill-Queen's University Press.

1970. Schwartz, Mildred A. Attachments to Province and Region in the Prairie Provinces. In *Proceedings of One Prairie Province? A Question for Canada and Selected Papers,* ed. D.K. Elton, 101-5. Lethbridge, AB: Lethbridge Herald.

Social Class

2004. Flap, Henk, and Beate Volker. *Creation and Returns of Social Capital: A New Research Program.* London: Routledge.

2002. Gidengil, Elisabeth. The Class Voting Conundrum. In *Political Sociology: Canadian Perspectives,* ed. Douglas Baer, 274-87. Don Mills, ON: Oxford University Press.

2001. Fearon, Gervan. Labor Union Political Contributions and Campaign Spending. *International Advances in Economic Research* 7(2): 269.

1996. Nakhaie, M. Reza, and Robert Arnold. Class Position, Class Ideology, and Class Voting: Mobilization of Support for the New Democratic Party in the Canadian Election of 1984. *Canadian Review of Sociology and Anthropology* 33(2): 181-212.

1996. Langford, Tom. The Politics of the Canadian New Middle Class: Public/Private Sector Cleavage in the 1980s. *Canadian Journal of Sociology* 21(2): 153-83.

1993. Lambert, Ronald D., and James E. Curtis. Perceived Party Choice and Class Voting. *Canadian Journal of Political Science* 26(2): 273-86.

1992. Nakhaie, M. Reza. Class and Voting Consistency in Canada: Analyses Bearing on the Mobilization Thesis. *Canadian Journal of Sociology* 17: 275-99.

1991. Langford, Tom. Left/Right Orientation and Political Attitudes: A Reappraisal and Class Comparison. *Canadian Journal of Political Science* 24(3): 475-98.

1991. Johnston, Richard. The Geography of Class and Religion in Canadian Elections. In *Voting in Canada*, ed. J. Wearing, 108-35. Toronto: Copp Clark Pitman.

1991. Blais, André, Donald E. Blake, and Stéphane Dion. The Voting Behavior of Bureaucrats. In *The Budget-Maximizing Bureaucrat: Appraisals and Evidence*, ed. A. Blais and S. Dion, 205-30. Pittsburgh: University of Pittsburgh Press.

1990. Fletcher, Joseph F., and H.D. Forbes. Education, Occupation, and Vote in Canada, 1965-1984. *Canadian Review of Sociology and Anthropology* 27(4): 441-61.

1990. Blais, André, Donald E. Blake, and Stéphane Dion. The Public/ Private Sector Cleavage in North America. *Comparative Political Studies* 23(3): 381-404.

1989. Gidengil, Elisabeth. Class and Region in Canadian Voting: A Dependency Interpretation. *Canadian Journal of Political Science* 22(3): 563-87.

1989. Brym, Robert J., Michael W. Gillespie, and Rhonda L. Lenton. Power, Class Mobilization, and Class Voting: The Canadian Case. *Canadian Journal of Sociology* 14(1): 25-44.

1987. Pammett, Jon. Class Voting and Class Consciousness in Canada. *Canadian Review of Sociology and Anthropology* 24: 269-89.

1987. Lambert, Ronald D., James E. Curtis, Steven D. Brown, and Barry J. Kay. Social Class, Left/Right Political Orientations, and Subjective Class Voting in Provincial and Federal Elections. *Canadian Review of Sociology and Anthropology* 24(4): 526-49.

1986. Lambert, Ronald D., Steven D. Brown, James E. Curtis, and Barry J. Kay. Canadians' Beliefs about Differences between Social Classes. *Canadian Journal of Sociology* 11(4): 379-99.

1982. Zipp, John F., and Joel Smith. A Structural Analysis of Class Voting. *Social Forces* 60(3): 738-59.

1982. Ogmundson, Rick, and M. Ng. On the Inference of Voter Motivation: A Comparison of the Subjective Class Vote in Canada and the United Kingdom. *Canadian Journal of Sociology* 7(2): 141-60.

1982. Hunter, Alfred A. On Class, Status, and Voting in Canada. *Canadian Journal of Sociology* 7(1): 19-39.

1981. Erickson, Bonnie H. Region, Knowledge, and Class Voting in Canada. *Canadian Journal of Sociology* 6(2): 121-44.

1979. Myles, John F. Differences in the Canadian and American Class Vote: Fact or Pseudofact? *American Journal of Sociology* 84(5): 1232-37.

1979. Lambert, Ronald D., and Alfred A. Hunter. Social Stratification, Voting Behaviour, and the Images of Canadian Federal Political Parties. *Canadian Review of Sociology and Anthropology* 16: 287-304.

1977. Kay, Barry J. An Examination of Class and Left-Right Party Images in Canadian Voting. *Canadian Journal of Political Science* 10(1): 127-43.

1976. Ogmundson, Rick. Mass-Elite Linkages and Class Issues in Canada. *Canadian Review of Sociology and Anthropology* 13: 1-11.

1975. Ogmundson, Rick. Party Class Images and the Class Vote in Canada. *American Sociological Review* 40(4): 506-12.

1975. Ogmundson, Rick. On the Use of Party Image Variables to Measure the Political Distinctiveness of a Class Vote: The Canadian Case. *Canadian Journal of Sociology* 1(2): 169-77.

1975. Ogmundson, Rick. On the Measurement of Party Class Position: The Case of Canadian Federal Political Parties. *Canadian Review of Sociology and Anthropology* 12: 565-76.

1971. McDonald, Lynn. Social Class and Voting: A Study of the 1968 Canadian Federal Election in Ontario. *British Journal of Sociology* 22(4): 410-22.

Women and Politics

2005. Gidengil, Elisabeth, Elisabeth Goodyear-Grant, Neil Nevitte, and André Blais. Gender, Knowledge, and Social Capital. In *Gender and Social Capital*, ed. B. O'Neill and E. Gidengil, 241-72. New York: Routledge.

2005. Gidengil, Elisabeth, Matthew Hennigar, André Blais, and Neil Nevitte. Explaining the Gender Gap in Support for the New Right. *Comparative Political Studies* 38(10): 1171-95.

2003. O'Neill, Brenda. On the Same Wavelength? Feminist Attitudes across Generations of Canadian Women. In *Women and Electoral Politics in Canada*, ed. M. Tremblay and L. Trimble, 177-91. Don Mills, ON: Oxford University Press.

2003. Gidengil, Elisabeth, André Blais, Richard Nadeau, and Neil Nevitte. Women to the Left? Gender Differences in Political Beliefs and Policy

Preferences. In *Women and Electoral Politics in Canada*, ed. M. Tremblay and L. Trimble, 140-59. Oxford: Oxford University Press.

2002. O'Neill, Brenda. "What Do Women Think?" *Horizons* 16(2): 20-23.

2002. Everitt, Joanna. Gender Gaps on Social Welfare Issues: Why Do Women Care? In *Citizen Politics: Research and Theory in Canadian Political Behaviour*, ed. B. O'Neill and J. Everitt, 110-25. Don Mills, ON: Oxford University Press.

2002. Erickson, Lynda, and Brenda O'Neill. The Gender Gap and the Changing Woman Voter in Canada. *International Political Science Review* 23(4): 373-92.

2001. O'Neill, Brenda. A Simple Difference of Opinion? Religious Beliefs and Gender Gaps in Public Opinion in Canada. *Canadian Journal of Political Science* 34(2): 275-98.

2001. Demarais, Serge, and James Curtis. Gender and Perceived Income Entitlement among Full-Time Workers: Analyses for Canadian National Samples, 1984 and 1994. *Basic and Applied Social Psychology.* 23(3): 157-68.

2001. Black, Jerome H., and Lynda Erickson. Similarity, Compensation, or Difference? *Women and Politics* 21(4): 1-38.

2000. Banducci, Susan, and Jeffrey Karp. Gender, Leadership and Choice in Multiparty Systems. *Political Research Quarterly* 53(4): 815-48.

1998. O'Neill, Brenda. The Relevance of Leader Gender to Voting in the 1993 Canadian National Election. *International Journal of Canadian Studies* 17(Spring): 105-30.

1998. Everitt, Joanna. Public Opinion and Social Movements: The Women's Movement and the Gender Gap in Canada. *Canadian Journal of Political Science* 31(4): 743-65.

1995. O'Neill, Brenda. The Gender Gap: Re-evaluating Theory and Method. In *Changing Methods: Feminists Reflect on Practice*, ed. S. Burt and L. Code, 327-55. Peterborough, ON: Broadview.

1995. Gidengil, Elisabeth. Economic Man – Social Woman? The Case of the Gender Gap in Support for the Canada-US Free Trade Agreement. *Comparative Political Studies* 28(3): 384-408.

1992. Lenton, Rhonda L. Home versus Career: Attitudes towards Women's Work among Canadian Women and Men. *Canadian Journal of Sociology* 17(1): 89-98.

1988. Kay, Barry J., Ronald D. Lambert, Steven D. Brown, and James E. Curtis. Feminist Consciousness and the Canadian Electorate: A

Review of National Election Studies 1965-1984. *Women and Politics* 8(2): 1-21.

1987. Kay, Barry J., Ronald D. Lambert, Steven D. Brown, and James E. Curtis. Gender and Political Activity in Canada, 1965-1984. *Canadian Journal of Political Science* 20(4): 851-63.

1983. Bashevkin, Sylvia. Social Change and Political Partisanship: The Development of Women's Attitudes in Quebec, 1965-1979. *Comparative Political Studies* 16(2): 147-71.

1979. Black, Jerome H., and Nancy E. McGlen. Male-Female Political Involvement Differentials in Canada, 1965-1974. *Canadian Journal of Political Science* 12(3): 471-97.

Religion

2005. Blais, André. Accounting for the Electoral Success of the Liberal Party in Canada. Presidential Address to the Canadian Political Science Association. *Canadian Journal of Political Science* 38(4): 821-40.

1997. Mendelsohn, Matthew, and Richard Nadeau. The Religious Cleavage and the Media in Canada. *Canadian Journal of Political Science* 30(1): 129-46.

1991. Brym, Robert J., and Rhonda L. Lenton. The Distribution of Anti-Semitism in Canada in 1984. *The Canadian Journal of Sociology – Cahiers Canadiens de Sociologie* 16(4): 411-18.

1985. Johnston, Richard. The Reproduction of the Religious Cleavage in Canadian Elections. *Canadian Journal of Political Science* 18(1): 99-113.

1979. Lijphart, Arend. Religious vs. Linguistic vs. Class Voting: The "Crucial Experiment" of Comparing Belgium, Canada, South Africa, and Switzerland. *American Political Science Review* 73(2): 442-58.

1974. Irvine, William P. Explaining the Religious Basis of the Canadian Partisan Identity: Success on the Third Try. *Canadian Journal of Political Science* 7(3): 560-63.

1969. McDonald, Lynn. Religion and Voting: A Study of the 1968 Canadian Federal Election in Ontario. *Canadian Review of Sociology and Anthropology* 6: 129-44.

1967. Meisel, John. Religious Affiliation and Electoral Behaviour: A Case Study. In *Voting in Canada*, ed. J. Courtney, 481-96. Scarborough, ON: Prentice-Hall.

Age

2005. Gidengil, Elisabeth, André Blais, Joanna Everitt, Patrick Fournier, and Neil Nevitte. Missing the Message: Young Adults and the Election Issues. *Electoral Insight* 7(1): 6-11.

2004. Rubenson, Daniel, André Blais, Patrick Fournier, Elisabeth Gidengil, and Neil Nevitte. Accounting for the Age Gap in Turnout. *Acta Politica* 39(4): 407-21.

2004. Blais, André, Elisabeth Gidengil, and Neil Nevitte. Where Does Turnout Decline Come From? *European Journal of Political Research* 43(2): 221-36.

2003. O'Neill, Brenda. Examining Declining Electoral Turnout among Canada's Youth. *Electoral Insight* 5(2): 15-9.

2003. Howe, Paul. Where Have All the Voters Gone? *Inroads Journal* 12: 74-83.

2003. Adsett, Margaret. Change in Political Era and Demographic Weight as Explanations of Youth "Disenfranchisement" in Federal Elections in Canada, 1965-2000. *Journal of Youth Studies* 6(3): 247-64.

2001. O'Neill, Brenda. Generational Patterns in the Political Opinions and Behaviour of Canadians: Separating the Wheat from the Chaff. *Policy Matters* 2(5).

1997. Martinez, Michael D. Losing Canada? Generation X and the Constitutional Crisis. In *After the Boom: The Politics of Generation X*, ed. S.C. Craig and S. Bennett, 145-66. Boulder, CO: Rowman and Littlefield.

1992. Johnston, Richard. Political Generations and Electoral Change in Canada. *British Journal of Political Science* 22(1): 93-115.

Other Socio-Demographics

2005. Byrne, Joseph M., and Thomas Rathwell. Medical Savings Accounts and the Canada Health Act: Complimentary or Contradictory. *Health Policy* 72(3): 367-79.

2004. Wilson, J. Matthew, and Michael Lusztig. The Spouse in the House: What Explains the Marriage Gap in Canada? *Canadian Journal of Political Science* 37: 979-95.

2004. Walks, R. Alan. Place of Residence, Party Preferences, and Political Attitudes in Canadian Cities and Suburbs. *Journal of Urban Affairs* 26(3): 269-95.

2003. Gidengil, Elisabeth, and Joanna Everitt. Talking Tough: Gender and Reported Speech in Campaign News Coverage. *Political Communication* 20(3): 209-32.

2003. Blake, Donald E. Environmental Determinants of Racial Attitudes among White Canadians. *Canadian Journal of Political Science* 36(3): 491-510.

2003. Andersen, Robert, and Anthony Heath. Social Identities and Political Cleavages: The Role of Political Context. *Journal of the Royal Statistical Society Series A* 166(3): 301-27.

2001. Turcotte, Martin. Did the Rural/Urban Opposition Do Its Time? The Case of Moral Traditionalism. *Canadian Journal of Sociology* 26(1): 1-29.

2001. Cutler, Fred, and Richard Jenkins. Where One Lives and What One Thinks: Implications of Rural-Urban Opinion Cleavages for Canadian Federalism. In *Canada: The State of the Federation 2001: Canadian Political Culture(s) in Transition*, ed. H. Telford and H. Lazar, 367-390. Montreal: McGill-Queen's University Press for the Institute for Intergovernmental Relations, Queen's University.

1994. Simpson, J.H. The Structure of Attitudes toward Body Issues in the American and Canadian Populations: An Elementary Analysis. In *Abortion Politics in the United States and Canada: Studies in Public Opinion*, ed. T.G. Jelen and M.A. Chandler, 145-60. Westport, CT: Praeger.

1992. Langford, T. Social Experiences and Variations in Economic Beliefs among Canadian Workers. *Canadian Review of Sociology and Anthropology* 29(4): 453-487.

1991. Chui, Tina W.L., James E. Curtis, and Ronald D. Lambert. Immigrant Background and Political Participation: Examining Generational Patterns. *Canadian Journal of Sociology* 16(4): 375-96.

1988. Lambert, Ronald D., James E. Curtis, Barry J. Kay, and Steven D. Brown. The Social Sources of Political Knowledge. *Canadian Journal of Political Science* 21(2): 359-74.

1982. Black, Jerome H. Immigrant Political Adaptation in Canada: Some Tentative Findings. *Canadian Journal of Political Science* 15(1): 3-27.

1978. Blake, Donald E. Constituency Contexts and Canadian Elections: An Exploratory Study. *Canadian Journal of Political Science* 11(2): 279-305.

Short-Term Factors

Issues

2005. Matthews, J. Scott. The Political Foundations of Support for Same-Sex Marriage in Canada. *Canadian Journal of Political Science* 38(4): 841-66.

2005. Lusztig, Michael, and J. Matthew Wilson. A New Right? Moral Issues and Partisan Change in Canada. *Social Science Quarterly* 86(1): 109-28.

2005. Endersby, James W. Nonpolicy Issues and the Spatial Theory of Voting. *Quality and Quantity* 28(3): 251-65.

2004. Noel, A., J.P. Therien, and S. Dallaire. Divided over Internationalism: The Canadian Public and Development Assistance. *Canadian Public Policy* 30(1): 29-46.

2004. Blais, André, Mathieu Turgeon, Elisabeth Gidengil, Neil Nevitte, and Richard Nadeau. Which Matters Most? Comparing the Impact of Issues and the Economy in American, British, and Canadian Elections. *British Journal of Political Science* 34(3): 555-63.

2003. Fournier, Patrick, André Blais, Richard Nadeau, Elisabeth Gidengil, and Neil Nevitte. Issue Importance and Performance Voting. *Political Behavior* 25(1): 51-67.

2002. Blais, André, Richard Nadeau, Elisabeth Gidengil, and Neil Nevitte. The Impact of Issues and the Economy in the 1997 Canadian Federal Election. *Canadian Journal of Political Science* 35(2): 409-21.

2001. Nadeau, Richard, André Blais, Elisabeth Gidengil, and Neil Nevitte. Perceptions of Party Competence in the 1997 Election. In *Party Politics in Canada*, 8th edition, ed. H. Thorburn and A. Whitehorn, 413-30. Toronto: Prentice-Hall.

2001. Mendelsohn, Matthew. Probing the Aftermath of Seattle: Canadian Public Opinion on International Trade, 1980-2000. *International Journal* 56(2): 234-60.

2000. Alvarez, R.M., J. Nagler, and J. Willette. Measuring the Relative Impact of Issues and the Economy in Democratic Elections. *Electoral Studies* 19(2-3): 237-53.

1997. Blake, Donald E., Neil Guppy, and Peter Urmetzer. Canadian Public Opinion and Environmental Action: Evidence from British Columbia. *Canadian Journal of Political Science* 30(3): 451-72.

1993. Johnston, Richard, André Blais, Henry E. Brady, and Jean Crête. Free Trade in Canadian Elections: Issue Evolution in the Long and the Short Run. In *Agenda Formation,* ed. W. Riker, 231-54. Ann Arbor: University of Michigan Press.

1991. Johnston, Richard, André Blais, Henry E. Brady, and Jean Crête. Free Trade and the Dynamics of the 1988 Canadian Election. In *The Ballot and Its Message,* ed. J. Wearing, 315-39. Toronto: Copp Clark Pitman.

1990. Nadeau, Richard, and André Blais. Do Canadians Distinguish between Parties? Perceptions of Party Competence. *Canadian Journal of Political Science* 23(2): 317-33.

1989. Blais, André. Public Opinion on Free Trade in the 1988 Election Campaign. In *The Free Trade Agreement of 1988: Implications for the Future of Canadian-American Relations,* ed. J. Jenson. Cambridge, MA: Center for International Affairs, Harvard University.

1985. Archer, Keith, and Allan Kornberg. Issue Perceptions and Electoral Behaviour in an Age of Restraint, 1974-1980. *American Review of Canadian Studies* 15 (Spring): 68-89.

1977. Pammett, Jon H., Lawrence LeDuc, Jane Jenson, and Harold D. Clarke. The Perception and Impact of Issues in the 1974 Federal Election. *Canadian Journal of Political Science* 10(1): 93-126.

Economic Voting

2005. Duch, Raymond M., and Randy Stevenson. Context and the Economic Vote: A Multilevel Analysis. *Political Analysis* 13(4): 387-409.

2002. Godbout, Jean-François, and Éric Bélanger. La dimension régionale du vote économique canadien aux élections fédérales de 1988 à 2000. *Canadian Journal of Political Science,* 35(3): 567-88.

2002. Duch, Raymond M., and Harvey D. Palmer. Heterogeneous Perceptions of Economic Conditions in Cross-National Perspective. In *Economic Voting,* ed. H. Dorussen and M. Taylor, 139-72. New York: Routledge.

2002. Cutler, Fred. Local Economies, Local Policy Impacts, and Federal Electoral Behaviour in Canada. *Canadian Journal of Political Science* 35(2): 347-82.

2001. Hellwig, Timothy T. Interdependence, Government Constraints, and Economic Voting. *Journal of Politics* 63(4): 1141-62.

2000. Royed, Terry J., Kevin M. Leyden, and Stephen A. Borrelli. Is "Clarity of Responsibility" Important for Economic Voting? Revisiting Powell and Whitten's Hypothesis. *British Journal of Political Science* 30(4): 669-85.

2000. Nadeau, Richard, André Blais, Neil Nevitte, and Elisabeth Gidengil. It's Unemployment, Stupid! Why Perceptions about the Job Situation Hurt the Liberals in the 1997 Election. *Canadian Public Policy* 26(1): 77-94.

1998. Guérin, Daniel, and Richard Nadeau. Clivage linguistique et vote économique au Canada. *Canadian Journal of Political Science* 32(3): 557-72.

1993. Nadeau, Richard, and André Blais. Explaining Election Outcomes in Canada: Economy and Politics. *Canadian Journal of Political Science* 26(4): 775-90.

1992. Happy, J.R. The Effect of Economic and Fiscal Performance on Incumbency Voting: The Canadian Case. *British Journal of Political Science* 22(1): 117-30.

1991. Brander, J.A. Election Polls, Free-Trade, and the Stock-Market: Evidence from the 1988 Canadian General Election. *Canadian Journal of Economics – Revue canadienne D'économique* 24(4): 827-43.

1989. Uslaner, Eric M. Looking Forward and Looking Backward: Prospective and Retrospective Voting in the 1980 Federal Elections in Canada. *British Journal of Political Science* 19(4): 495-513.

1989. Happy, J.R. Economic Performance and Retrospective Voting in Canadian Federal Elections. *Canadian Journal of Political Science* 22(2): 377-87.

1988. Erickson, Lynda. CCF-NDP Popularity and the Economy. *Canadian Journal of Political Science* 21(1): 99-116.

1988. Archer, Keith, and Marquis Johnson. Inflation, Unemployment and Canadian Federal Voting Behaviour. *Canadian Journal of Political Science* 21(3): 569-84.

1986. Happy, J.R. Voter Sensitivity to Economic Conditions: A Canadian-American Comparison. *Comparative Politics* 19(1): 45-56.

1978. Munton, Don, and Dale H. Poel. Electoral Accountability and Canadian Foreign Policy: The Case of Foreign Investment. *International Journal* 33(1): 217-47.

Strategic Voting and Preference Maximization

2005. Kedar, Orit. When Moderate Voters Prefer Extreme Parties: Policy Balancing in Parliamentary Elections. *American Political Science Review* 99(2): 185-99.

2005. Justice, J.W., and David J. Lanoue. Strategic and Sincere Voting in a One-Sided Election: The Canadian Federal Election of 1997. *Social Science Quarterly* 86(1): 129-46.

2005. Blais, André, Robert Young, and Martin Turcotte. Direct or Indirect? Assessing Two Approaches to the Measurement of Strategic Voting. *Electoral Studies* 24(2): 163-76.

2004. Blais, André, and Mathieu Turgeon. How Good are Voters at Sorting Out the Weakest Candidate in Their Constituency? *Electoral Studies* 23(3): 455-61.

2002. Blais, André. Why Is There So Little Strategic Voting in Canadian Plurality Rule Elections? *Political Studies* 50(3): 445-54.

2001. Blais, André, Richard Nadeau, Elisabeth Gidengil, and Neil Nevitte. The Formation of Party Preferences: Testing the Proximity and Directional Models. *European Journal of Political Research* 40(1): 81-91.

2001. Blais, André, Richard Nadeau, Elisabeth Gidengil, and Neil Nevitte. Measuring Strategic Voting in Multiparty Plurality Elections. *Electoral Studies* 20(3): 343-52.

2000. Johnston, Richard, Patrick Fournier, and Richard W. Jenkins. Party Location and Party Support: Unpacking Competing Models. *The Journal of Politics* 62(4): 1145-60.

1998. Lanoue, David J., and Shaun Bowler. Picking the Winners: Perceptions of Party Viability and Their Impact on Voting Behavior. *Social Science Quarterly* 79(2): 361-77.

1996. Nieuwbeerta, Paul. The Democratic Class Struggle in Postwar Societies: Class Voting in Twenty Countries, 1945-1990. *Acta Sociologica* 39(4): 345-83.

1996. Blais, André, and Richard Nadeau. Measuring Strategic Voting: A Two-Step Procedure. *Electoral Studies* 15(1): 39-52.

1994. Koop, Gary, and Dale J. Poirier. Rank-Ordered Logit Models: An Empirical Analysis of Ontario Voter Preferences. *Journal of Applied Econometrics* 9(4): 369-88.

1992. Bowler, Shaun, and David J. Lanoue. Strategic and Protest Voting for Third Parties: The Case of the Canadian NDP. *Western Political Quarterly* 45(2): 485-99.

1978. Black, Jerome H. The Multicandidate Calculus of Voting: Application to Canadian Federal Elections. *American Journal of Political Science* 22(3): 609-38.

Media

2004. Bastien, Frédérick. Branchés, informés et engagés? Les Canadiens, Internet et l'élection fédérale de 2000. *Politique et Sociétés.* 23(1): 171-91.

2003. Dobrzynska, Agnieszka, André Blais, and Richard Nadeau. Do the Media Have a Direct Impact on the Vote? *International Journal of Public Opinion Research* 15(1): 27-43.

1999. Jenkins, Richard W. How Much Is Too Much? Media Attention and Popular Support for an Insurgent Party. *Political Communication* 16(4): 429-45.

1999. Antecol, Michael, and James W. Endersby. Newspaper Consumption and Beliefs about Canada and Quebec. *Political Communication* 16(1): 95-112.

1996. Mendelsohn, Matthew. Television News Frames in the 1993 Canadian Election. In *Seeing Ourselves: Media Power and Policy in Canada,* 2nd edition, ed. H. Holmes and D. Taras, 8-22. Toronto: Harcourt Brace.

1996. Mendelsohn, Matthew. The Magnification and Minimization of Social Cleavages by the Broadcast and Narrowcast News Media. *International Journal of Public Opinion Research* 8(4): 374-89.

1996. Mendelsohn, Matthew. The Media and Interpersonal Communications: The Priming of Issues, Leaders, and Party Identification. *The Journal of Politics* 58(1): 112-25.

1996. Blais, André, and M. Martin Boyer. Assessing the Impact of Televised Debates: The Case of the 1988 Canadian Election. *British Journal of Political Science* 26(2): 143-64.

1994. Mendelsohn, Matthew. The Media's Persuasive Effects: The Priming of Leadership in the 1988 Canadian Election. *Canadian Journal of Political Science* 27(1): 81-97.

1993. Mendelsohn, Matthew. Television's Frames in the 1988 Canadian Election. *Canadian Journal of Communication* 19(2): 149-71.

1991. Barr, Cathy Widdis. The Importance and Potential of Leaders' Debates. In *Media and Voters in Canadian Election Campaigns,* ed. F.J. Fletcher, 107-56. Toronto: Dundurn.

1988. Wagenberg, R.H., W.C. Soderlund, W.I. Romanow, and E.D. Briggs. Campaigns, Images, and Polls: Mass Media Coverage of the 1984 Canadian Election. *Canadian Journal of Political Science* 21(1): 117-29.

1985. LeDuc, Lawrence, and Richard Price. Great Debates: The Televised Leadership Debates of 1979. *Canadian Journal of Political Science* 18(1): 135-53.

Electoral Campaigns

2004. Fournier, Patrick, Richard Nadeau, André Blais, Elisabeth Gidengil, and Neil Nevitte. Time of Voting Decision and Susceptibility to Campaign Effects. *Electoral Studies* 23(4): 661-81.

2004. Blais, André. How Many Voters Change Their Minds in the Month Preceding an Election? *PS: Political Science and Politics* 37(4): 801-3.

2003. Blais, André, Elisabeth Gidengil, Richard Nadeau, and Neil Nevitte. Campaign Dynamics in the 2000 Canadian Election: How the Leader Debates Salvaged the Conservative Party. *PS: Political Science and Politics* 36(1): 45-50.

2002. Jenkins, Richard W. How Campaigns Matter in Canada: Priming and Learning as Explanations for the Reform Party's 1993 Campaign Success. *Canadian Journal of Political Science* 35(3): 383-408.

2002. Gidengil, Elisabeth, André Blais, Neil Nevitte, and Richard Nadeau. Priming and Campaign Context: Evidence from Recent Canadian Elections. In *Do Political Campaigns Matter? Campaign Effects in Elections and Referendums*, ed. D. Farrell and R. Schmitt-Beck, 76-91. London: Routledge.

2001. Johnston, Richard. Capturing Campaigns in National Election Studies. In *Election Studies: What's Their Use?* ed. E. Katz and Y. Warshel, 149-72. Boulder, CO: Westview.

2001. Andersen, R., and J. Fox. Pre-Election Polls and the Dynamics of the 1997 Canadian Federal Election. *Electoral Studies* 20(1): 87-108.

1999. Carty, R.K., and Munroe Eagles. Do Local Campaigns Matter? Campaign Spending, the Local Canvass, and Party Support in Canada. *Electoral Studies* 18(1): 69-87.

1999. Blais, André, Richard Nadeau, Elisabeth Gidengil, and Neil Nevitte. Campaign Dynamics in the 1997 Canadian Election. *Canadian Public Policy* 15(2): 197-205.

1989. Coyte, Peter C., and Stuart Landon. The Impact of Competition on Advertising: The Case of Political Campaign Expenditures. *Canadian Journal of Economics* 22(4): 795-818.

1984. Black, Jerome H. Revisiting the Effects of Canvassing on Voting Behaviour. *Canadian Journal of Political Science* 17(2): 351-74.

Leaders and Candidates

2004. Blais, André, Elisabeth Gidengil, Neil Nevitte, and Richard Nadeau. Do (Some) Canadian Voters Punish a Prime Minister for Calling a Snap Election? *Political Studies* 52(2): 307-23.

2003. Blais, André, Elisabeth Gidengil, Agnieszka Dobrzynska, Neil Nevitte, and Richard Nadeau. Does the Local Candidate Matter? Candidate Effects in the Canadian Election of 2000. *Canadian Journal of Political Science* 36(3): 657-64.

2002. Johnston, Richard. Prime Ministerial Contenders in Canada. In *Leaders' Personalities and the Outcomes of Democratic Elections*, ed. A. King, 158-83. Oxford: Oxford University Press.

2002. Cutler, Fred. The Simplest Shortcut of All: Sociodemographic Characteristics and Electoral Choice. *The Journal of Politics* 64(2): 466-90.

2000. Blais, André, Neil Nevitte, Elisabeth Gidengil, and Richard Nadeau. Do People Have Feelings toward Leaders about Whom They Say They Know Nothing? *Public Opinion Quarterly* 64(4): 452-63.

1999. Mendelsohn, Matthew, and Richard Nadeau. The Rise and Fall of Candidates in Canadian Election Campaigns. *Harvard International Review of Press/Politics* 4(2): 63-76.

1991. Lanoue, David J. Debates That Mattered: Voters' Reaction to the 1984 Canadian Leadership Debates. *Canadian Journal of Political Science* 24(1): 51-65.

1988. Brown, Steven D., Ronald D. Lambert, Barry J. Kay, and James E. Curtis. In the Eye of the Beholder: Leader Images in Canada. *Canadian Journal of Political Science* 21(4): 729-55.

1982. Irvine, William P. Does the Candidate Make a Difference? The Macro-Politics and Micro-Politics of Getting Elected. *Canadian Journal of Political Science* 15(4): 755-82.

1982. Clarke, Harold D., Jane Jenson, Lawrence LeDuc, and Jon Pammett. Voting Behaviour and the Outcome of the 1979 Federal Election: The Impact of Leaders and Issues. *Canadian Journal of Political Science* 15(3): 517-52.

1970. Winham, Gilbert R., and Robert B. Cunningham. Party Leader Images in the 1968 Federal Election. *Canadian Journal of Political Science* 3(1): 37-55.

Miscellaneous (not counted in totals for Appendix figures)

2005. Tellier, Geneviève. *Les dépenses des gouvernements provinciaux: l'influence des partis politiques, des élections et de l'opinion publique sur la variation des budgets publics.* Sainte-Foy, QC: Presses de l'Université Laval.

2005. Parent, Michael, Christine A. Vandebeek, and Andrew C. Gemino. Building Citizen Trust through E-Government. *Government Information Quarterly* 22(4): 720-36.

2005. Matthews, J. Scott, and Lynda Erickson. Public Opinion and Social Citizenship in Canada. *Canadian Review of Sociology and Anthropology* 42(4): 373-401.

2004. Young, Lisa, and Joanna Everitt. *Advocacy Groups.* Vancouver: UBC Press.

2002. Beaulieu, Eugene. Factor or Industry Cleavages in Trade Policy? An Empirical Analysis of the Stolper-Samuelson Theorem. *Economics and Politics* 14(2): 99-132.

2002. Archer, Keith, Roger Gibbins, Rainer Knopff, Heather MacIvor, and Leslie A. Pal. *Parameters of Power: Canada's Political Institutions*, 3rd edition. Scarborough, ON: Nelson.

2000. Clarke, Harold D. Refutations Affirmed: Conversations Concerning the Euro-Barometer Values Battery. *Political Research Quarterly* 53(3): 477-94.

2000. Bashevkin, Sylvia. Rethinking Retrenchment: North American Social Policy during the Early Clinton and Chrétien Years. *Canadian Journal of Political Science* 33(1): 7-36.

1997. Balistreri, Edward J. The Performance of the Heckscher-Ohlin-Vanek Model in Predicting Endogenous Policy Forces at the Individual Level. *Canadian Journal of Economics* 30(1): 1-17.

1993. Brym, Robert J., and Andrei Degtyarev. Anti-Semitism in Moscow: Results of an October 1992 Survey. *Slavic Review* 52(1): 1-12.

1990. Meng, Ronald A,. and Douglas A. Smith. The Valuation of Risk of Death in Public Sector Decision-Making. *Canadian Public Policy/ Analyse de Politiques* 16(2): 137-44.

1986. Johnston, Richard. *Public Opinion and Public Policy in Canada: Questions of Confidence.* Toronto: University of Toronto Press.

1971. Van Loon, Richard, and Michael Whittington. *The Canadian Political System: Environment, Structure, and Process.* New York: McGraw-Hill.

Contributors

Éric Bélanger is an associate professor of political science at McGill University. His research interests are in the areas of Quebec and Canadian Politics, political parties and party systems, and public opinion and voting behaviour.

Antoine Bilodeau is an associate professor of political science at Concordia University. His research focuses on the political integration of immigrants and attitudes toward immigration and ethnic diversity.

André Blais is a professor of political science at the Université de Montréal, where he holds a Canada Research Chair in electoral studies. His research interests include electoral participation, electoral systems, electoral behaviour, and methodology. He is the leader of the Making Electoral Democracy Work project and chair of the planning committee of the Comparative Study of Electoral Systems.

Harold D. Clarke is Ashbel Smith Professor in the School of Economic, Political, and Policy Sciences at the University of Texas at Dallas, and an adjunct professor in the Department of Government at the University of Essex. His research focuses on electoral choice and the political economy of party support in Great Britain, the United States, and Canada, as well as statistics, survey research, time series analysis, structural equation modeling, public opinion, and political attitudes and behaviour.

Elisabeth Gidengil is Hiram Mills Professor in the Department of Political Science at McGill University and director of the Centre for the Study of Democratic Citizenship. Her areas of interest include voting behaviour and public opinion, media and politics, political engagement, and biopolitics.

Richard Johnston is a professor of political science at the University of British Columbia. His interests are in the area of electoral politics, and he currently holds a Canada Research Chair in public opinion, elections, and representation. He is also the Marie Curie Research Fellow at the European University Institute, Florence.

Mebs Kanji is an associate professor of political science at Concordia University. His current research interests focus mainly on the study of values and value diversity and their implications for social cohesion, political support, and democratic governance.

Barry J. Kay is an associate professor of political science at Wilfrid Laurier University. His research interests are in public opinion and elections, the politics of policy making, Canadian and American politics, and research methodology.

Allan Kornberg is Norb F. Schaefer Professor of Political Science at Duke University. His research concentrates on political parties, legislatures, and comparative political behaviour.

Lawrence LeDuc is a professor of political science at the University of Toronto. His research interests are in Canadian and comparative political behaviour, political parties, elections, and research methods and design.

John Meisel is a professor emeritus of political science at Queen's University. His research interests include Canadian elections and political parties, questions of national cohesion and identity, Quebec politics, science policy, and cultural policy. His memoir, *A Life of Learning and Other Pleasures: John Meisel's Tale,* is to be published in the spring of 2012 by Wintergreen Studios Press.

Richard Nadeau is a professor of political science at the Université de Montréal. His research interests include electoral behaviour, public opinion, political communication, and methodology.

Jon H. Pammett is a professor of political science at Carleton University. His interests lie in the fields of voting behaviour, declines in voter participation, political education, and socialization.

Andrea M.L. Perrella is an associate professor of political science at Wilfrid Laurier University. His research interests include political behaviour, electoral politics, political communication, and Canadian politics.

Mildred A. Schwartz is a professor emerita at the University of Illinois at Chicago and a visiting scholar in the Department of Sociology at New York University. Her wide-ranging research interests have generated influential work on various dimensions of parties and the political process in Canada.

Thomas J. Scotto is a reader in government at the University of Essex. His research interests include American and Canadian voting behaviour, foreign policy attitudes, public opinion, and latent variable modeling.

Index

The letter f after a page number indicates a figure; t after a page number indicates a table; individual Canadian Election Studies are styled as "CES (1965)," "CES (1968)," and so on. CATI stands for computer-assisted telephone interviews; NDP stands for New Democratic Party; PC stands for Progressive Conservative; ROC stands for rest of Canada.

Printed and bound in Canada by Friesens

Set in Futura Condensed and Warnock
by Artegraphica Design Co. Ltd.

Copy editor: Stacy Belden

Proofreader: Lara Kordic

Indexer: Cheryl Lemmens

ENVIRONMENTAL BENEFITS STATEMENT

UBC Press saved the following resources by printing
the pages of this book on chlorine free paper made
with 100% post-consumer waste.

TREES	WATER	ENERGY	SOLID WASTE	GREENHOUSE GASES
6	2,665	2	169	591
FULLY GROWN	GALLONS	MILLION BTUs	POUNDS	POUNDS

Environmental impact estimates were made using the Environmental Paper Network
Paper Calculator. For more information visit www.papercalculator.org.